India and Israel
Against Islamic Terror

Old Nations New Leaders

India and Israel
Against Islamic Terror

Old Nations-New Leaders

Brigadier B.N. Sharma

Manas Publications
New Delhi-110 002 (INDIA)

MANAS PUBLICATIONS
(Publishers, Distributors, Importers & Exporters)
4858, Prahlad Street,
24, Ansari Road, Darya Ganj,
New Delhi - 110 002 (INDIA)
Ph.: 23260783, 23265523 (O); 27131660, 27143052 (R)
Fax: 011-23272766
E-mail: manaspublications@vsnl.com

First Published 2003

ISBN 81-7049-169-X

Typeset at
Manas Publications

Printed in India at
Shree Balaji Arts
and Published by Mrs Suman Lata for
Manas Publications, 4858, Prahlad Street,
24, Ansari Road, Darya Ganj,
New Delhi - 110 002 (INDIA)

Introduction

Empires have risen, prospered, declined and fell into oblivion, states and countries came into being and disappeared. The sands of history trickled down the hour glass of time as hordes of restless nomads from lands of scanty came from nowhere and destroyed mighty empires, cultures and civilizations, softened by affluence of agrarian existence. These same conquerors after settling down were in turn invaded by fresh waves of the more virile nomads, and the cycle of history continued. But amidst the cataclysms of recorded history only two cultures and civilizations endured. Down the fifteen millennia of known human development and ten millennia of recorded history, two but only two cultures, the most ancient of them survived the onslaughts of sword and destruction and still retain a large part of their original form and essence, Hinduism and Judaism. Strictly speaking, most major religions of the world have lived but the same cannot be said about the cultures and civilizations. The present inheritors of other cultures hardly remember their ancestry and their ancient and original cultural forms. A European does not have to look back very far, the two Americas still less, barely half a millennium, Africans with the exception of Egypt, even less. But even the present inhabitants of the land of Nile,

Akkad, Sumeria and even Iran do not remember their roots of origin. Ask an Iraqi or a Syrian about Sargon of Akkad, Assyrian war chariots, or an Egyptian about the Medianites. They shall look puzzled. But the Jew would remember the story of Abel and Cain, Abraham, Moses and Joshua and the kingdoms of Israel and Judea. A Hindu would with equal ease quote the trinity of his principal God and the panthean of gods and goddesses, the lays of ancient epics, *Puranas*, the story of *Ramayan* and *Mahabharat*, the rituals of marriage that are dateless and the *shlokas* to be recited at various occasions. The two people most attached to their past and their land who derive inspiration from their old cultures even today are the Hindus and the Jews. It is not entirely fortuitous that these happen to be the oldest religions and cultures of recorded history. Both religions are to an extent inward looking, seek fulfillment in the elevation of the soul and direct communion with their maker Jehovah or Brahma. Both feel bounden to follow their commandments, strive for purity of being, rather than adhere to mere rituals and outward forms of worship. Distortions have indeed crept in with time, as in all other religions, by a shifting of emphasis from essence to form, but by and large the wise and the learned of each of these two religions are fully aware of the original essence of their culture and religion.

Zionism is as old as the concept of Zion in the Jewish mind. Stress on God, His creation of man as an instrument for ushering in the Kingdom of God on this land, the sanctity of land as such and the Holy land, the land of the Book in particular with Jerusalem at its heart. The Hindu thought goes back to God, the one Brahma, the eternal, timeless, formless, creator and creation itself and enjoins upon man to reach Him through his deeds on this land; be of and one with this earth (*Dharati/ Thal*) and reach perfection through spiritual and material actions and means. More special is the emphasis on God, man and the land. Zion and the land of Zion compares with Brahma and Bharat. The striving for perfection and God's Kingdom on Earth by a Jew matches the striving for spiritual perfection and salvation by a

Hindu. The term Hindu here is used in a generic sense denoting the believer in the oldest thought, call it religion, which is *Sanatan* (eternal and unchanging), popularly called Sanatan Dharm. The Jew receives God's commandment and dictates through various prophets from Abraham to Moses. In the Hindu thought the wisdom of Vedas, their commentary in Upanishads and the Lord's message through sages and saints and the Rishis of yore continues till He incarnates Himself as Lord Krishna, and at the battle field of Kurukshetra, He preaches in the *Bhagwad Gita* His Last gospel and Message to mankind.

Both people produced great prophets, sages and saints, kings and patriots and established a secular kingdom of repute. Both had to face invaders who tried to destroy their carefully nurtured culture and civilization. In the case of Jews they passed through conquests, pogroms and Diaspora and still, Phoenix-like rose from the ashes of their past again and again. The Jews could never live permanently on their land and were homeless for long periods in history. But in India land was not lost. However, the invaders slaughtered, converted and ruled but could not snuff out the spirit of the ten millennia old culture. The land was the same but kingdoms appeared, and reappeared, people suffered privations and slavery but the spirit of Bharat endured. Both in the case of India and Israel, it can truly be said that what is amazing is not how both civilizations were constantly attacked and suffered, but how inspite of heavy odds they retained their identity, the spirit of their culture and essence of their spirituality.

To quote Dr. K.M. Munshi, "Generation after generation, during their school or college career, were told about the successive foreign invasions of the country, but little about how we resisted them and less about our victories. They were taught to decry the Hindu social system; but they were not told how this system came into existence as a synthesis of political, social, economic and cultural forces; how it developed in the people the tenacity to survive catastrophic changes for millennia; how it protected life and culture in times of difficulty by its conservative strength and in favourable time developed an elasticity which made ordered progress possible; and how its vitality enabled the national culture to adjust its central ideas to new conditions."

Jews and Hindus clung to their past and culture. Both looked to their God and took up arms to resist invaders and suffered and died fighting. But those that remained carried the torch and the struggle, and simply refused to be wiped out of existence. Israel and its heart Jerusalem were attached by scores of tribes and nationalities, who ruled for a while and then were thrown into the dustbin of history. But Israel endures. Likewise India was invaded by the Greeks, Huns, Shakas, Mongols, Moslems, Turks, Afghans, Moghuls and the British, but India, that is Bharat, survives.

Past is the mother of present and a foundation for the future. Nations that have achieved eminence in history have imbibed pride in their past. India and Israel are the two leading nations which not only take pride in the knowledge of their past, but without being retrogressive use this impulse to propel them forward to achieve new levels of excellence. The people who take pride in their antiquity and pedigree are naturally more advantaged in their future achievements. Indians and Israelies could rightly be proud of their glorious past and are better placed to build their future. As someone has so wisely put it—"Past must act as a spring-board, not a hammock." Equally wise Capt. Liddel Hart, the profoundest military writer of our age, has put it very succinctly—"Come to the point but do not camp on it". Thus it behoves Indians not to live permanently on their past glory, but to act in the present to achieve a glorious future.

There are certain striking similarities between these two ancient civilizations. Their antiquity being the first and foremost which gives them depth, maturity and an immanence, all their own. This inevitably gives these people a strength to forbear and a detachment from immediacy of events and immunity against temporary reverses. They have imbibed the wisdom that the times change and history inflicts it's cruel nemesis on upstart prophets and those who believe that every thing can be changed merely by the power of the sword. That sound ideas are more important than catchy slogans; that substance outlives the shine and that the struggle of a people does not merely lie in the might of its armies but it stays deeper in its steeled determination to resist wrongs and injustice and that ultimately it is the strength of character that endures and prevails.

Both "Hindutva" or the essence of Hinduism which is not a straight jacketed religion, and 'Zionism' have fostered strengths and released forces that have not been defeated, howsoever overwhelming the odds. And they will survive till the last syllable of recorded time. Both believe in abjuring violence as far as possible, but enjoin upon their people to take up arms for what is right and stand up and fight when forced by oppressors. In the history of the Chosen people time and again their Lord God speaks to the prophets, judges, kings, and the leaders to smite the hand that spoils the holy land and Jewish shrines or oppresses its people. In Hindu lore Lord Krishna commands Arjun to pick up the gauntlet thrown by Kauravas and wage a Dharm Yudh in the cause of justice and righteousness. Both religions believe in the universality of human values and brotherhood of man "Vasudhaiv Kutumbakam". Very few know that Judaism in its original form like Hinduism was not exclusivistic but all embracing, calling man to rise to the level of God's best creation. Both embrace all shades of opinion and permit dissent; both believe in cosmic eternity and enjoin a very high moral code. The rituals are unimportant, the spirit is all. In some religions even as they were born, the emphasis on outward form was all important, such as the postures at prayers, the direction to face, the number of prayers a day, and even inanities and details of everyday life. Their's was a total system, holistic and rigid, where not a line could be erased nor a new word added.

Both nations suffered invasions and oppressions; the Hindus invasions, forcible conversions, destruction of their temples, slaughter and devastation. So did the Jews suffer the sword, the destruction of their shrines, forcible conversions, devastation of their land, pillage, slavery and above all pogroms, that have shaken the conscience of the world.

Many triangulation marks of great events on the geodetic map of history have disappeared in the sands of time, but two enduring edifices exist, India and Israel. They shall continue to exist on this planet and these two civilizations are destined to lead.

Contents

Part II

From Diaspora to the Establishment of a Jewish Home

Part III

India: Past and Present

Part IV

The Future

PART - 1

From Jewish Genesis To The Beginning Of Modern Era

Chapter 1

Outline of Historiography

There are several ways of looking at history, each under a different paradigm. The first is the "unhistoric" or "Henry Ford" way who declared history to be bunk and a confusion of dates, names and battles with little to learn. We shall reject this approach for obvious reasons.

The next one is one of "political interpretation", looking as it does, on dynasties, kings and battles in a chronological order, the type which is taught in schools. Yet another way is the geographical one in which the land and the climate determine human character and social institutions through physical environments. In the case of the Jews, as for the Hindus, this approach is not tenable, since the Jews, just like the Hindus, have survived in almost every climate without losing their ethnicity and cultural identity. This can be seen in today's Israel where people from all over the world have coalesced into one homogeneous entity, just like the Hindus in different parts of this Sub-continent have retained their cultural roots.

A different way of viewing history is the economic or Marxian model, where all events are determined by the way the goods are produced, and the perpetual clash of social classes is historically ordained, till the state withers away and a utopia prevails. The other method is the one founded by Prof. Sigmund

Freud in the early twentieth century, holding that all events are the result of suppression of man's unconscious hostilities. The primary determinant in this psychoanalytic process is the libido, unbridled sex, murder, violence, incest and sadism. It is only after man overcomes these impulses that he can achieve creative thinking and civilised impulses.

The next is the philosophical way. Its chief proponents were the German philosopher George Wilhelm Friedrich Hegel, the Prussian philosopher-historian, Oswald Spengler, and the British historian Arnold Toynbee. This method views history as a series of isolated events in some semblance of continuity with each civilization following a predictable pattern which is like the development of a man from infancy to old age and death. According to this view, the life of a civilization depends upon the ideas and ideals by which it lives. Spengler suggests that the civilizations pass through the youth of its spring, mature to the summer of their achievements, reaching the apex of their intellectual pinnacle in the autumn, and finally decline into the winter and die. In contrast, Toynbee's theory holds that civilizations evolve from a lower to a higher form as long as it responds correctly to the challenges it faces. Somehow, history of the Jews and the Hindus does not fit either into the Spengler or Toynbee system.

Another view is that of the cult of personality, holding forth that great individuals shape history, quoting Washington as the architect of the American Revolution, Robespierre of the French and Lenin of the Russian Revolution.

The last approach to history is the religious one in its oldest and newest concept. The Bible for the Jews and the Vedas and Indian epics such as *Ramayana* and *Mahabharata* for Hindus have moulded their character and history, emerging out of a struggle between good and evil, morality and immorality. Jewish history mainly has been written from this viewpoint. With rapid strides in science and development of the scientific temper, these "existential theologians" are in disrepute. Thus the circle is complete with God as the maker of history and human effort of viewing history as a series of events, a philosophical one as a series of purposive events, the economic one with its productive methods as the prime force, the psychological one based on unconscious drives, the theory of "great man" as the centre piece, and the master of his historic destiny and finally back to God as the centre of all. To our chronology of events we shall add colours of most of the viewpoints as appropriate.

It would be a Herculean task to condense within the confines of these pages, the history of these two civilizations. What is attempted here is to trace out the physical contours of development of these cultures and nations through historical records, objectively studied to bring out the essence of these two most ancient human societies. A brief record of kings, battles and ever-changing shape of political state is essential to put this study in the right perspective. Since the book is addressed to both the western and Indian readers, due emphasis is needed to be given to both the histories. However, Indian history and Hindu thought is much more vast and diffused, deriving as it does from innumerable sources. Though few in number, and described in what is properly called written historiographic texts and sources, these texts serve as a useful guide to understand our civilizational history. The history of Israel on the other hand is basically confined to definitive sources in the Bible and later research and commentaries, and is easier to describe. Its uniqueness is less known to the Christian world. Thus Judaic history would occupy a larger coverage than our own which, it is hoped, is better known to Indian public.

The Jewish history has been described first, serving as it does, a reference matrix to Indian history that follows thereafter. Further our history is well-known to Indian readers. What is aimed in this book is only to highlight those aspects of our civilizational history which are not commonly known to western readers by choice or prejudice and even our own people nurtured on western media sharing the same prejudices. The western ignorance about Zion, the Jew and the Judaic history is matched only by a similar ignorance by Indians of our own history and culture.

Chapter 2

History of Israel

Section 1: People of the Book

A little land thrown up by a geographical accident during the early Diluvial period, blocking the expansion of the Mediterranean sea eastwards, later called Palestine did not have much to recommend it to a present day tourist. A wandering ground for the nomads, a poor cousin to the greener Egypt and Babylon it had little grace or scenic beauty, consisting as it did of barren hills punctuated by a few fertile oases, located next to the Dead Sea depression and separated by an inhospitable desert eastward. Who could imagine that one day this little drab land will become one of the most important spiritual centres of the world. The little green patches coveted by the nomads attracted hordes of vandals and despoilers who repelled by the desert wastes flocked to this land in search of food and shelter. Invaders came and went but some made it their home. Placed at the crossroads of ancient world, little Palestine not only became a refuge for the homeless but also a haven for the more enterprising, and always remained at the hub centre of the civilised world west of India.

The Amonites, the first recorded settlers in the third millennium B.C. who conquered the land upto the district of Lebanon, were hedged between two great powers—the

Babylonians on the north and Egyptians on the south—whose influence and sovereignty alternated over the land. Of the two, the Babylonian influence in the early period was deeper. Lugalzaggisi, the first Babylonian Emperor, spread his empire westward upto the sea, followed by Sargon of Agad around 2600 B.C., which name figures in fables along with Moses a century later. Sargon completed the conquest, and finally Hammurabi by the end of third millennium B.C. formalized the assimilation of Palestine into the Babylonian Empire. Lightly controlled, fairly taxed and wisely and benevolently ruled and administered, Palestine was culturally transformed with its country's customs, laws and even myths, acquiring a Babylonian hue.

Abraham and Hebrew Genesis

Instead of treating the slow and tortuous route of chronology of events, fairly well documented by more competent authorities, an attempt is made here to emphasise events and personalities as they shaped the Jewish nation. Simply stated the Jews in some form existed as early as 4500 B.C., the beginning of the Pagan period, as a historiologist would like to describe. This was the time of proto-history when pre-Mohenjodaro and Indus Valley culture existed in India contemporaneous to Sura and Kest in Babylon and the pre-dynastic period of Egypt. By 3600 B.C. Sumerian civilization was fairly well-known and by 3500 B.C. the first dynasty in Egypt came into being. Before 2800 B.C. Akkad had established a great kingdom around Saragon. Later, uniting the kingdom of Sanana and Akkadia he laid the foundation of Babylonian supremacy. The Middle Kingdom in Egypt is dated around 2400 B.C. and the period 2000 B.C. to 1200 B.C. can roughly be described as the era of wandering for the Chosen people. Around 2000 B.C. Abraham, the father of the Jews, and Sarah, his wife, left Ur in Chaldea within Babylonia. The time of Noah and the great flood according to many historians is much earlier than Abraham and is placed around the time of Manu, the first man who appeared on the soil of Bharat through water, ice and flood.

As per Genesis Chapter 7 to 9, Noah was six hundred years old when the great flood came which lasted a hundred and fifty days. After that he lived another three hundred fifty years. This gives him a total life span of nine hundred fifty years. Noah's sons and the new generation of Nimrod and Babel feature thereafter till in Chapter 11, the whole world became of one tongue. The last progeny of Noah's lineage Terah begot Abraham, Nahor and Haron. Haron begot Lot and the story of Abraham and his wife Sarah starts then in Ur in the land of Chaldea. It would be imprudent to put too fine a point on the time span of Babylonian account since that would upset the applecart of historical time frame. So we come straight to the time of Abraham and take as read the story of Abraham's journey from Ur to the land of Canaan and from there to Haran, where he lived for some time till God ordered him out to a new land, blessed him and promised to make his seed a great nation. Thereupon, Abraham left Haran with his coveted Sarah who was fair, and a plague descended upon the land forcing Abraham to leave Egypt till he reached Bethal and Hai and built an altar to his Lord. Later Lot under entreaties from his uncle Abraham left the overcrowded habitat of Cannanite and the Perizzite and journeyed east to Jordan. And then in Chapter 13, Para 14 ibid "And the Lord said unto Abram, after that Lot was separated from him, Lift up now thine eyes, and look from the place where thou art northward, and southward, and eastward, and westward:

"15 For all the land which thou seest, to thee will I give it, and to thy seed forever.

"16 And I will make thy seed as the dust of the earth: so that if a man can number the dust of the earth then shall thy seed also be numbered.

"17 Arise, walk through the land in the length of it and in the breadth of it; for I will give it into thee.

"18 Then Abram removed his tent and came and dwelt in the plain of Mamre, which is in Hebron, and built there an altar unto the Lord."

We hear of the word Hebrew associated with Abraham for the first time in Chapter 14 Para 13 ibid "And there came one that had escaped, and told Abram the Hebrew; for he dwelt in the plain of Mamre the Amorite, brother of Eshcol, and brother of Aner: and these were confederate with Abraham."

Later Abraham on insistence from Sarah fathered a child named Ishmael from his Egyptian maid servant Hagar, and then the Lord entered into Covenant with Abraham and blessed him. He promised that he shall be the father of many nations and his seed shall multiply on the earth. Then Sarah in old age bore Abraham a son named, Isaac, while the Lord as part of His covenant bode Abraham to get every eight days old child and himself circumcised. The story thereafter of Abraham's willingness to sacrifice Isaac and the intervention of the Angel is well known and told elsewhere. Now we come to the story of Essau and Jacob, twin sons of Isaac. The treachery of Jacob to steal the blessings of his father at the behest of his mother, Sarah, offering of fresh blessing on Essau by Isaac and ordering away of Jacob to a distant place whose subsequent flight and wanderings took him to East and finally his entry into Egypt are chronicled elsewhere. We leave the proto-history of the dynasty of Abraham into two main branches, one of Jews and the other born out of Ishmael who bore a new race which embraced the religion of Islam, and return to the other momentous events in the life of the Israelites.

During the Egyptian exile around 2000 B.C. Palestine prospered well, its figs and grapes were plentiful. Water and honey abounded and wheat and barley crops nourished its people and it's cattle wealth. Baked bricks were used in frail houses and huts, the art of amulets and wine presses and potteries prospered and long tunnels at Gezar led to a flowing spring, mythologically linked to the great Flood. Politically, the land was undeveloped with constant clan feuds making it easy for the invaders to subdue the warring tribes. By the beginning of 2nd millennium, B.C., the Canaanites and Semetic tribes probably came to inhabit the land and gradually overpowered the earlier Amonites. Simultaneously, the Babylonian influence gave way to Egyptian paramountcy, helped by an invasion of the Kassites from the East which distracted the Babylonian state and its own dynasty lasted for 600 years.

Egyptian King Thutomose III (1501 to 1447 B.C.) ransacked Palestine and enriched his coffers with the tributes and spoils of the land, letting his soldiers live off the countryside and carried the children to Egypt for education in order to completely Egyptianise the country. The Canaanites lived by agriculture, their produce being plundered by the king's soldiers, they toiled hard to cultivate the land and maintain a rather workable economy. Arts and crafts flourished but the land was still riven by petty jealousies and torn by rivalries of petty princes. The Tel El Amara letters of 1887 throw considerable light on the period of Canaanite survival under the Pharoah's rule, which reduced them to a state of utter servility and humiliation, constantly prostrating before the king, seeking help against the invaders from the north and east. Troubled as the land of Canaanites was and the Egyptian king Amenhotep IV, preoccupied with his own kingdom, the Hittites, a virile northern tribe, took control of Canaanites as far as south Palestine and even challenged by now the nominal Egyptian king. Ramses managed to contain any further Hittite' advance southwards and in 1271 B.C. signed a treaty of peace. These were troubled times. Pressed by rapacious hordes from the desert in the east, and the sea in the west, the Canaanites fought almost half a dozen enemies living from crisis to crisis.

A fog now descends on the story of the land and little is known till it lifts five centuries later. By then, Egyptian power declines, Hittites lose control, Babylon and Assyria busy themselves fighting each other and little Palestine left uncared got a reprieve. The vacuum is soon filled by the Philistines moving in from the sea and the Armeans from north penetrating upto Syria. And in this confused kaleidoscope of racial movements the Hebrews eager for a piece of land in the fertile crescent make their appearance. As the fog clears after these five centuries, records begin with the Biblical narration where the Hebrews and their ancestors have long ago been settled in the land of Palestine, named after the latest entrants, the Philistines. They occupy important places, ruled by monarchy and worship a strange new God, Yahweh. The early period of Hebrew arrival is shrouded in mystery, folk- lores and fables resulting in an accomplished miracle of scattered tribes arriving from different directions into this land, metamorphosed into a unique national religion.

Moses and Exile in Egypt

Less of myth and more of a fact as generations to come later believed the Egyptian bondage left a permanent scar on the Jewish psyche and burned into their consciousness a hatred for oppression and tyranny. This found place in many of their laws, some of them preambling "Remember your bondage in Egypt." Even if people forgot, their Prophets constantly reminded them that they had been oppressed and a Semitic fervour ordained them to show consideration and compassion to the orphan, widow, slave or an alien. These exhortations transformed the soul of the Jewish nation to practise and preach the gospel of freedom, its meaning and responsibilities.

The saga of exodus revolves round one man, unique in Jewish history. Moses, who according to Napoleon, was even a greater Biblical figure than Jesus, and to Heine, even greater than Mount Sinai. Moses created the Jewish Nation. Leader, preacher and prophet rolled into one he reorganised Hebrew religion and thought. A moral Titan with immense influence over his folk, he created the Hebrew people by binding them through the laws of religion. Though of uncertain scientific historicity based on evidence till date, Moses according to Bible was born during the height of Pharaos' oppression. Escaping the child slaughter ordered by the Pharaos, cleverly hidden by his mother in the Nile and discovered by the King's own daughter, Moses was brought up in royal luxury. But his heart wept for the misery of his people. Having slained the tormentor of a Jew, he fled to escape the wrath of the Pharaos, seeking shelter with the wandering Medianites in the desert and married the daughter of their Priest Chief. In the solitude of the desert, Moses came face to face with Yahweh, His first revelation to a man. Fortified and inspired he returned to Egypt to save his people. The story of the exodus is well documented in the Biblical account and by later day historians. He consecrated the freedom of his people at Sinai through a covenant with Yahweh and gave to successive generations the laws and religion based on the immortal Decalogue, better known to the world as The Ten Commandments. A masterful leader and law giver, through his wanderings in the desert, he schooled his flock in hardships, trials and tribulations. Striving for the Promised Land, fighting desert tribes like the Amalekites, overcoming strifes and dissensions within he steeled his people into a formidable, virile and bedouin nation capable of winning a home for themselves. Thus, leading and preaching, he brought them to Canaan, the land he only saw from a distance, never reaching there, as God gave him to death and "no man knoweth of his sepulchre". Moses, myth or fact, left a legacy that profoundly influenced the Hebrews on the threshold of history. Emulated by their Prophets, "a pillar of light" as described by philosopher Ahad Ha'm, the greatest Hebrew who lived as the quintessence of the best in the Hebrew genius, Moses through his influence catalysed into unity one Semitic tribe after another, bound by laws, and moulded them into a Nation.

In Mosaic faith, Yahweh is an inseparable part of the lives of man and the spirit of universal order. He is the source and sanction for all secular laws made, not for convenience of man, but to accomplish a higher divine purpose. To break laws was not merely the sin against society but against Yahweh Himself and His wishes. This resulted in a unique bond between Hebrews and their God Yahweh, who sought to help, teach and protect his chosen seed. He helped his children in destroying their enemies but punished them all the same for their trespasses and breach of the moral code. Unlike other religions his code was rigid and there were no laxity or extenuating circumstances to allow deviations. He helped his Chosen people when they were right but smote them with vengeance when they erred. This magnetic austerity and unfailing adherence to the principle of law depicted in a Michaelangelo masterpiece puts Moses in a unique position amongst world's religious leaders.

Steeped in the spirit of the desert Moses wove his people, Yahweh and the moral law in a sublime trinity. Yahweh, loving, cold, hard, extremely jealous of his rights, filled his people with awe and demanded of them a very high standard of moral code. The law of Moses in various modes, spread through the pages of Pentateuch and the simple Decalogue of Exodus XXXIV, 14-26, being the oldest suited to the needs of a nomad people. The code demanded only the worship of Yahweh and forbade graven images and idols. Sacrifices and some rituals, however, were added and Sabbath made a day of rest. Deuteronomic code owed its essence to the genius of Moses and his remarkable document called for the suppression of baser passions, forbade stealing, adultery, murder, being false witness and coveting. It thus went far beyond the narrow compass of ancient morality. Though many heathen customs and distortions crept in Hebrew worship with time and the Israelites fell into wicked ways due to alien influence, these were checked by the Prophets, and the religion of Moses remained unsullied, purified by the fire that scorched his soul when he was in communion with his God.

The Return

The nomad Jews who entered Palestine were not savages who descended upon a settled populace. Some of them had lived a settled existence earlier, while the others moved from one harvesting place to another. But they were strangers to the ways of the settled people. Divided and ignorant even from Canaanite standards, they were to produce men of piety and prophets who hallowed the soil; where they spread the gospel and gave a religion of tremendous force and vitality with a corpus of high spirituality, mirroring the biography of a God drunk people. Biblical accounts speak eloquently of Joshua's conquests and occupation of Palestine by his people through well-organised military expeditions that transgressed Jordan and divided the land among twelve tribes who consolidated his victory and laid a permanent hold over Palestine. Romanticised in Deuteronomy by the priestly historians, a picture emerges of a united Hebrew people by the grant of a land by a fatherly Yahweh to his obedient children. The "Book of Judges" gives a different historical account nearer to truth, of a slow filling in of people through successive pushes, tribe by tribe, of a land hungry people slugging it out with local people to gain a foot-hold and then enlarge their possessions through settlement, battles, inter-marriages, and assimilation, and generations after generations sending permanent roots into the conquered soil. A tide from the east of Joseph's client Ephram, Manasseh and Benjamin from Trans Jordan pushed westward across the river fighting for a more fertile land, mingling with other settlers till around 1200 B.C. Judah came with his client such as Lovi, Simon and Kenites who pushed south into the desert bringing with them the worship of Yahweh and the memory of Moses.

With the process of transformation of the nomadic Hebrews as they came across the ways of the Canaanites, with their settled ways of agriculture, hamlets, towns, walled fortresses, fertile fields with abundant products, instruments of war with fast moving chariots and artefacts of peace, there took place a slow melting of identity of Yahweh and Baal, the Canaanite God. While they learnt to produce corn, oil, wine and figs and traded with Tyre and Sidon the new plenty of the land increased their population. They learnt the alphabet carved in stones, learnt to record and produced a folklore of legendary heroes, court bards and scribes, described in the Biblical records of King David. The Jews could not long remain unaffected by the religious rites of Canaanites and their central God figure Baal. Influenced by the old Semitic poly-demonism and polytheism of Babylon and Egypt, by the time of Tell el Amara period the Canaanites had evolved a heady mix of nature worship, akin to the Aryans, where all natural forces represented a god. Wind, storm, lightning, rain, sun, trees, stones all represented the power of gods to be propitiated to ward off evil effects. Thus Baal was a god of nature and life; health and happiness depended on his favour. The Jews took readily to the new God Baal and his symbols of power over nature. The female counterpart of Baal, the Baalith was not long in coming and much to Yahweh's anguish his people revelled in such worship. Baal was more visible and in daily contact, associated with agriculture, while Yahweh the desert god was forgotten, and then the final transformation of Yahweh into Baal took place as Canaanite shrines were taken over by the Hebrews. The Shecheam height, long devoted to Baal worship was converted into a Hebrew shrine under the pretext that it was here that Yahweh had promised Canaan to the seed of Abraham.

The old Canaanite sanctuary at Bethel, of Jacob's dream became a Hebrew shrine in the days of Kings. The Hebrews consecrated it as the burial place of the Patriarchs and the cave of Machpelah is today a hallowed place for the three faiths of Judaism, Christianity and Islam. Canaanite sepulchres were turned into holy resting place for the dead Hebrews and celebrated as a fitting revenge to the conquered. The process of assimilation thus went on inexorably. Nothing of the Hebrew rites remained untouched. To the Passover of lamb offer now was added the agricultural festival of unleavened cakes marking the corn harvest "when thou putteth the sickle into the Corn" and so on it went. Divinities, rites, festivals, altars, all were transformed through a Canaanite local colour. The process was the same as was to be repeated later, where a great corpus of pagan rites was absorbed into early Christianity. Ceremonies, dogmas and doctrines were borrowed from pagan temples and incorporated as events and happenings in the life of Jesus with the march of Christianity. Synthesis is a natural phenomenon in the fusion of religions, but the free ingress of Baalith practice with its lasciviousness, sex practice and destructive polytheism led the gullible Hebrews into orgies and such sexual indulgence as invited the wrath of Yahweh, their desert God. Then the early prophets appeared angry and inflamed to pull their folk out of degradation by demanding total reformation, removing all alien influences and set the course straight for the Chosen people.

Before the Hebrews could settle and make history in their new found land, some time in the Twelfth century B.C., the bete noire of Hebrew life, the Philistines, a new Semitic people migrating from their Greek abode of Crete and Mycenaen island burst upon the new comers. While one arm of their southern invasion into Egypt was checked by Rameses III in 1180 B.C., they were more successful in their north and eastward advances, meeting feeble resistance of small tribes. They conquered, built and prospered, establishing big towns like Gaza, traded with Bedouin caravans and built magnificent temples to Dagon and other gods, and finally fell upon the Hebrews. The first to face the onslaught was the small tribe of Dan and the legend of Samson was born. This Biblical giant of a genial Hebrew stood to defend his people, slew the enemy by the thousands, using his skill and tremendous strength. Despite the saga of his individual valour and the legend that grew around him, the weakness of his tribe forced a retreat to the north to Phoenicia where they remained as an outpost of Hebrew presence in Palestine. The Philistinic juggernaut rolled on sweeping before it Ephram and Manaseb and won resounding victory at Aphek near Benjamin, leaving countless dead. They then crushed the last desperate effort of the Hebrews at Shiloh who fought under the presence of the Ark of Yahweh with its sacred palladium planted in the battlefield.

Their God having failed the Hebrews, the Philistines carried the Ark to their own temples leaving behind a burning Shiloh and occupied the whole land, garrisoned and heavily taxed. With the Philistine repression, the Ark of Lord in the pagan sanctuary under the lustful glare of Dagon, Shiloh a ghost town, the country ravaged, the Hebrew cup of woe was full. But the suffering did not snuff out their spirit. The Philistine fire and hammer blows forged them into a nation. The persecuted retaliated with sword and the obscure son of Benjamin was the flag bearer. As the Ammonite hammered at Gilead, Saul, the young farmer turned the tide and with a motley warriors of his tribe turned upon them and routed them. The people were electrified and Saul became the saviour of the Hebrews and crowned king at Gilgal. He now struck at the Philistines and after many vicissitudes the king of Benjamin clan drove out the enemy.

With Saul began the origins of monarchy. Biblical accounts are conflicting but the main events are sound. Said to be a choice of the Saint Samuel, a farmer's son, he is told of his historic destiny and anointed as Yahweh's instrument of Salvation.

Saul's great victories raised him to the level of glorified judgeship. His exploits were numerous. His kingship was consecrated by the Prophets who persistently effected the choice of kings and monarchy. He united all Hebrew tribes, and proved the prophets' blessings true. His life was devoted to fighting the Philistines. Having lost the initial skirmish against the Philistines at Aphek, the Amphictyonic shrine of the Ark was fetched from Shiloh to guarantee the presence of their God among the hard pressed Israelis in the second battle. Finally, it was transported to a camp. But the Philistines returned again and again with greater numbers. Never could Saul sheath his sword. While he fought, the other jealous tribes like Moab, Edom and Ammon, slunk for spoils. He held court in camp and was always battling till the end of his life as battle cries echoed from the Palestinian hills.

Living an austere and democratic life Saul assuaged the feelings of his people, not used to kingly despotism. He met his Councilors frequently and his royal table consisted only of four members—himself, Jonathan, his son, his minstrel David and Abner, his cousin the "Captain of the host". No ceremonial trappings of royal authority were present. Later, in his reign internal dissensions surfaced up with differences with the prophets. Unlike the ugly picture painted by Judean chroniclers, Saul was a simple and sincere man. But the historians, to show David in a better light, have often been unjust to this simple warrior King. The prophets then sought David's assistance to get rid of Saul. Engaged in battles on all sides Saul died, as he lived, by the sword in the battle of Mount Gilboa, fighting the now reinforced Philistines, let down by some of his own tribes and priests, and defended only by his three stalwart sons, who surrounded him.

King David

Saul was succeeded by his own warrior David, a trend setter in Jewish folklore, mythical, romantic and epitomising all possible virtues of a king, bravery and skill in war not being the least of them. It was he who fired the world imagination to this day as the virtuous little boy with a sling who defeated the evil Philistine giant Goliath, and became a legend for all times to come. David was a Judaen from Bethlehem (the modern Betlahm) 5 miles north of Jerusalem and later became the "king of Judah and Israel." He combined every happy talent with human quality and wisdom; rising from reverses to grab success, he is the only Biblical figure with so many legends woven round him.

Let us see how Bible treats this great warrior king who wrote Psalms, his discovery from obscurity by Samuel, his encounter with Goliath, his anointment by the Lord, and finally His order to David to build Him a house in Jerusalem.

I Samuel (Chapter 16)

"10. Again, Jesse made seven of his sons to pass before Samuel. And Samuel said unto Jesse, The Lord hath not chosen these.

11. And Samuel said unto Jesse, Are here all thy children/ and he said, There remaineth yet the youngest, and, behold, he keepeth the sheep. And Samuel said unto-Jesse, Send and fetch him: for we will not sit down till he come hither.

12. And he sent and brought him in. Now he was ruddy, and withal of a beautiful countenance, and goodly to look to. And the Lord said, Arise, anoint him: for this is he.

13. Then Samuel took the horn of oil, and anointed him in the midst of his brethren: and the Spirit of the Lord came upon David from that day forward. So Samuel rose up and went to Ramah.

14. But the Spirit of the Lord departed from Saul, and an evil spirit from the Lord troubled him."

*****

I Samuel (Chapter 17)

Now the Philistines gathered together their armies to battle, and were gathered together at Shochoh, which belongeth to Judah, and pitched between Shochoh and Azekah, in Ephes-dammim.

2. And Saul and the men of Israel were gathered together, and pitched by the valley of Elah, and set the battle in array against the Philistines.

3. And the Philistines stood on a mountain on the one side, and Israel stood on a mountain on the other side: and there was a valley between them.

4. And there went out a champion out of the camp of the Philistines, named Goliath, of Gath, whose height was six cubits and a span.

5. And he had an helmet of brass upon his head, and he was armed with a coat of nail; and the weight of the coat was five thousand shekels of brass.

*****

14. And David was the youngest: and the three eldest followed Saul.

15. But David went and returned from Saul to feed his father's sheep at Beth-lehem.

16. And the Philistine drew near morning and evening, and presented himself forty days.

*****

32. And David said to Saul, Let no man's heart fail because of him; thy servant will go and fight with this Philistine.

33. And Saul said to David, Thou are not able to go against this Philistine to fight with him: for thou art but a youth, and he a man of war from his youth.

34. And David said unto Saul, Thy servant kept his father's sheep, and there came a lion, and a bear, and took a lamb out of the flock:

35. And I went out after him, and smote him, and delivered it out of his mouth: and when he arose against me, I caught him by his beard, and smote him, and slew him.

*****

43. And the Philistine said unto David, Am I a dog, that thou comest to me with staves? and the Philistine cursed David by his gods.
44. And the Philistine said to David, Come to me, and I will give thy flesh unto the. fowls of the airs, and to the beasts of the field.
45. Then said David to the Philistine, Thou comest to me with a sword, and with a spear, and with a shield: but I come to thee in the name of the Lord of hosts, the God of the armies of Israel, whom thou has defied.
46, This day will the Lord deliver thee into mine hand; and I will smite thee, and take thine head from thee; and I will give the carcases of the host of the Philistines this day unto the fowls of the air, and to the wild beasts of the earth; that all the earth may know that there is a God in Israel.
47. And all this assembly shall know that the Lord saveth not with sword and spear for the battle is the Lord's, and he will give you into our hands."

*****

25. And now, O Lord God, the word that thou has spoken concerning thy servant, and concerning his house, establish it forever, and do as thee has said.
26. And let thy name be magnified for ever, saying, The Lord of hosts is the God over Israel: and let the house of thy servant David be established before thee.

Reverting to the Davidic odessy. Attached as a youth to the king's entourage and later outlawed by Saul, he fled to Judean hills with a small band of followers. He won fame at the battle-fields and appreciation in the camp for his amiable manners. Chased by the king's hordes he went over to the Philistines, raiding and freebooting there. It was while steeled in adversity and hemmed in by enemies, that David received his initiation into warfare and kingship. At the time of Saul's death he was controlling Judah and surrounding districts and was on amicable terms with shepherds of the South. Crowned king in Hebrew he had to contend with Abner, Saul's faithful general from North, and old rivalries flared up again with the advantage of numbers and strength lying with the latter. David's tiny kingdom was in peril as Philistines watched gleefully the two Hebrews slugging it out. But they reckoned without David. Resourceful, patient, supremely confident, using diplomacy, tact. flattery and bribes, accidental but timely murders removed all obstacles. Abner died in a vendetta, Ishbual's head was severed through a treacherous plot and at the end of ten years David rises as a new star out of the bloodshed and mire of treachery; victorious and happy, admired by all, controlling a much wider area than Saul ever did, and a ruler in his own right. He united the scattered tribes into a nation providing religious and national symbols by conquering a centrally located town from a Jebusite clan, high up in the Judean hills, called Jerusalem.

History of Jerusalem

Having gained the Kingdom and the unification of all the tribes under his leadership, David now decided to give a religious and political focus to his Kingdom. The place found most suitable was Jerusalem. While the boundary of Israel lay north of Jerusalem that of the Northern Judah lay South. Thus Jerusalem lay on the overlap of both the kingdoms. This was reason enough for its selection. Further, Jerusalem lay on a hill within the hollow of a valley in a strong position, though not commanding a large area but at a height of 2500ft., on the rather inaccessible southern part of the hills, west of Jordan.

Jerusalem, the capital city of David, has probably the most chequered history of all the cities in this world. Possibly, no other city in the world has suffered as much arson, carnage, destruction and warfare as Jerusalem. In three thousand years of its' recorded history, Jerusalem has been attacked forty times. It has been successively conquered and occupied by Egyptians, Assyrians, Babylonians, Persians, Seleucids, Greeks, Romans, Muslims, Arabs, Seljuks, Crusaders, Seracens, Mamelukas and Ottomon Turks. Not mentioning the earlier inter and intra tribal wars for the occupation of Jerusalem before David, a brief but not comprehensive chronology of some major conflicts for Jerusalem is given below:

	Time	Events
1.	587 or 586 B.C.	Destruction by Babylonians.
2.	198 B.C.	Seleucid Conquest.
3.	170 B.C.	Capture by Antiochus Epiphanes.
4.	164-141 B.C.	Hasmonean Revolt, Occupation, Defeat & Reoccupation
5.	63 B.C.	Pompey's Siege.
6.	37 B.C.	Conquest by Herod.
7.	70 A.D.	Destruction by Romans.
8.	132-135 A.D.	Bar Kochba Revolt.
9.	614 A.D.	Persian Conquest.
10.	638 A.D.	Muslim Conquest.
11.	1071, 1076 A.D.	Seljuk Conquest.
12.	1098 A.D.	Fatmid Conquest.
13.	1099 A.D.	First Crusader Siege and Conquest.
14.	1187 A.D.	Siege of Saladin.
15.	1229 A.D.	Third Crusader Siege.
16.	1244 A.D.	Conquest and Sacking by Tartars.
17.	1917 A.D.	Starvation relieved by Allenby's Entry.
18.	1920, 1929, A.D.	Arab Mob Outbreaks in Old City.
19.	1944-1946 A.D.	Jewish Underground Violence.
20.	1947 A.D.	Arab-Jewish Conflict.
21.	1948 A.D.	Arab Siege and Conflict.
22.	1967 A. D.	Jewish Conquest of East Jerusalem.

The name Jerusalem is derived from two Hebrew words—"Yara" and "Shalom" the former meaning city and the latter stands for peace· in other words a city of peace. Another interpretation could be the combination of "Yara" with "Salome", a local goddess. In Egyptian hieroglyphs, the city is referred to as Urushamem, in Akkadian tongue as Urusalim. Another school of thought relates to the belief in Hebrew connotation as "City of Peace" born out of two Hebrew words "Ir" meaning city and "Shalon" meaning peace. Modern historians, however, consider the derivation of this name from the two words "Yara" meaning "Founded" and "Salem" the name of the local God. Thus the city was supposed to be founded by the God "Salem". Thus the word Jerusalem had it's roots in antiquity. The city of shalom was conquered three millennia ago by David from the Jebusites, just after the onset of 10th century B.C. But the establishment of David's capital in the city of the House of Lord came much later. As described in Bible II Samuel (Chapter 7), the Lord spoke to David thus:

5. Thus saith the Lord, Shalt thou build me an house for me to dwell in?
6. Whereas I have not dwelt in any house since the time that I brought up the children of Israel out of Egypt, even to this day, but have walked in a tent and in a tabernacle.
7. In all the places wherein I have walked with all the children of Israel spake I a word with any of the tribes of Israel, whom I commanded to feed my people Israel, saying, Why build ye not me an house of cedar?
8. Now therefore, so shalt thou say unto my servant David, Thus said the Lord of hosts, I took thee from the sheepcote, from following the sheep, to be ruler over my people, over Israel."

*****

Thus the Lord's message to David through Samuel:

13. He shall build an house for my name, and I will establish the throne of his kingdom forever.
14. I will be his father, and he shall be my son. If he commit iniquity, I will chasten him with the rod of men, and with the stripes of the children of men:
15. But my mercy shall not depart away from him, as I took it. from Saul, whom I put away before thee."

*****

In obedience to the aforesaid word of the Lord, David purchased a ground site for the Temple from the local tribesmen for fifty shekels of silver at the same spot where Abraham had prepared an altar for the sacrifice of his son to please the Lord of Israel. Earlier called 'Mount Moriah' the place was subsequently named the 'Temple Mount', which also later became Haram-esh-Sharief, the existing site of Al-Aqsa Mosque and the Dome of Rock. The Israelies even today refer to the Temple site as 'Mount Moriah'.

Impregnable and strong, a bastion of Hebrew honour, Jerusalem served the emotional needs of the Hebrew people. Starting from modest beginnings David turned it into a great capital city, enlarging, reconstructing, uniting it to the fortress of Zion on a nearby hill and surrounding both with a strong wall. And then with great pomp and fervour he brought here the Holy Ark of Yahweh that had passed through troubled times earlier. Thus consecrated and hallowed, Jerusalem became a focal point of Hebrew faith, their kingdom and unity. Its marts and markets overflowed, its sanctuaries crowded with pilgrims and old Hebrew history was revived and relived, firing countless generations of bards and patriots, while the enigmatic bandit warrior, the founder of the city became a pious religious figure, a favoured son of Yahweh. Esconsed there in his new capital the restless soul of David struck everywhere fighting the surrounding foes and fired by his unquenchable thirst for conquest, he founded a kingdom that stretched from Lebanon to the Red Sea. Feared by the Syrians he beat back the Philistines, occupying their capital Goth, and avenged the indignity of Mount Gilboa. Moabites were routed, the Ammonites, Edomites. Armeans and Amalekites were crushed in a ruthless and brutal manner symptomatic of the times, desperation for life and home marking his exploits. These achievements unified and consolidated the Hebrew life around its kingdom with David as the law giver, arbitrator. and warrior king.

Jerusalem has never been the seat of Moslem empire. Earlier it was Damascas which was the seat of the Caliph, which later moved to Baghdad. Moslems never built a single town in Palestine except Ramalah, built by Abd-el-Malik, the second son of

Suleiman. This name too is derived from the name of the Jewish king Soloman, who founded Ramalah near the international airport of Lod. As far as the the Dome of Rock or Mosque of the Dome is concerned, it was initially a ramshackle wooden structure built by Omar and only later improved to its present shape by the Caliph. The site is, as Moslems believe, where Prophet Mohammed made his mystic flight to heaven on his legendary steed el-Burak. However, the Rock within is the site of an improvised altar on which Abraham was commanded by the Lord to sacrifice his son Isaac. The rock or Mount of Moriah as well as the site of Holy of Holies is part of the Jewish Temple made by king David.

The great shrine built later by Abd-el-Malik (682 to 705 A.D.) stands at the highest point of the Jewish Temple compound, renamed by the Arabs as Haram-esh-Sharief, meaning Noble Sanctuary. Al-Aqsa Mosque or the Dome of Rock was subsequently improved by Abd-el-Malik's son. It was later reconstructed with building material of the columns and remains of churches destroyed in the area. The mosque of Al-Aqsa later became the headquarters building for the Knights known as the 'Order of Templars' and named 'Palatium Solomanis', the place of Solomon, considering it to be the site of his residence built south of Solomon's Temple. During the Crusaders' occupation of Jerusalem (1099-1187 A.D.) the Dome of Rock was converted into a Christian church, known as 'Templum Domini' due to the association of the site with the Jewish Temple.

David moved into his new capital Jerusalem, the ancient tribal relic of the Ark, in order to give this city the dignity due to this central relic of the confederation of the tribes. In the process, he boldly linked it to the ancient tradition which bound the tribes together and made it a central point for all the Jews. 'Mount Zion, the name of the hill top on which Jerusalem's place of worship stood, became a concept in Israel's religious vocabulary. Around Jerusalem developed all the trade and prosperity of Israel. Construction and development followed the establishment of the city. Ancient trade routes were revived.

Trade developed as exchange of goods and services took place; roads were constructed, houses built and good governance provided to the children of Israel. Commerce and wealth flowed. Wells were dug where possible and resting place for the pilgrims constructed to shelter the pious visiting Jerusalem for worship and sacrifice.

Trade flowed from neighbouring lands along highways and the Hebrews, the scattered little nomads, became a strong force of the East. This was the peak of David's glory and then the decline began. He fell prey to the weaknesses of unbridled power, and developed into a medieval despot, his harem overflowing with women and hangers-on, the military austerity replaced by adulterous deeds and court intrigues. Rebellions broke out and the aging David lost most of his prestige and halo. His son rebelled and was killed by Jacob, his faithful general. His son's quarrels and endless intrigues among his concubines made his last years miserable. One of his famous concubines, Bathsheeba got her son propped up as the next king. This last phase of degeneration notwithstanding, David was the maker of Israel, a statesman and warrior king. Inheriting a dispirited and divided people, he raised a kingdom battle by battle. A succession of diplomatic coups pushed forward and secured the frontiers to establish a kingdom. He brought back the Holy Ark and created Jerusalem, a capital and a shrine. David, a king at 30, ruled in glory for forty years and his kingdom prospered. His rule stretched along the sea from Dan in the north to Beersheba in the south, while its eastern borders lay along the Judean hills and the river Jordan. His muster roll for battle included eight hundred thousand men from Israel and a hundred thousand from Judah. History remembers the man not for his foibles but his achievements. A genius in war and diplomacy, he holds a unique position in the Hebrew lore. A king poet in shining armour, he holds the unique distinction of being the maker of the Jewish nation. The star of David on Israel's flag is well deserved.

Solomon, the Wise

His son, Solomon, inherited the genes of his father. He improved upon them by his own winning charm, a keen wit, worldly wisdom, and a searching mind, appealing to Eastern instincts. Aware of human frailties. he grew into a shrewd judge of men. Seeing through intrigues, perfidy and obsequiousness, he saw through his hangers-on and became known for his wisdom. He could read hearts of men as he could the speech of birds and the trees. With time his reputation grew and he became the blessed son of Yahweh and the wisest among men. To him were attributed much of the Biblical wisdom, the proverbs, the cynical Ecclesiastes and portions of Appocrypha. Eulogised by some historians and equally criticised by others for his pomp and extravagance by despoliation of his subjects, his genius has never been in doubt, known not for his spirituality but earthiness, a characteristic of his times. As his fame in the Hebrew and Arab world grew, he opened the Hebrew culture to new influences and extended his boundaries while executing new projects. Wreaking vengeance on some of David's compatriots like Adonijah and Abiathar, he secured his position and sent a clear message that beyond sophistry of phrases he was a stern ruler of men. Having inherited a secured kingdom through his father's victory he turned from the problems of war to those of peace. He was not overtly concerned about the loss of territory of Edom and Moab or Aramaeans at Damascus to the rebellion of Rezon. Forgoing the lure of controlling troublesome aliens and their lands, he decided to consolidate his own kingdom by dividing it into twelve districts regardless of tribal loyalties under an overarching national unity. His efforts in evolving a national consciousness succeeded to a degree. He was a builder par excellence and had a passion for constructing big cities and palaces, well defended marts overflowing with trade that could equal his neighbours, and finally he built a grand temple to Yahweh over the site of David's temporary handiwork. The cost to his subject was high. His great construction odessey made a great state out of a nomad people as all material and architectural assistance came from his friend and neighbour Hiram of Tyre, a sea-faring Phoenician state. Israeli fleets took to sea and commerce for the first time through Tyre in return for supply of corn and oil. All population including non-Hebrews like Gibeonites and Jebusites and Canaanites, contributed to the building activities, sometimes under duress. With tremendous national effort, exaction of the people and unpopular taxes, at last a great temple was built to Yahweh at David's site. Splendid and majestic the structure bore testimony to Solomon's greatness, in spite of adverse home weather and cost. His palace was equally decorous and awe inspiring.

So far the visit of Queen Sheba, the black beauty from Africa, to the wise and powerful Israelite ruler, remained in the realm of a Biblical myth. However, the latest excavations of the ruins located 80 miles east of Yemen's capital Sana, just a few miles from the citadel of Marib at the edge of the Arabian desert, have validated the story of Queen Sheba. 'Black Minerva' to the Greeks, 'Makeda' or greatness to the Ethiopians and 'Bilqis' (a religious honorific title) to the Arabs, Queen Sheba ruled around 950 B.C. in a Middle East royalty, mentioned mainly in religious texts. The latest excavations in the north Yemen also shed light on a 3500 years old temple to Mahram Bilqis.

A custom grew up in the nation to resort to the capital on religious festivals and bring gifts to the holy shrine as the Temple became the heritage of the Hebrews and Jerusalem the centre of their religious lives. As generations passed, the Temple overshadowed Jerusalem and meanings read into every stone and artifect. The use of iron, a symbol of war was scrupulously avoided in the construction and then legend grew. For better or worse the Temple became the centre of sacerdotal faith, with all its rituals, priests, prayers, and sacrifices and even equated with Sinai in its religious importance. In all this show and glitter, the clean-simplicity of faith was the first casualty. Jerusalem grew and glittered, while Solomon built, secured and consolidated his kingdom with weapons of war and fortresses. New roads catalysed commercial development and military mobility, while the influence of the surrounding Semitic world permeated into the land through treaties and marriages further securing Jerusalem.

Solomon's large harem included princesses from lands all round such as Moab, Edom and even Egypt, leading to new religious practices and diluting the old. The cost of splendour meant increasing taxes and this was met by an expansion of trade overseas upto as far as India. The fiscal deficit grew and excessive prodigality led to an almost bankrupt treasury. Forty years of Solomon's momentous reign led to the greatness of his nation, Jerusalem its capital, and the rise in the dignity of the Temple. In the social order, an acquisitive rich aristocracy lorded it over a poverty ridden proletariat. This led to a class dichotomy in early history which resulted in a bitter harvest later. Despite all his splendour and profligacy Solomon's statesmanship and innovations more than made up for the hardships of his people by breaching the barriers around Palestine by developing Yahweh into an idea that outranged Israel's little Hebrew world.

The Prophets

The same tolerant policy towards dilution of the pristine Yahweh faith was continued by Ahab, the next king in the series of monarchy. The subordination of religion to diplomacy did not amuse the prophets and purists. Though broadmindedness had a civilising effect, in reality it preyed on religious uniqueness and national unity. Anger simmered against the house of Omri. Baal worship and other heathen practices that stole in Hebrew life were the ultimate straw. The Prophets revolted against what they called the blasphemy and apostacy. A long war followed, intolerant and ruthless and amidst this chaos of religious crises, rose the towery figure of Prophet Elijah, a popular and the most romantic figure in Jewish history; who was harsh, severe, and intolerant of existing corruption in the civilised life of the Hebrews.

With time his austere and uncompromising image got softened into a champion of the oppressed, and a true interpreter of Jewish faith, who could show the path of salvation through martyrdom. A deity at rituals, such as circumcision and Pass over feast, he is known as the gate keeper to Heaven and a messiah to open a new world. Challenging mainly the Tyrian nibbling into Yahweh's greatness, he suffered no compromise.

Battling for long on the peaceful slopes of Mount Carmel, Elijah won spectacular victory against prophets of Jezebel through Yahweh's miracles and nourished the roots of old Judaism while Judah became the guardian of Hebrew faith. Simultaneously began its division through internecine quarrels. While some states became pliable, Judah remained isolated from the Asiatic world and bore the brunt of attacks through a non-compromising stance and lost to Assyria. Judean King Hezekiah was more pragmatic. His kingdom prospered even while he retained the true faith of Yahweh. As the situation around changed rapidly in their favour, the believers abandoned their policy of supplication. Encouraging news from Egypt of Syrian decline catalysed an alliance of coastal countries against the Syrians who were now also threatened by the Chaldeans of Babylon. But this premature attempt at insurrection was stymied by a bold preemptive blow by Sargon who inflicted heavy casualties on the conspirators. Hezekiah kept a low profile and waited till his chance came in 705 B.C. when the mighty Sargon of Assyria fell. Even though it offered a temporary relief, in which Egypt and the league of the Palestinian States and Judea hoped to prey on the remains of Assyria, the march was halted. Inspite of Isaiah's remonstrance advocating wisdom of temperance, the hotheaded amongst Judah actively conspired. Vindicating Isaiah's fears, the successor king Sennacherib ruthlessly eliminated his Babylonian rivals and wreaked heavy vengeance on Philistine cities of Edom and Moab and then destroyed Judah sparing no one, burning and pillaging. Jerusalem was ruined and Hezekiah lost most of his territories; even his daughters were herded to the conqueror's harem. Sennacherib now turned to Egypt, but strangely, though assured of success, he abandoned the invasion and turned back baffling all reason and Biblical historians. Possibly it was the outbreak of the Bubonic plague and mice that destroyed all his weapons. However, Assyria retained its power. Under its conquering heels Judah was kept under total heathen subjugation by their greatest conquerors, Essar-Haddon and Assur-Bani-Pal, and Judah was ruled for 45 long years under their king Manasseh who turned to heathen practices to the extent of total apostasy.

However, materially the people prospered as the long period of peace healed the scars of earlier devastations and they abandoned the earlier Puritanism of Hezekiah's day. While Assyria remained in power, peace reigned in Judah. And then new threats appeared from Median and Scythian tribes and the Chaldean power now in possession of Babylon challenged the thousand years of Assyrian dominance of the Semitic world. The Scythians ravaged Syria and swept on to Egypt leaving Judah unscathed and then met a reverse at the Nile. The Egyptians emboldened by a weakened Assyria, and a powerful Navy struck back at Judah in the battle of Meggido. The young king Josiah died fighting gallantly and Judah became a principality of Egypt paying tribute to the suzerain who now occupied the throne of David. But these were turbulent times. The Chaldean leader of Babylon, Nebuchadnezzar, the greatest Eastern potentate since Hammurabi, having mopped up the remains of Assyria now assisted by the Medianites inflicted a crushing defeat on Egypt in the battle of Carchemish in 601 B.C. and Babylon now wrote a new world order with the new arts of life and construction. Judah now submitted to the inevitable. As long as it acquiesced Judah stayed out of trouble. But the King ill advised by the prophets defied Chaldean potentate and resorted to minor skirmishes, and guerrilla attacks. Incited by Judah's surrounding enemies, Nebuchadnezzar finally struck and devastated the land. He invaded Jerusalem in 579 B.C. and occupied the little capital. He plundered and sacked and carried into captivity large number of warriors and artisans and craftsmen leaving Zedekiah, the last Hebrew king exhausted and miserable. In spite of all this ruination, fire still burnt among the Judeans and inspired by everyday news trickling in from abroad, Zedekiah defied the mighty sovereign and ceased to pay tribute. Thereupon, an impatient and enraged Nebuchadnezzar once again swooped upon Judah, destroyed all that stood before him. The valiant little people defended Jerusalem till the end. When that also fell, the Temple was destroyed, the princes and priests slaughtered and Zedekiah, blinded and chained, was carried back to Babylon.

On the ruins of Judah Nebuchadnezzar placed Gedaliah as a royal governor ruling from Mizpah. Gedaliah ruled well and wisely but some malcontents assassinated him and fearful of Babylonian reprisals fled to Egypt carrying with them the old prophet Jeremiah. Despite the exile abroad and devastation at home, the spirit of Judea refused to die. And there from the ashes of political upheavals arose, phoenix like, the generation of prophets who combined all that was best in Hellenic art, Roman law and their own ancient culture. Innately pious and uncompromising they rose above narrow parochialism, greed and rituals, acted as guardians to the people and fearlessly defying even the king, they awakened amongst the Judeans a new moral zeal. The prophets of three centuries ending 600 B.C., Amos, Hosea, Isaiah, Micah, Zephaniah and Jeremiah, great geniuses, persecuted while alive, gave Hebrew religion a progressive thought combining a strict moral code with prevalent rituals; keeping conscience above law and became an example for successive generations, raising religion from its heathen depth to the height of spiritualism. It was this inspiration that enabled the Jewish nation to survive all onslaughts and stick to their faith, a phenomenon unseen in history. The Jews, a people who survived the destruction of their state, and in spite of persecution through ages, the Diaspora and pogroms, kept their spirit alive which refused to be extinguished. Not tied to any temple, city, sacra, or rituals they attained a religious solidarity which no power could destroy.

Then came the time of Jeremiah, when the temple was resurrected and Jerusalem rebuilt in spite of the hostility of Ammonites, Edmonites, and the surrounding Arabs. Encircled by the heathen there was a real possibility of dilution of the Jewish faith. But a zealous Babylonian scribe Ezra took charge and reinforced his people through immigrants from Babylon. Armed with royal authority from the Persian king he along with Jeremiah brought about a reformation and purified the faith. Despite doubts about Ezra's historicity, the purified reformation was an undeniable reality. The scribes, the forerunners of Pharisees, interpreted the law and became natural leaders in the

Synagogues. Centered round Torah and the Mosaic law, strict religious discipline was observed. Torah, preserved orally for generations, was scripted and the Jews gladly responded with complete devotion. Generalities of Torah were subjected to great details of interpretation, application and practice, leading to the foundation of Talmud. Devoid of orthodoxy and practicable in real life for later generations, the laws were humane. The useful principles of civil laws, later modified in Mishnah were an improvement over Biblical injunctions and religious practices whereby Sabbath became a day of useful rest. Some of the laws of Bible, such as prohibition on eating torn meat and washing the baby in the mother's milk, though based on sound principles of health, became embroiled in religious dialectics. Elaborate and difficult rituals regarding slaughter were evolved and prevention of drinking and eating meat at the same table became a taboo. Such narrow and stifling rituals set a reaction among free thinkers and the scribes had a hard time getting their way. The Allegory of Jonah of these times illustrates the points very well.

The central theme throughout was that in a special relationship with His Chosen people God wants the Jews to preach the gospel and improve the lot of the heathens as well, much beyond the boundaries of Palestine. Another example of protest is the Book of Ruth. Ruth was born of alien tribes and absorbed in the faith, and she begot heir to the throne of David and the Temple, thus negating the concept of exclusiveness. In Judaism, as in all religions, the dichotomy of revealed faith, a rigid law with its stifling and uncompromising adherence to the Book and the liberal, rational and inquiring religiosity of its adherents bound only by universal values, has been a permanent phenomenon The scribes adhered to the rituals and their own interpretations of the laws of the Lord, while other inquiring and liberal minds with equal attachment to their religion, fought for more freedom and less exclusivism. Yet the scribes performed a profound service to Judaism by giving coherence and a distinct identity to their religion, the greatest gift after Torah, and the prophecy for a Messiah that linked together Jews all over the world.

The Greeks

Judaism, that for a century after the building of the Temple consolidated itself under the Mosaic law and the rigidity of its religious rites, now faced a great onslaught of values and new gods after the conquest of Alexander and subsequent Hellenism. Their very rigidity gave them firm roots and the people survived the passing storm. From centuries of struggle for survival against the Greeks and later the Romans, though influenced by both, Judaism emerged distinct and militant even after the destruction of their Temple and the state. And then the Syrians took over the task of destroying Judaism. This was a time when the Book of Daniel was written to reassure the Jews that Judaism will survive all assaults as it had done in the past. And then came the Greeks with their capital at Antioch in Syria, led by Antiochus. His main contribution was to exacerbate the feelings of the Jews by imposing Greek culture and symbols on the people and trying to transform Jerusalem into a Greek metropolis. Feared and hated by the Hasidim, the Jewish reaction to his depredations was prompt. His persecution began in 169 B.C with a ban on the reading of Torah, a death sentence for a Jew observing the Sabbath or circumcising his children and forcing them to participate in pagan temple sacrifices and the abhorrent eating of pig's meat. He ordered the statue of Zeus to be established in the Holy of Holies, where the Ark of the Covenant reposed, "abomination which makes desolation" (Daniel 9:27). This continued persecution set the Jewish nation afire in the year 167 B.C., the spark being the sight of a Jew offering sacrifice on a pagan altar. Matthias Hasmon from the village of Modein took up the torch of rebellion and slew the Greek officer and the obedient Jew. He organised a small band of dedicated followers including his five sons and struck the first blow for freedom. Living hardly for two years, the torch was passed to the ablest of his five sons, Judas, nicknamed Maccabee, or the "Hammerer" so described for his military zeal. Judah continued the guerrilla revolt with fanatic zeal against Antiochus, now preoccupied in the east, and won four battles, crowning it all with a decisive victory at Emmanu pass, the gateway to Jerusalem, the same site where earlier Joshua had defeated the Amonites. He again won the battle of Mizpah. He with his brothers Jonathan and Simon, rallied the people against the Seleucids, and by 163 B.C. Judah, Samaria and the Galilee,were re-conquered and Jerusalem cleared of all Greek forces with the Temple finally cleansed of all abominations.

The struggle which began continued from the hills overlooking Lydda and ended by the consecration of the Temple in Jerusalem as the sacred candelabrum was lit. This was an epochal moment of religious and political significance prominently etched in the festival calendar of the Jews to be celebrated thereafter as 'Hanukkah', the Feast of Dedication. The territorial expansion of the Jewish state by the Hasmonean, dynasty which stretched' from the sea coast to TransJordan led to the consolidation of the new Jewish state by including Idumea, Samaria and Moab in TransJordan. Later his son Alexander Jannacus (103-76 B.C.) extended the Jewish kingdom to Gaza and Dor, equaling the size of the Jewish state to that under King David. Jerusalem also expanded five-fold and its population stood at 30,000. While the territorial expansion provided a degree of military security, the internal troubles and quarrels between Hellenizers and Hasidim persisted and did not end even after the successes of the Hasmonean leaders. A quarrel broke out between the Pharisees, the orthodox and purists, and the Sadducees, calling themselves the descendants of King David's chief priest, Zadok, all as a result of their differences in the theological interpretation of the Torah. With the passage of time, the conflict reduced itself to the opposition of Sadducees forming a pro-monarchy party with Hellenic influence against the Pharisees, who called themselves the teachers in Torah's academies. The quarrel between the two later took political colour after the death of Judas Maccabeus in 161 B.C. His succession by his brother, Jonathan, was followed by Simon, both claiming the title of high priest. This internecine turmoil led to what was perceived at the time as the usurpation of the royal title by John Hyrcanus in 135 B.C. Unsure of his Davidic lineage, and a king on purely political reasons, Hyrcanus, supported by the Hellenizers and opposed by the Pharisees, never won the confidence of his subjects. His despotic tendency further infuriated the Pharisees, as Israeli army was filled with the Greek mercenaries who owed no loyalty to the Jewish land. The puritanical Essenes also took offence to the tyrannical rule of the king, fled Jerusalem to the caves of Qumran near the Dead Sea, praying and fasting for the next two hundred years for the arrival of the Messiah until they were destroyed by the Romans in 68 B.C. In his fanatic zeal Alexander Jannacus who succeeded his father, Hyrcanus, while quelling the six-year old rebellion of the Pharisees, ordered 800 Pharisees to be executed and the throats of their wives and children slit open before their eyes. Merely 13 years after the death of king Jannacus, the Hasmonean state came to an end, the last ruler being Alexandra, the wife of Jannacus who ruled for nine years (76-67 B.C.). Cursed by her two incompetent sons, Hyrcanus II and Aristobulus II who fought a constant civil war of succession, the land of Judea opened the gates of Jerusalem to Roman forces in 63 B.C.

The Roman Invasions

History now meanders till we find the Romans come to power with Palestine as an outer province where the emperor appointed a pro-curator. Their policy towards Jewish religion was more tolerant and the Sanhedrin, the supreme judicial body of the Jews, was allowed to handle freely its domestic affairs and religious practices. But the taxes continued and so did the practice of leaving behind offensive Roman images. Some efforts at Romanising the Jews continued and later intensified by Pontious Pilate, not realising the backlash of such measures on the Jewish' religious mind, until a five-day siege by the priests and a general uprising in the whole nation forced him to yield ground. His diversion of Temple funds for secular use again infuriated the masses, and his cruelties and stringencies of taxes turned even the moderates into zealots, while public hangings created vengeance. Driven to desperation, the procurators became more barbarous. Slaughter, crucifixion of Jewish leaders, wholesale razing of villages fanned further frenzy when every Jew stood up to die mocking the Romans. The Romans were bewildered. Never before had they seen such national and religious frenzy. National rebellion broke out, ending only by the fall of Massada where three thousand Roman cavalry rushed to avenge the slaughter of Romans and protect the Roman fortresses. But they were disarmed and driven out by a people now fully aroused. Even the Roman soldiers in the fortresses were slaughtered to a man. The Pagan was to be wiped out. All the country was afire with reprisals against the rulers. A desperate people suddenly tasted revenge. Cestious Gullus, realising the gravity of the situation, ordered a force of twenty thousand cavalry and the same number of auxiliaries to crush and subdue Jerusalem. The siege lasted six months but the Jews held on and ultimately won, killing six thousand soldiers with Cestious retreating with haste and ignominy. There were no moderates left now in Palestine and the state was cleared of Romans.

Nero now sent Titus, one of his ablest generals, with fifty thousand men and immense war materials to finish the Jews once and for ever. Titus set about his task meticulously and gained successive victories till he came to the Holy City, the last remaining bastion of the Jewish state, now crammed with a million people with dissensions within. He used ballistas, slinging one hundred and twenty five pounds shots into the city and battering rams to force open the doors. We now take a few steps back in history. During the times of Hyrcanus II, the ethnarch of Judah, who was merely a titular head, the real power lay in the hands of a half-Jewish, Rome appointed Governor named Antipater. He was succeeded by his son, Herod, the most controversial figure in Jewish history. He served his Roman masters well, kept influential leaders in good humour with lavish presents, and in real Graeco-Roman style constructed gymnasia, pagan temples, amphitheaters, hyppodromes and baths. A new deep water harbour at the site of old Straton's tower was constructed and renamed Caesarea to propitiate Augustus. Herod also built massive fortresses to protect Judah from all sides, including the north-western approach to the Temple Mount, the last being named Antonia after Marc Antony, his benefactor. The gifts and constructions needed money and Herod enforced a strict system of tax collection leading to numerous plots of unsuccessful rebellions. He kept his spies alert to report on any sign of discontent. His important fortresses were Herodion near Bethlehem and Massada a highly emotive name in Jewish history, overlooking the Dead Sea. A tyrant, a murderer, a Hellenizer and an instrument of Roman repression against the Jews, he also introduced some pro-Jewish policies to gain acceptance from the population at large. He seldom interfered in Jewish ritual practices and to put a stamp on his Jewish origin he married Mariamne, the grand-daughter of Hyrcanus II; though eventually he had her killed. Antipater and his son Herod ruled Judah from 40 B.C. onwards while Herod became the king in 37 B.C. and died in 4 B.C. after a reign of 33 years.

While on the one hand he insisted circumcision of any prince marrying into the Herodian family, on the other he encouraged scriptural study of the Pharisees, the scholars of Torah. He won the support of the Sadducees by ordering the reconstruction of Jerusalem's Temple by the priests themselves which starting in 20 BC was completed in 64 A.D., 68 years after his death and only six years before its destruction in war. Herod, the last great king of Judah described by some as strong and statesman like, who brought prosperity, was never liked by the hardcore of Zealots for his half Jewish and half Idumean breed. "The blood of Edon flowed through his veins" goes a saying. Hated by the Jews, he earned the dubious epitaph "He stole along to the throne like a fox, he ruled like a tiger and he died like a dog". With the ascension to the throne of his son Archelous, with Roman blessing, the kingdom of the Jews came to an end. As mentioned earlier the fortress of Massada was the key to the capture of Jerusalem. It was here that a desperate fight took place between the Jews and the Romans. The fortress occupied by the Jews held out against all odds due to the tenacity of the Jews who fought till the last man was slaughtered. This episode is chronicled in the history of Jews in golden letters and acts as an exhortation to the Jews to revenge past defeats. Even now in every Jewth home a common prayer goes "Massada shall be avenged". The battle for Jerusalem continued.

Dying by the thousands, starving and sick, the Jews held out and brushed aside every demand for surrender. Ultimately, after six days all the three walls broke and the Romans rushed in, and a killing spree began. With weapons or bare hands every Jew fought till death. The remaining few withdrew into the Temple and continued resistance. In spite of a restraint order by Titus on the Temple, the angry Roman soldiers set it to fire and butchered all Jews within. However, the district of Herod stood intact and fighting continued for one more month, before the defenders were all cut to pieces. Thousands of survivors were sent in to captivity and the most valiant Simon bar Giora was hurled from the Tarpein rock to customarily propitiate the Roman Gods. Titus struck coins to celebrate Roman holiday and his victory with an inscription "Judaea Devicta" or "Judaea Capita". The Torah was taken to the palace of the emperor, and a victory arch erected, that survives to this day to commemorate not the Romans but the heroic Jews who outlived their conquerors.

Then passed four centuries of Roman rule after Pompey's capture of Jerusalem with all its cruelty and cussedness while the Jews continued to wait for the advent of the Kingdom of God and rise of the Messiah. There were pretenders for this coveted role till Jesus finally came. With a voluminous corpus of theological quibblings and the circumstances of his birth and the miracles attributed to him, it is well nigh impossible to establish the historicity of Jesus. Nevertheless, in the name of this Prince of Peace and Son of God the zealots of Christianity perpetrated every conceivable outrage on the cursed race that begot him; the cross bearing crusaders, plundering their homes, destroying their properties and ravishing their women. In Spain Torquemada burnt, and pillaged, and drove 200,000 peaceful Jews out of their homes to exile. So also, Russian Tzar solved the Jewish problem by baptizing, expelling and destroying the Jews and compelled them to live in filthy ghettos. Forced to wear degrading badges, robbed of the right of existence as human beings, right to work and play, despised and spat upon all under the name of the Savior, these miserable people had little reason to like the Son of God. This tale is told in Toldos Yeshu, the Jewish book chronicling these perversions of Christian bigotry during the middle ages.

An effective effort is afoot now both by liberal Jews and Christians to learn the truth about the prophet, the doctrinal content of the Gospels and the Acts and the meaning and message of Jesus, the Jew converted into Christianity long after his death. The early life of Jesus is shrouded in obscurity. Except for canonical Gospels, no authentic records exist either in the Hebrew lore nor Roman records, except for Tacitus and Suetonius who mention the word "Christo" attributed to his crucifixion. Jesus did not write nor did his disciples, who were entrusted to spread his message. It was only after his death when the need arose to teach the gospel to new Christians and spread it worldwide, that the first accounts were compiled, leading to the development of the Gospel of Mark, Matthew, Luke, and John from 65 A.D. to the beginning of the second century A.D. Mathew was originally a Jew, bitterly critical of those who rejected the Messiahanic claim of Jesus. The sources reveal little while concealing a lot, and the synoptic problems have not yet been solved in the absence of authentic material. For paucity of facts the treatment of Jesus remains essentially subjective. However, certain facts about Jesus and Christianity are so well chronicled that it will be futile to dwell on these. What is proposed to be done is to shed some new light on some relatively less known facts in this literature.

Section 2: Jesus and Thereafter

Born around 4 B.C. of humble parents in Bethlehem, a part of Galilee, his paternal origin through Joseph goes to the royal stock of David. The concept of virgin birth was developed much later after his death. Deprived of the rigid Jewish training of the Pharisees, he still loved Biblical heroes, the psalms and the message of the prophets. The myth of Pontius Pilate's unwillingness to punish Jesus to save a "just man being persecuted through his righteousness" is a creation of late 1st century A.D. aimed at enlarging the base of Christianity through the goodwill of gentiles rather than the Jews. To implicate the enlarged Roman empire in the execution was impolitic, since the new faith could not antagonise the mightiest empire yet known. Pilate unconcerned with the blasphemy charge executed Jesus as a Roman rebel due to his Messianic claims. The Romans were experts in the art of torture, and crucifixion was a natural consequence at Golgotha, outside Jerusalem where Jesus died carrying the derisive words "The King of Jews" scratched on his forehead. Even in his agony, he cried out in the words of the Psalms, he so loved:" My God, my God, why hast Thou forsaken me." The martyred Prophet lived and died a Jew not wishing to desert his people. He endeavoured to enrich them spiritually and not chart out a new religion inimical to his own inherited one. He once remarked "I was not sent except to bring back the lost sheep of the house of Israel." After his death as the belief in his Messianic powers grew amongst the humble folk, the Jew in Jesus was forgotten, and affected by the Graeco-Roman culture, a new faith grew up subordinating the Mosaic law. Stripped of his humanity, and adorned by imagined miracles, Jesus became a divine figure while Christianity strode out to conquer the world. Since there is much controversy about the sin of the Jews against the Christians, earning them the dubious sobriquet of " the suckers of Christian blood and Crucifiers of Jesus," we shall revert to certain facts of recorded history.

As Jesus grew up, he became aware of the brutality of the Romans in the persecution of the Jews. He had known about the apocalyptic literature regarding the Messiah, but he never dreamt of a Jewish state completely free from worldly oppression, till John, the Baptist, the fiery Hebrew prophet turned Christian, inspired him to a different path. His sharp tongue and intolerance of moral lapses reached far and wide, and he sincerely believed that he was destined to pave the way for the future Messiah. With his magnetic personality and appeal to the masses, people flocked to him for Bapitization. Starting from Judaea, his influence spread far beyond Galilee. He was to change the course of history and civilization by his preparation for the arrival of Christ as the much awaited Messiah. Jesus imbibed much of John's single-minded pursuit of his goal but his method was milder. His shining personality, simplicity of preaching with charm and conviction, his humility and tenderness drew large crowds. Gifted with a lucid tongue, and vivid imagination his parables spread far and wide and his message spread from mouth to mouth even though some what exaggerated. What Jesus said did not in the least clash with the Jewish thought, even that of the Pharisees. He preached in the synagogues but emphasized seeking of a new God devoid of many pretentions of the orthodox. Though liberalism was not new to the Jews, his message was simpler and different from the early ones.

He healed the sick on the sabbath-day, mixed with the sinners and the publicans and made them repent for the sins, something unusual in the Jewish lore, but not enough to infuriate tradition, or repudiate Judaism. The criticism of Jesus as mentioned earlier, was aimed at the fanatics. However, later as the division between Christians and Jews grew, the new Christians spew venom and hatred against the Jews with a self-righteousness denounced by Jesus himself. They revolted against the Jewish faith which they felt difficult to supplant. Unwittingly Jesus also rubbed another raw nerve of the Jews, when he proclaimed his gospel emanated from himself and was not the message of the Lord. All his teachings are full of pronouncements like," But I say unto you...". Thus Jesus replaced God himself and slowly he was convinced that he himself was the long-awaited Messiah in the form of God's proclaimed son and his task was to prepare the people for the Kingdom of Heaven.

Jesus deliberately journeyed to Jerusalem during Passover time almost alone with a very few disciples and rode in the Holy City on the back of an ass, in keeping with the Messianic tradition. Thus embellished his great entry was celebrated by shouts of "Hosannah". Now Jesus came into his own and criticised almost everything that the Jews and the priests stood for. He called the scribes and Pharisees hypocrites and cursed them. He even physically got removed the money and the vendors out of the premises of the temple. The act though well-meant, the priests and the Levites were outraged by the violence. He alarmed the Sadducee high priest who kept the peace of the community.

Fearing violence Pontius Pilate, the Roman Procurator, brought additional troops to keep peace in anticipation of the Barabbas rebellion. For the Jews it was only reviving old memories of slaughter and they insisted that Jesus, the disturber of peace, must be restrained or removed. Thus by his guileless talks on the Pharisees, Jesus forced them into an uncompromising position, and the rest is history. The method of betrayal by Judas, arrest of Jesus and the role of Sanhedrin, the highest body of the Jews, and Roman governor is still full of controversy.

To quote Thomas A. Idinopulos in his book *Jerusalem Blessed, Jerusalem Cursed* :

> "In Jesus' day the Temple was not only the central religious shrine, it was also the major industrial and banking facility of the nation. It received the annual Temple tax payed by Jews throughout the world. Great sums of money were deposited at the Temple by wealthy families and by the hundreds of elderly Jews who had come to retire in the Holy City. The daily sale of sacrificial animals was routinely conducted in the Temple area. At the Passover, with the city's population bloated by pilgrims from its normal 25,000 to as many as 125,000, one can imagine the congestion of pilgrims, priests, beasts, blood, and money. Conduit's carried blood drained from the sacrificed animals down the southern side of the Temple into the Kidron Valley, where it was used as fertilizer for vegetable gardens. The Temple itself gleamed from the sheer amount of gold, marble, and bronze used in its construction. And outside the walls of the Temple were artisan shops of gold and silver, and other shops of incense and shewbread catering directly to Temple needs. One need not have had so lofty a view of religion as Jesus to have found himself nauseated by such sights in a city whose ritual purity was promptly restored at sunrise each morning by an army of street cleaners."

And further,

> " It was Jesus' preaching of the coming kingdom at the Temple that drew the adverse reaction of Temple officials,

who may have warned Roman police authorities about him. Messianic preaching at the Temple site during the Passover would have been interpreted as an incitement to revolt. Jewish Temple officials guarded against nationalistic expressions, particularly at festival time, lest the permanently stationed Roman garrison act against people and priests alike. Possibly Jerusalem's Jewish leaders had heard of the troubles Jesus had encountered in the Galilee with the Pharisees and officials of Herod Antipas." A source thus describes the last supper:

"The eve of the Passover Festival approached. It was marked then, as it is to this day by Jews all over the world, by a ritual meal called the 'Seder' when the story of the exodus from Egypt is recited and certain foods are taken which symbolise the dramatic events of that liberation. The bread eaten (matzah) is unleavened—to symbolise the haste of the Israelite departure so that there was no time for the dough to rise; the tasting of bitter herbs is a reminder of the harsh life and labour suffered by the Israelite slaves; a shank bone represents the slaughtered paschal lamb whose blood was sprinkled on the doorposts of Israelite dwellings just before the exodus so that the angel of death would 'pass over' them when he went to slay the Egyptian first-born. Four glasses of ritual wine are drunk during the recital. Such was the Passover meal celebrated by the Jew, Jesus, and his disciples, the meal that was to be known very much later, with the rise of Christianity as The Last Supper, and out of which was to grow the ritual of the Mass."

And the narrative goes on:

"In any event, Jesus was arrested for committing a civil offense of sedition, and was subsequently executed ; a common punishment for this offense according to Roman practice by crucifixion. He was not the first nor the last Jew to be so arrested and executed. The tragedy of Jesus' death is that he seems to have underestimated the effect of his messianic preaching in Jerusalem at the Passover. He expected to be heard. He did not expect to be arrested, and he did not intend to die. The story of Jesus' sorrow at Gethsemene ('Abba, Father, all things are possible, to thee; remove this cup from me...') and the final words attributed to him on the cross ('My God, my God, why hast thou forsaken me?')—these expressions of human vulnerability suggest a man who went to Jerusalem in the same idealistic and innocent spirit that guided his ministry in the Galilee. In that respect it was understandable for the Gospel writer Matthew, in denouncing Jerusalem for the crime of executing Christ, to put into Jesus' mouth words of condemnation: 'O Jerusalem, Jerusalem, killing the prophets and stoning those who are sent you!" (Luke 13:34)."

And further:

"If the arrest and execution were essentially political, what are we to make of the two dramatic scenes in which Jesus is interrogated about his messianic claim by Jerusalem's high priest Caiaphas, and later by the Roman procurator Pontius Pilate? The first thing to be said is that it is doubtful that either event, certainly in the form presented, ever took place. Both scenes were shaped by later Christian attitudes at a time when it was in the interest of the church to shift blame for Jesus' death from the Roman state authority to Jewish religious leadership."

"According to Mark, it is the charge of blasphemy which prompts Jewish officials to turn Jesus over to Roman authorities. But if it is unlikely that Jesus ever appeared before a Jewish court (Sanhedrin) in Jerusalem, it is equally unlikely that he was ever charged with blasphemy. The technical Jewish charge of blasphemy was directed not against a claim of messiahship but rather for using the sacred, unutterable name of God, the tetragram YHWH (Yahweh). Nowhere in the Gospel is Jesus depicted as so blaspheming."

" The point of the scene in which Pilate interrogates Jesus about his messiahship is to absolve Pilate of direct responsiblities for Jesus' execution by the device of allowing a Jewish mob to make the decision."

"And Pilate again said to them,' Then what shall I do with the man whom you call the King of the Jews?' And they cried out again,' Crucify him'. And Pilate said to them,' Why, what evil has he done?' But they shouted all the more,' Crucify him.' So Pilate, wishing to satisfy the crowd, released for them Barabbas: and having scourged Jesus, he delivered him to be crucified."

"If there is a kernel of historical truth in this scene, it lies in the reference to Barabbas, who supposedly belonged to the anti-Roman revolutionary party of the Sicarii. If so, it is conceivable that Jesus was arrested in a police roundup of any number of persons taken to be political agitators."

"The belief in Jesus' resurrection took shape among the disciples soon after his death. They were convinced of the miraculous powers of God who in the messianic era would judge the wicked and rouse the righteous from their graves. The Pharisees held strongly to a belief in the resurrection, sharply disagreeing with the Sadduceean Temple priests who rejected it. Jesus believed in physical resurrection. And the disciples, convinced that Jesus was the messianic agent of God's redemption, could not accept his death as anything more than a prelude to his resurrection and second coming. With this attitude Mark, at the conclusion of his Gospel, provided reports of the apparitions of Jesus which appeared to the disciples after the discovery of the empty tomb."

And finally:

"Upon the death of Jesus, the disciples, fearing arrest and a fate similar to their leader, now branded a criminal, fled Jerusalem. Undoubtedly they were disappointed that Jesus' prophecy of the coming kingdom had not immediately been fulfilled, and that the prophet himself had come to an ignominious end. We cannot be certain what made them overcome disappointment and return to Jerusalem to preach the message of Jesus' lordship and the coming kingdom. The magnetism of his personality, the authority of his teachings, the wonder of his healing, his personal courage in the face of opposition—all these must have played a role in keeping the memory of Jesus alive in their minds."

" To the disciples, the Resurrection meant that the condemnation of Jesus by his fellow Jews and his death by crucifixion were not a human defeat but a divine revelation, stages in the fulfillment of God's plan to judge and forgive human sins through the suffering and death of his chosen son. As Saint Paul was later to preach to the gentile community of Antioch: "For those who live in Jerusalem and their rulers, because they did not recognize him nor understand the utterances of the prophets which are read every Sabbath, fulfilled these by condemning him."

It is an irony of history that Jesus born a Jew and died as one, should have caused the birth of a religion which perpetrated the maximum attrocities on its mother religion. There are many commonly, forgotten facets of the life of Jesus which had put the fringe fanatics of the Pharisees against him. Jesus was inspired by a radical and Messianic zeal to reform Judaism, which inevitably created enemies around. The temple priests had their vested interest in collecting taxes from the visitors to the temple and charged usurious prices on the sale of animals meant for slaughter and sacrifice. This priestly class got so much enmeshed in the rituals, outdated customs and minutiae of worship that any improvement suggested seemed to them a challenge to their authority and worldly interests. Jesus' teachings were simple and rational. He spoke vehemently about the abolition of such rites and levy of taxes. He also challenged certain rigidities and distortions which had crept in the Jewish religion. This enraged the Jews whose only asset and driving force during the centuries of oppression and persecution was a rigid adherence to the Mosaic laws, the Torah and the Talmud. It was but natural for this section of Jewry to view with suspicion this new upstart claiming to be the son of God. Jesus contributed to the confusion by not giving a categorical answer to the question often thrown at him whether he was the son of God or the Messiah prophesised by Isiah the last of the Jewish prophets.

While upbraiding the Jews he adopted a soft attitude towards the Roman governors, and exhorted them to pay taxes to Rome through his famous dictum" Give unto Caesar what belongs to Caesar". Thus he did cause a confusion by equating temporal power with that of God and His Kingdom. He also enjoined the Jews to accept the Roman Emperor as their worldly head. While he distinguished the temporal from the spiritual, to the Jews the life on earth and hereafter was their Lord's command. It accepted no temporal authority but Yahweh, and non-payment of taxes to the Roman pagans and refusal to worship their idols was a natural corollary. Thus possibly unintentionally, Jesus allowed the perpetuation of the Roman supremacy on earth while talking of a Kingdom of Heaven. It was totally against the faith of the Jews. Even the circumstance of the death of Jesus is shrouded in mystery. It was not the Jews in general but only the fanatic fringe who protested against the heresy of Jesus, whom they considered as much of an enemy as the Romans at whose hands they had suffered for the last four centuries.. His trial on heresy, as is commonly believed, was demanded not by the Jews as such but these fringe fanatics of the Pharisees. This dissension between the Jewery and the followers of Christ suited the Romans eminently, since to them a growing Christianity posed a greater threat than the small band of Jews accustomed to subjugation and oppression. Thus the crucifixion blame does not lie alone with the Jews in general and even the Pharisees in particular, but was connived at by the Romans keeping in mind their long term interests. This was to be proved later when the Christians suffered the same persecution as the Jews had suffered earlier, and were burnt at the stakes and thrown to the wild animals in the Roman amphitheatres.

We shall now rejoin the mainstream of history and pick up the threads of the narrative of the fortune of the Jews in medieval Europe. The Jews enjoyed a comparative era of peace and opportunity for professional development at par with their Christian friends in French and German cities. On the other hand the comparative peace allowed the flowering of Talmudic studies and development of Jewish thought by Gershom of

Mayence, the learned Jew, popularly known as the" Light of the Exile". After the death of Gershom in 1040 A.D. another Jewish scholar Rabbi Solomon ben Isaac, later known as Rashi, furthered the cause of Biblical and Talmudic studies with his commentaries and achieved great intellectual heights. But the age of Gershom and Rashi was short-lived and another period of oppression was in waiting. In France, Philip Augustus refined the art of Jewish oppression during the 3rd crusade and expelled all Jews from his dominions around Paris, though Richard, the Lion-Hearted, the gallant king and co-crusader with Philip, showed some compassion towards the Jews.

But as soon as he crossed the Channel, five hundred Jews of York were besieged in a castle and starved to the point where they took their own lives. Then came the age of Magna Carta, the enlightened Frederick II, the gentile St. Francis and the vigorous St. Dominic, with Dante's immortal literary work and philosophical works of Aquinas. But for the Jews this period meant further intensification of the torments, which had started in the 11th and 12th centuries. Degraded in body and spirit, they were forced to wear a shameful badge and witnessed the public destruction of their sacred books. Stripped of self respect, degraded in mind and spirit they truely represented Byron's famous lines: "The wild-dove hath her nest, the fox his cave, Mankind their country - Israel but the grave!"

The next century opened with Pope Innocent III, young eloquent in speech, sublime in thought, a great statesman and a fitting successor to Emperor Constantine.

Aiming at Christian unity, he excelled in his zeal for purification of Jews by conversion, if possible, and threatened excommunication and penalties otherwise. An inspired fanatic he saw his duties in the persecution of error which was translated through his 'Constitutio Judaecorum' and which indirectly meant conversion of Jews. In spite of his 'Constitutio Judaecorum', prohibiting attack on Jews or conversion by force, the oppression of Jews continued. He always considered Jews to be, a lower form of human being. Later on, however, he changed and summed up his policy.

> "The Jews, like the fratricide Cain, are doomed to wander about the earth as fugitives and vagabonds, and their faces must be covered in shame. They are under no circumstances to be protected by Christian princes, on the contrary, to be condemned to serfdom."

Thus began the tale of 400 years of Jewish persecution. Hounded by all crusaders, disenfranchised by the Church Councils, accused of ritual, murder and blasphemy, persecuted by Jew-baiters, as the cause of Black Death, the Hussite war and Capistrano the Jew became a poor, homeless broken man. The death penalty and other horrors forced a large number of Jews to conversion into Christianity. This has an echo in the Indian history during the Moslem conquest when countless Hindus were converted to Islam or slaughtered. This revolted the conscience of Martin Luther, who exclaimed:

> "Our fools, the popes, bishops, sophists, and monks, have hitherto conducted themselves towards the Jews in such a manner that he who was a good Christian would have preferred to be a Jew. And if I had been a Jew and had seen such block-heads and louts ruling and teaching Christianity, I would have become a swine rather than a Christian, because they have treated the Jews like dogs, and not like human beings."

While all this was happening in Europe, Spain, where the Jews had earlier enjoyed comparative peace, also turned against them. In the later half of 14th century, the persecution commenced. On Ash Wednesday of 1391 at Seville the Jewish quarters were burnt down, and an orgy of bloodshed led to the butchery of several thousands Jews, baptism of those who had escaped death, while the rest were sold as slaves to Moors. In Cordoba once the proudest city of Jews 2000 were slaughtered and left in heaps in the streets. Toledo the largest centre of Jews in Spain was ravaged on the ninth of Ab, the anniversary of Jerusalem's downfall. Seventy cities of Old Castile were destroyed leaving broken homes and broken hearts; the land from Castile to Aragon, the province of Valencia and the sea-port of Barcelona meeting the same fate. After three months of this blood-letting thousands of Jews lost their lives and tens of thousands converted to Christianity. In comparison Germany and Austria seemed to be a distant paradise. While the ferocity of the Christian zealots can be understood, what was more baffling was even the greater crimes perpetrated by the converted Jews, a leading light of whom was Paul, a brilliant Talmudic scholar, freshly converted to Christianity. This is again reminiscent of similar action by converted Hindus perpetrated on their own Hindu brethren during the Moslem period. Paul's zeal to bring the Jews to Christian fellowship was unrivalled He wrote, debated, exploited and persuaded non-Christians to turn to the purity of his new creed. He led his hooligans into the synagogues, to spread his gospels of love and brotherhood. Cross in one hand and the Torah in the other, he told the Jews to convert and achieve salvation. This led to a large exodus from Judaism to Christianity in which 35,000 Jewish souls were rescued and the people of the book, forced beyond endurance, lost all self-respect.

Contrary to the prevalent theory that persecution and hardship steel a people and bring forth vitality and a tensile strength hitherto unknown, the same did not happen to the Jews. During the medieval ages already referred to above, the Jews just managed to survive without exhibiting excellence in any field of human endeavour. This phenomenon has a striking similarity with the utter degradation of the Hindu society under perpetual foreign invasions starting from 1000 A.D. down to the entire span of the British Empire. With a few happy exceptions, such as showing the gems of Bible to the humanists amongst the gentiles, and serving as a bridge between Christian and Semitic culture, little can be attributed to Jews. They lost their vigour, resilience of mind and power of judgement. In such a spiritual darkness imposters and charlatans took over promising a way out; some even claiming to be the Messiah sent by God, to usher a new world order.

Mysticism has always been a permanent feature of the Jewish philosophical and religious thought. This continued during the dark medieval ages. The search to define God without limiting Him, as it is with the Sanatan Dharma of Hindus, reinforced through their unhappy temporal experiences brought out the Cabalists who tried to reinvigorate the Jewish religion. The Book of Creation written in Hebrew language is one such effort which had a great influence in the development of the Jewish mind during these harsh times. Thus continued the inexorable march of time till we reach the age of Baruch Spinoza, whom Renan described as the greatest Jew of modern times. Born in Amsterdam in 1632, of parents exiled from Portugal, he along with his basic Jewish education had a keen interest in every type of human learning. Delving deep into the works of Ibn Ezra, Hasdai Crescas, Maimonides, and other Jewish philosophers, he was greatly influenced by the mellow wisdom of Van den Ende, martyred for his radical thoughts. Devoted alike to the natural sciences and the logic of Descartes, he also imbibed the thoughts of philosopher Bruno and his defiance of the Church. On his rationalism, he rose above superstition and gradually became a non-conformist to Talmudic Judaism. His radical views challenging the tenets of Bible, the notions about God and denial of immortality alarmed the Jews and the Christians alike. Fearing the spread of such blasphemies the Jews pleaded with Spinoza to be more discreet, and even threatened him with ex-communication. One thing led to another and ultimately Spinoza was exiled. Happy in his isolation, he was offered a post in the University of Heidelberg with a total freedom to think and write. His efforts were not recognised in his lifetime by the hardcore Jews, but ultimately, they resulted in enriching and liberalising Jewish religion and philosophy. He died in 1677, forty-four of age, a frail frustrated man but he contributed in the largest measure to the Jewish culture and thought, which was resurrected by later generations. A monument was raised in his memory at The Hague in 1882.

The three centuries following the Jewish expulsion from Spain, are marked by a constant decline in the spiritual and mental fibre of the Jewish race. A people groping in the dark believing in fanatics and imposters, who masqueraded as Messiahs, they narrowed their spiritual horizon and cocooned themselves in the rigidities of their code. Much to the glee of the persecuting

Christians the 18th century Jewery was a bent, broken, superstitious and ignorant mass.

At the dawn of modern history in the eighteenth century, the Jews were dispersed to almost all corners of the globe. Of the three million Jews at that time of history who survived the epidemics and the harsh economic restrictions of the medieval times a large portion remained static, confined to limited areas and specific occupations, forced by the societies. A large portion of this population driven by the atrocities of the crusades in Western Europe, moved to East, of which Poland alone accounted for more than one and a half million. After the partition of Poland, the hapless Jews came under the despoiling powers of Russia, Prussia and Austria. A few remained in Romania and some under the Turkish rule, amounting to about 100,000, mainly in Constantinople. A few refugees from Spain also moved out to Egypt, carrying with them their Sephardic way of life. The centre of Jewish repression, however, remained the heart of Western Europe around German Austria. Here the Jewish population was confined to the largest cities of Berlin, Hamburg, Frankfurt and Main, squeezed between the two grinding wheels of the Catholics and the Protestants. Smaller communities of these also existed in England, France, Italy and Holland. The twenty-two thousand Jews living in Amsterdam took up the diamond and precious stones industries and did reasonably well as importers and exporters. The Jewish population in America was negligible and the Marranos in the Spanish colonies could not evade the inquisition. A few Jews also were scattered in Africa and inner Asia. Those settled in Abyssinia called Falashas, an ancient community living by pure Mosaism, were proud to trace their descent from the Menelek, the son of Queen of Sheba and King Solomon. The Jewish dispersion extended even to the Great Wall of China.

A unique feature of the Middle Ages is the development of the ghetto and its consequences. Shunned by the societies in general, cut off from political, social and intellectual life, deprived of citizenship, the Jews were forced to live in isolated societies away from the gentiles. The papal bulls handed out punishments to those who dared put the Jews in positions of trust. The Municipal councils also insisted that the Jews wear a distinguishing badge, while the Church barely tolerated them, keeping them away from the Christians to keep their faith pure. But for some exceptions, such as the friendship between the Hebrew poet Immanuel of Rome and the great Dante and the influence that the Jewish writings had on some famous Christians such as on Albertus Magnus from Maimonides's thoughts, the divide between the Christians and the Jews was complete. Even Albertus with all his respect for Maimonides did not raise a finger at the burning of the Talmud, and Pico saw no harm in the Jews being driven away from Spain.

Ghetto was a clearly marked area in a city beyond which the Jews were not to venture. While this completely alienated the Jews from the society at large, it had some advantages too, such as collective living, the feeling of security and a spirit of solidarity within the helpless victims enclosed in these cages. Sixteenth century may well be called the Ghetto age. These enclosed communities festered with illness, and unhygienic conditions, devastated by fires, congested and swelling to capacities, full of graveyards, in different stages of degradation showed every facet of Jewish declension almost amounting to struggle for death. The Ghetto was a symbol of the worst in papal bigotry. Some ghettos in Frankfurt and Main and Prague set the typical examples, though the latter was less fouling and more liberated, forming a township of its own for the Jews. No medieval institution led to a greater degeneration of Jews, divorcing them from nature, society and aesthetics. This encysting of the Jews led to more prejudice among the Christians against them, magnifying the horrors of their rituals in fusty places hidden from public eyes. Being thus insulated, the Jews were hardly expected to develop a sense of patriotism to the country they lived in. Left to their own devices, the Jews developed their own languages, such as Yiddish, a cross between Hebrew and other East European languages, while in the Sephardic communities a language called the Ladino, a corrupted Spanish-Hebrew was the spoken dialect. The worst part of the Ghetto psyche was the loss of self-respect among the Jews. This segregation finally led to the spirit of the" worthless worm that never dies". There emerged in the community an esprit de corps, defying death. The home with its high moral values became a fortress against time and adversity. Folk-life and folk-ways developed within the Jewish consciousness an unconquerable spirit, so virile that these people separated from their land and denied a place under the sun, stood stead-fast for centuries to come.

The Jews were treated as a separate and inferior class, in all countries. In Germany there were special state legislations for the Jews. This, however, did not cow them down and they developed their own organisations, educational systems, a code of laws, and law courts and even separate prisons. The distinctive locations of the ghettos made it easy for the state to collect taxes from the Jews, such as poll-tax, communal tax, special tax and protection tax. In Spain there was even a hearth tax and a tax for the king's dinner, while in France there was a coronation tax too, and in England heavy tax was levied on the renewal of charters. There were also taxes to build and to demolish, taxes for self-conduct, participation in fairs, tax for even acquiring the ground to bury the dead and to top it all, the tax for the burial. Thus there were taxes for all things in heaven, earth and the waters of the sea. In England, before their expulsion, the taxes from the Jews amounted to one twelfth of the national income. In other countries, the proportion was even higher.

Thus hemmed in from all sides, the Jews met in synods to discuss their affairs while each community usually had its "Bet Din", a court presided over by a rabbi. To keep the fold together this court had jurisdiction in all cases involving the Jews and even meted out physical punishments; some times even excommunication, whose milder form was the 'niddiu'. Montesquieu, one of the outstanding political philosophers of the eighteenth century, blasted Christianity in Europe for its hatred of the Jews in the following words: "If any of our descendants should ever venture to say that the nations of Europe were cultured, your example will be adduced to prove that they were barbarians." Another shining example of a fighter for the

Jewish rights was Mirabeau, the most powerful statesman and orator of France on the eve of the Revolution. A friend to several Jews of intellect he was particularly fond of Mendelssohn, and a frequent visitor to the Jewish salons. His booming eloquence forced the Revolutionary National Assembly to advocate the complete political equality for the Jews. However, such events were merely a flicker of light in the all pervading darkness of Christian Europe. The prejudices against the Jews were high. The Christian children were brought up from their birth, in the belief that the Jews were moral-lepers, outcasts and deemed to damnation due to their unforgiveable crime at the crucifixion of Jesus 2000 years ago. Egged on relentlessly by the fanatical priests the Christian laity had no inclination to abandon this belief. In England, the situation brightened a little due to the liberalist Walpole who noticed that the Jews were naturalised in the American colonies and advocated a policy of" let sleeping dogs lie". Consequently in 1753 Prime Minister Pelham introduced a Naturalization law which was passed by both the Houses of Parliament. However, the stiff resistance and mob fury by the Christians forced Pelham to withdraw this legislation in 1754. Things were no different in Central Europe where mob hysteria against the Jews overtook the town of Alsace where fourth-fifths of the French Jewish population lived. In Prussia anti-Jewish literature appeared and further fanned the misgivings about Jews, spreading the canard that "in order to limit their increase, the second male child of each Jew should be castrated."

Even Frederick the Great of Prussia, known for his liberal views and tolerance of the Jews, followed this pattern of Jew bashing. His *General Privilege* written in 1750 echoed the medieval spirit of intolerance. The king with all his virtues swam with the anti-Jew tide. Even a more astonishing example is that of Voltaire, a man of great learning, a crusader against the prevalent abuses and superstitions, the defender of the weak, who while denouncing the bigots, reserved his biting pen and tongue, to pillory the Jews as a greedy and selfish race, whose only ideals were more money and more children. It was a hopeless situation. Even the great Goethe with all his profound thoughts and works looked upon the Jews with a jaundiced eye. He is quoted to have said: "The only way I see by which civil rights can be conceded to them is to cut off all their heads in one night and to set new ones on their shoulders, which should contain not a single Jewish idea. The only means of protecting ourselves against them is to conquer their promised land and send them there." Herder, another great philosopher, followed in the footsteps of Goethe.

The French Revolution was the first silver lining for the Jews in this anti-Jewish world. By granting them political emancipation, it was the almost impossible Jewish dream fulfilled, when for the first time in 1000 years they became the citizens of the states where they lived. The economic conditions changed completely and opened vistas of opportunities for the persecuted people. However, it took some more time for the theory to become a practice when the Jews could wield more economic power. There were flips and flops in the Jewish fortunes in these turbulent days of French Revolution when it was commonly believed, that no riot is ever complete which does not involve the Jews. As France emerged from the revolutionary turmoil, with the Declaration of the Rights of Man, one of the noblest document in history, Jews were afforded equality before the law. The practicality of this proposition, however, took some time, as Mirabeau, Abbe Gregoire, Robespierre and others championed the Jewish case for equality. Things now moved faster when late in January 1790, the Portuguese and Avignonese Jews of southern France received full citizenship, followed by similar privileges all over France. The Jews were no longer aliens. The Jews in turn reciprocated with great fervor by their devotion to the State and "la patrie". They enlisted in the armed forces and even sold candelabra of synagogues to contribute to the war fund.

With rapid industrialization and mass production of goods manufacturers became the kingpins of the market. The industrialization ushered a levelling process between communities; enterprise, profit and quick turnover became the key-words. Individuals with capital and a spirit of enterprise came to the forefront and the Jews' industrial talents, capacity for hard work and possession of capital put them in the forefront of economic activities and power. Gradually industrial power replaced the landed aristocracy. The Jews broke through the old feudal restrictions and with the expansion of capitalism old prejudices gradually faded away, bestowing political equality on the Jews. Noted among the great Jewish entrepreneurs were the Rothschilds, the House of Shammai and the House of Hillel. Snide remarks were often heard that a small Jewish clique was controlling the International finance and dominated the class of capitalists and bankers. This financial clout bestowed political powers to the Jews as they rose up in the social ladder. These financial giants were no selfish preachers but they did their best to improve the lot of the remaining Jews the world over. The Montefiores, the Goldsmids, the Salomons in England, the Pereires in France, the Bischoffsheims in Germany and the Rothschilds everywhere in Europe, contributed actively and decisively towards the emancipation of the Jews all over the world. Rothschild, in particular, became the jewel in the crown of his race as he obtained a seat in the Parliament leading to a remark by Lord Macaulay," How was it possible to deny a Rothschild a seat on the grounds of his race when his signatures on the back of a piece of paper was worth more than the royal word of three kings!" Towards the end of 19th century the great Jewish middle class came into being, and the enormous Jewish enterprise, abandoning its old degraded means of livelihood, occupied the centre stage in the world industry and finance, and no effort of reactionary governments could reverse this process.

The revolutionary spirit in France which had so far helped the Jews, however, died down after Nepoleon's defeat at Waterloo. The conservatism returned and the Jews resigned themselves to a low intensity struggle for democratic reforms of 1830-1848. However, this period produced some eminent Jews who did their community proud. Disraeli, though a converted Jew by confession, rose from the lowest rank to become the Prime Minister of England. After a bright career in Victorian history he became a liberal Tory of distinction. He indirectly helped the cause of the Jews and improved their living conditions, remarking jocularly" Sanitas, sanitatum, omnia sanitas". Another outstanding Jew later 'converted' was the great poet and philosopher Heinrich Heine. He broke away from the sedate literary style of his contemporaries and contributed in a very large measure to the political discourse of the times. He described himself as a soldier in the war for liberalism. A fitting tribute to the man was the following famous epigram from Matthew Arnold:

"The spirit of *the world*
Beholding the *absurdity of men,*
Their vaunts, *their feats,*
let a sardonic *smile,*
For one short moment, *wander o'er his lips.*
That smile was Heine!"

Heine loved Jewish lore and denounced the" chiropody" of the so called nationalists. His "Confessions" ' is a vibrant testimony to his loyalty and genuineness to the Jewish cause. Regarding his conversion he often said that" I was merely baptized, not converted". This" German Aristophanes" rebelled against the existing institutions with a sharp tongue mainly targeting the religious hypocrites. Of profound thoughts, he could be fervently flippant, as he wrote," An Englishman loves liberty like his lawfully wedded wife. She is a possession; he may not treat her with much tenderness, but he knows how to defend her. A Frenchman loves liberty like his sweetheart, and he will do a thousand follies for her sake. A German loves liberty like his old grandmother". The greatest influence in politics and literature on the new liberal Germany was of one man alone and that man was Heine. Another prominent Jew of the post-Waterloo era was Karl Ludwig Borne who like Heine, had a keen incisive pen and a vigorous style of literary writing, devoted to the cause of freedom. He too like Heine was a converted Jew, but fumed against the inequalities heaped on his people when he said," What you call human rights, which, it must be conceded, you grant Jews, are only animal rights. The rights of seeking food, of devouring it, of sleeping, of multiplying, are enjoyed also by the beasts of the field, until they are slain, and to the Jews you grant no more". The French Revolution inspired him to write, in 1830, his famous "Letters from Paris" in which he made war on social and intellectual abuses of the times.

In Hungary the Jews rebelled with the local population against Austrian rule in 1848 and were treated decently by the Hungarians. Soon political rights were granted to them but the freedom was short-lived as Russia and Austria again combined to suppress Hungary. This bondage continued for a period of two decades, until autonomy was granted by the Ausgleich, and official equality was proclaimed in 1895-96. However, in Italy freedom came to the Jews piecemeal as Italy struggled to free itself from the domination of Austria. The great statesman Count Cavour and the fighter Garibaldi, the heroes of the freedom struggle, greatly helped the Jewish cause.

The Jews in England, however, did not suffer severe restrictions as in other countries, though denied admissions to the bar, high rank in the armed forces or positions in municipal offices, admissions to Oxford and Cambridge and the right to a seat in the Parliament. Struggle went on till 1837 when at the time of coronation of Queen Victoria, except for a seat in Parliament, other restrictions were gradually removed. This mainly was due to the efforts of Macaulay, Russell and Disraeli. At last, after a decade the Jews were allowed to become members of the House of Commons and Lionel Rothschild became the first Jewish member of Parliament. Later, his son was admitted to the peerage. The Conservatives of the Victorian period were pleasantly surprised when Lord Reading, formerly Sir Rufus Isaacs, became the Viceroy of the Indian empire, while Sir Herbert Samuel, as High Commissioner in Palestine, was appointed Arbitrator on the disputes of races and religions. Upheavals in social and economic order changed the lives of men. A number of inventions came up to tame nature and provide machines to replace human labour.

After the American Civil War in the eighties a large Russian population migrated to the States bringing their philanthropic and educational institutions with them. But the tide really started later when after the May laws and violent pogroms tens of thousands of Jews fled Russia seeking a sanctuary in the United States. Around twenty thousand Jews entered America each year and after the enunciation of the policy of wholesale expulsion, wave after wave of Jews reached the American shores. Between 1881 and 1900 about 600,000 Russian and Romanian Jews reached the United States soaring their population to more than a million, and by the violent pogroms, consequent to the Russian Revolution and slaughter by the Black Hundreds, the wave turned into a torrent and about a million more Jews reached the shores of United States. Thus America became a safe haven and one of the most important settlements of the Jews in their entire history. The early settlers, two hundred thousand Sephardic and German Jews, were literally submerged in the two million migrants from the eastern Europe. While assimilation was easier for the earlier tricklers, the new waves had to settle in their own ghettos in the larger towns of the East. Alarmed by this mass scale of migrants, the American Administration from 1906 to 1913 legislated certain restrictive measures, such as literacy tests and certificates of character from the home country. The difficulty of obtaining these certificates slowed down the process of migration for some time but after its repeal in 1913 by President Taft and supported by President Wilson, the flow of the migrants remained unabated. Now tens of thousands of Jews passed by the Statute of Liberty freely and sought their living in this new land of opportunity; mostly as manual workers, middle men and as other artisans. Life remained a perpetual struggle, but the Jews never gave up. This was their Promised Land, full of opportunities. The Jewish talent and ambition could not be suppressed for long and almost the whole of textile industry passed into Jewish hands as the capitalisation in this sector rose from US $ 60 million by almost fifteen hundred percent between 1880 and 1916. Along with these industrial activities came the era of Trade Unions and movement towards fair wages and hygienic conditions at the shop floor. The Trade Union movement of the Jews, radicalism in politics, in economic outlook and religion, and 'compulsions of new industrial climate resulted in a loosening of religious hold and emancipation from rigidities of the Synagogue culture. In Russia. However, for nearly a century and a half things remained much as before under the pall of misery and despotic excesses. Hard as steel, not easy to assimilate, stubborn as ever, most of the Jews in Russia remained indigestible to the nationalists. Though the problem was understandably difficult, it did not demand the butchery that followed which further aggravated the hurt to the Jewish psyche and permanently alienated them from the Russian despotism.

A revolution in the religious thought of the world almost exploded like a bomb with the publication of Darwin's monumental work *The Origin of Species*. His thesis agitated all the countries in Europe and shook the foundations of genesis and the other allied subjects in the Bible, it was not a frivolous matter to a generation whose entire life was built around the Holy Book. The Jewish world was no exception and soon there was a conflict between those who believed in revelation and those who changed to the evolutionary view of religion. This churning of religious thoughts gave an impetus to scientific criticism of the Bible. Judaism, whose religious genius was perpetually unfolding itself, could now study the Bible from a new angle. It was inevitable that the Biblical instances and teachings had to be reviewed rationally, discarding all dogma and in the process, reconciling the temple of creed with the temple of science. Though parts of Bible were discarded under the new scientific scrutiny, its magnificent ethical writ remains a spiritual repository. While some miracles and stories were to be viewed in the proper perspective, the identity of Moses and his laws continued to inspire 'the Jewish religious system. The Haskalah actually remained a source of intense nationalism among the Jews, reinforced as it was by the cultural revival amongst the Jewish nationality in the Balkans, Italy, Hungary and Ireland. The central position of Haskalah during these turbulent times became the precursor of the later day 'Zionism'. As a sequel, the Jewish cultural renaissance inculcated amongst its youth a love for Hebrew language, and a sense of Jewishness. This phenomenon forms an interesting contrast with today's India's hybrid culture wherein the youth in their blind craze of aping Western values have lost all sense of national identity and culture. In his book *The Eternal People*, Smolenskin, in 1873, for the first time, made out a thesis that the Jews are a nation and Palestine was their natural home to develop their genius, and the Messianic dream could only be realised if the Jews achieved political and moral emancipation in their own land. Nahman Haym Bialik, the profoundest of Jewish poets, stirred the conscience of the Jews through Hebrew language as he gave voice to the painful longings of his times. The massacre of Kishinev incited him to his most radical work *City of Slaughter*, a strong denouncement of Russian barbarities and torture of his people.

Chapter 3

The Awakening

The closing years of the 19th century are fraught with achievements which equal almost the entire previous life of this planet in all fields of human knowledge. The towering figures of this period were Hegel, Schopenhauer, Mill, Darwin and Spencer. Illustrious paintings of Goya, Turner, Renoir and Gauguin were matched by the music of Beethoven, Schubert, Chopin, Wagner and the literary works of Goethe, Keats, Balzac and Bernard Shaw. With the invention of combustion engine, X-ray and Pasteur's theory science took gigantic strides in human development. In this galaxy of the distinguished the contribution of Jews is of no mean magnitude. The names that spring to mind are those of Marx, Freud, Bergson and Einstein in the field of science, that of Pissarro, Soutine, Chagall and Modigliani in painting, Mendelssohn, Offenbaach, Saint-Saens, Bizet and Mahler in music, while Heine, Froust, Maurois and Romains were the shining stars in the field of literature. Theoretical physics termed as "Judenphysik" was mainly the work of German Jews, while in medicine, Wassermann, Ehrlich and Schick achieved pre-eminence. The Jewish contribution was the largest in the field of mathematics, biology and chemistry as evidenced by the fact that more Nobel prizes in science were awarded to the Jews than any other nationality. The Jewish viceroys, prime ministers, generals and intellectuals shaped Europe and changed the course of world history; all this despite the fact that they formed less than half per cent of the populations of the entire west and central Europe, fighting the ghetto with one hand and anti-Semitism with the other.

Although mention has been made earlier of Spinoza's thoughts and philosophy the essence of his thoughts and the main strands of his philosophy still need a repetition. Not only had he contributed to ethics, politics and religion, but had his own well-reasoned principles for application to physics and mathematics which he could not apply as the cruel hands of death cut short his life at the age of 44. Influenced by Talmud and Kabala, he emphasised the need for piety, a passion for freedom and justice, a rational order of thought and a vision, of an all encompassing science of the universe. His last unfinished task was left to the four great modern Jewish thinkers: Leopold Zunz, Karl Marx, Sigmund Freud and Albert Einstein. Spinoza's combination of a rational piety with the science of faith had far-reaching influence on Jewish thoughts and life in the days to come. Zunz (1794-1886) on whom fell the task of consumating the embryonic Spinoza's thoughts successfully emancipated the Jew from his Ghetto psyche, into the new "Science of Judaism". He changed the Christian concept of the Jewish stereotype of a stagnant medieval individual to a scientific and intellectual human being who could not only defend his faith but also advance intellectual frontiers of mankind. His "Reform Judaism" was further enriched by the efforts of the remaining trinity. While Marx who died in 1883 introduced economics as the foundation of politics and human destiny, Sigmund Freud (1856-1939), the Austrian Jew, revolutionized human understanding of the effect of libido and sexual impulses on human behaviour. He opened the field of psychiatry with his theory of psychoanalysis which was to play a major role in later day medical science. The last in the Spinozian quartet Albert Einstein (1879-1955) a product of German-Jewish enlightenment, not only gave the modern theory of relativity, ideas of Brownian motion and photoelectric effect but also a synthetic view of time and space, and the nature of universe. He mentioned that "the logic of a theory must stem from an inner coherence, not because external evidence makes it the most logical over other theories." A Nobel prize winner, Einstein was an embodiment of all that is noble in man and his surrounding universe.

Before the Jews were driven out of Germany under Hitler's dictat of the superior Nordic Aryans to be purged of the impure Semitism, the Jews had contributed in the largest measure to the science of micro-organism as the cause of contagious diseases and had laid the foundation of modern heart therapy, bacteriology and clinical pathology, besides the discovery of chemical processes within cells causing glandular activity, suggesting serum immunity and pioneered chemistry of muscles, blood transfusion through discovery of blood types, treatment for venereal diseases through gonococcus and salvarsan. In the field of astronomy the work of Sir William Herschel needs no introduction. The development of German chemical and dye industry was entirely the work of the Jews. The list is endless including as it does the potash industry, vapor density, expansion of gases, theory of valencies, molecular theory and organic compounds.

In physics, the list is even longer. But to mention just a few, Hertzian photoelectric phenomena, gamma rays, isotopes and electron kinetics, revealed the secret of the atom. The future of the entire school of relativity led by Albert Einstein, paved the way for nuclear fission, which enabled Enrico Fermi and Leo Szilard along with Niels Bohr, to develop the first chain reaction system resulting into the atom bomb. All these Jews along with Meitner migrated to the U.S.A. giving them their first nuclear bomb. In arts and humanities the Jews were equally prominent. They performed concerts, conducted orchestras, staged great dramas and introduced new art forms, in addition to capturing headlines in the music world. Politics, finance and.industry were the natural forte for the Jew, and where permitted he dominated the financial structure of the country of his citizenship. He innovated in all financial fields and gave international finance and banking a new look. How did the Jew, handicapped, deprived and disenfranchised achieve such marvels on the world stage, baffles logic. The answer is not simple. But there could be three main reasons. First, the survival of education, in spite of centuries of pogroms and ghettos; second, he had to work twice as hard as his Christian competitor to be taken seriously, no matter how hopeless the task before; he studied every profession and devoured voraciously all knowledge of science, industry and commerce; and lastly an awareness of the destiny that awaited him. He stuck steadfastly to his religion, culture and heritage that respected learning and the value of natural justice.

The common concept of American law based upon the Roman system, is not entirely correct, since Roman laws themselves evolved from the Jewish jurisprudence of the Biblical days. It is not a mere coincidence that around the fourth century B.C. the Jewish legal system was based on equality before law and dignity of man. Law was conceived to be a vehicle for justice without which they were considered immoral. While the Jews at that time did not have a jury system, the trials and indictments of the accused were similar to those in present day American courts. Presumed to be innocent, till proved guilty, the accused had the right to counsel and of fair trial. He could call witnesses to rebut accusers and testify for him. He had the right not to testify against himself, immunity from jeopardy and permit to appeal on appearance of new evidence.

Eastern Europe

Before we commence a study of the modern Jewish history after the creation of the state of Palestine in 1917, under the Balfour Declaration, let us pause and take stock of the cultural and civilizational development of the Jews on the threshold of the twentieth century. The European Jewish culture was sharply divided into two streams, the West and the East. The Western culture had a strong scientific content based on knowledge and a technology driven enlightenment. But in Eastern Europe, the un-emancipated Jews created a culture based on Haskala, epitomising the basic Jewish values. It did not produce great scientists, musicians or painters which were decoratively studded in the edifice of the Christian achievements of the West. The Eastern humanistic culture based on Hebrew and Yiddish was of far more value to the Jewish survival in the difficult days to come. Despite Western Enlightenment, Haskala like the Freudian libido coursed through the veins of Judaism, synchronizing the old Jewish values with the new. Anchored as it was on Hebrew and Yiddish language it created a new culture. This core culture acting as an adhesive to the Jewish religion created Jewish existentialism and later gave birth to Zionism fusing Eastern and Western Jews including those in the United States in the creation of the new state of Israel. However Talmudic studies and Hasidistic thoughts forever ran like parallel strands in the history of Judaism. What is the historical perspective on this vexing saga of the Jewish survival? Is it a mere accident or a destiny shaped by deterministic forces? Did materialism play a part in Jewish history? or their deep adherence to the prophetic writings, a product of centuries of repression, or the sustaining force of Torah and Talmud, Karaism and Kabala, Hasidism and Zionism? Can Toynbee's "challenge and response" theory fully explain the Jewish phenomenon, or was it divine intervention? The most appropriate answer to these puzzling questions perhaps lies in a synthesis of two 'metahistorians' of the Twentieth century the "fatalistic" or "nonfree-will" theory of Spengler and the "free-will" theory of Toynbee.

The Jews have answered these mute questions of history for four millennia, defying all cut and dry theories. Since they did not fit into the customary definition of a civilization, envisaged by Spengler and Toynbee, they called Judaism an "arrested civilization". However, this so-called "arrested civilization" successfully responded to the challenges of history and therein lies the secret of Jewish survival. This can be better understood if we define Judaism as a "culture" and not a "civilization". To quote Amaury de Riencourt from his book *The Coming Caesars*

" Culture predominates in young societies awakening to life... and represents a new world outlook. It implies original creation of new values, or new religious symbols and artistic styles, of new intellectual and spiritual structures, new sciences, new legislation, new moral codes. It emphasizes the individual rather than the society, original creation rather than preservation and duplication, prototypes rather than mass production, an aesthetic outlook on the life rather than an ethical one. Culture is essentially trail-blazing. "Civilization, on the other hand, represents the crystallization on a gigantic scale of the preceding Culture's deepest and greatest thoughts and styles, living on the petrified stock forms created by the parent Culture, basically uncreative, culturally sterile, but efficient in its mass organization, practical and ethical, spreading over large surfaces on the globe, finally ending in a universal state...Civilization aims at the gradual standardization of increasingly large masses of men within a rigidly mechanical framework-masses of 'common men' who think alike, feel alike, thrive on conformism, are willing to bow to vast bureaucratic structures, and in whom the social instinct predominates over that of the creative individual."

Each successive blow to the Jewish existence brought forth a new energy for survival. The exile from Egypt resulted in the formation of a state in Canaan. Babylonian captivity invigorated the emerging civilization. The war with Rome dissociated them from the destiny of that declining civilization, as they dispersed into the Diaspora. Thus exiled to freedom into Diaspora, they carried their highly developed culture of prophets, saints and scholars. The Jews went down *under* and came up again with one civilization after another. This bred in the Jewish blood resilience of character, the tensile strength of mind and body. The firm belief that they were God's Chosen People, forever kindled the fire of survival. Jews would bend but could not break. The Diaspora in a sense was a blessing in disguise, shielding them as it did from the fate of other civilizations which rose and fell with time. The Diaspora remains the universal soul of Judaism. The question before history is - "Are the Jews like the Hindus, a divinely chosen people to fulfill a divine mission?" Does it follow the prophecy of Isaiah or the sages of Vedas and

Upanishads to create a brotherhood of man "Vasudhaiv Kutumbakam" and having fulfilled their pre-ordained mission disappear from the pages of history. The answer is a resounding "No". Jews like the Hindus have too much of a past, a potent culture and civilisation to give them an anchor in any deluge of future history. The Hindus like the Jews have suffered persecution through ages and still retain their faith and identity.

Down the lane of history, the trinity of Jehovah, Torah and Prophets by design or accident, evolved the laws not only to preserve the Jews as Jews but to preserve mankind as a whole. The Hindu sages in the past did the same. It will be a very faithful reproduction of the teachings of Hindu sages, Vedas and Upanishads as one views Jewish achievements not merely in material terms of a tiny people in a tiny land but their overall spiritual achievements. Removing the blinkers of prejudice and viewing the world not as a "thing" but as an "idea", the real truth shall reveal itself as two thirds of the civilized world is ruled by the ideas of Jews and their teachers like Moses, Jesus, Paul, Spinoza, Marx, Freud, Einstein along with Hindu sages whose words of wisdom lie scattered in un-discovered manuscripts. Will the world in the next two millennia imbibe the morality of Judaism and Hinduism? If so, Isaiah's words "Peace peace, to him that is far off and to him that is near" shall come true.

At the start of the modern age, prior, during and soon after the World War I, Jews were divided into two distinct groups: those belonging to the Western democracy under liveable conditions and the other half in the Eastern Europe and Russia in just the opposite. After the defeat of Russia, the World War I and the onset of the Bolshevik Revolution, the radicals were faced once again with the "Jewish question". Slavofile gave his description on this question as "one third conversion, one third migrants and one third starvation". These pogroms initiated as a diversion for the masses from the miseries, were later adopted in the whole of Russia despite world protests. This led to a Diaspora of Jews into various lands, leaving a miserable few in the Russian heartland. Then one day the worm turned. Having stayed away from politics for long, and tired of the train of Jewish funerals, the young Jews threw caution to the winds, abandoned the policy of appeasement and demanded their place under the sun, ready to fight for it, if necessary. Instead of begging, they now demanded liberties, entered politics and underground movements. Some Jewish liberals even joined the Red Army organised by Leon Trotsky to fight the invaders assisted by White Russians. The Eastern Jews even fought the Western Jews in German uniform not only on the battlefield but also in the battles between the Left and the Right in the fields of idea and theology. Thus modern Jewish history begins with an impatient Jew knocking on the closing doors of the eighteenth century for admission to full citizenship. Little did the Jews realise that there was even more savage racism waiting for them in the West. The word 'anti-Semitism' first came in the historical lexicon around 1879, coined by a German, and defined a new pattern of Jewish-Christian relationship. With the development of scientific age at the beginning of the nineteenth century and World War I, the Jews like their gentile counterparts became extroverts and developed a utilitarian and scientific temper. But the East European Jews remained introvert clinging to their Jewish past to seek affirmation in the future. As the two poles of civilization while the Western Jew acquired modern Western culture, the Jew in the East adhered to his old and true Jewish culture. A scholar of history has said:

> "An unhistoric people is acted upon by events. A historic people acts upon events. The Jews have remained a historic people through the centuries because they have always been active agents instead of passive bystanders. The Modern Age was no exception. The Jews were not only acted upon by historical forces but they themselves also acted upon history".

Chapter 4

The Foundations of Anti-Semitism

Before we describe the Jewish history in the early half of the twentieth century, it is time to pause and focus upon the clash between Judaism and Christianity, in particular and other states and religions in general. The second part has been adequately covered in our narrative thus far, but some points are worth mention.

The persecution of the Jews in Egypt and under the Graeco-Roman Empire has been described earlier. This was basically founded on a mistrust of the Jews by the pagans who believed in polytheism which was not in consonance with the Jewish theology of monotheism. However, the growth of resentment and suspicion of Christians against the Jews could not be so easily explained. The divide between Judaism and the teachings of Jesus has been explained earlier. Though Jesus differed from the Jews and their rigid observance of Judaism only in matters of details his firebrand disciple, Paul, his sharp tongue and loud denunciations did much to widen the chasm. The misunderstanding of his teachings by his Gentile successors, deliberate or unconscious, resulted in a big cleavage between Judaism and Christianity difficult to bridge. Once the Church rejected the Old Testament in its totality, acceptance of Jesus by

Jews became impossible, leading to bitter periods of hostility between the two in the early days of Christianity. This mutual hatred was exacerbated in the following two millennia described earlier in the book.

It should, therefore, cause no surprise that even Shakespeare, the greatest English playwright, created a Jew stereotype in Shylock, the money lender who demanded his pound of flesh from his debtor. The idea came from an episode between two knights, both Christians, one of whom was the creditor and had demanded a pound of flesh without any blood from the debtor knight. The legend dates back to 13th century. The substitution of the Jew for the Christian creditor was made later in a medieval poem in England after which the Jews were expelled from the realm in 1290. Marlowe, one source of this legend, puts the Jew in Malta, a big ship-magnet whose purpose in life was to kill Christians and gain wealth and power. The character along with a mix of Tamerlane out of Faust has portrayed the Jew as a poisonous liar, traitor, usurer and intriguer. Shylock of Shakespeare though no hero, is no villain either. While Marlowe calls him Barabbas—a loaded name, Shakespeare names him Shylock, whose aim in life is wealth for its own sake, and is parasitic.

We will revert to the first part shortly after mentioning the common struggle of Judaism and Sanatan Hinduism, based on Vedic culture, with other religions. With the brief exception of sundry nomad marauders from the Northwest, such as the Huns, Shakas, Mongols and the Turks upto the tenth century, the real and sustained cultural and religious invasion soaked in blood came from Islam from the eleventh century onwards. Thereafter, under the British rule it was a resistance to the Christian proselytisation under the patronage of British Imperial Government, closely coordinated with cultural invasion through English language, and activities of the Christian missionaries who strived to baptise the fringe sections of Hindu society such as the tribals and lower classes. Of the two, the Islamic invasion was more violent and widespread, with the result that today Islam claims 14 percent of the total Indian population while the other minorities together count for just 2.3 percent. The survival of the predominant Hindu majority culture speaks volumes about the power, endurance, universality, versatility and durability of the Hindu thought. As against this, the Jews were exposed to aggression from almost all pagan states and cultures of the Middle-East till the cultural and political conquest of the Greeks and the Romans. These have been well documented earlier. The clash with Christianity came mainly after the death of Jesus, the influence of his teachings and the Christian hatred.

Common to all European countries, the Jews suffered not only on the ground of religion but Christian greed and political expediency of the ruling kings and lords. In common with the Hindus, the Jews suffered throughout the tenth century at the hands of Islam and its fanatic followers. Both the cultures were the victims of Islamic doctrine interpreted from the Holy Quran over the world and divided into two clear domains. The one belonging to the faithful *Dar-ul-Islam* the benign one; and the unbelievers termed as 'Kafirs' constitute the second part, called Darul-Harab. Islam enjoins on its faithful to extend the limits of 'Darul-Islam' as far as possible and consummate a duty ordained by Allah by annihilation of *Dar-ul-Harab* and its subsequent merger into *Dar-ul-Islam*. It thus follows as a natural corollary from the tenets of Islam that it lies on the faithful to constantly wage a religious war called Jehad on the Kafirs. Temporary truces, treaties, compromises and expediencies notwithstanding,the ultimate aim shall always remain the annihilation of the Kafirs and the consummation of *Dar-ul- Islam*. Thus though the Hindus suffered mainly at the hands of Islam and to a lesser degree from Christians, the Jews with a minimalistic population confined to the small land of Palestine and spread in driblets in the Western world suffered from almost every state.

The origin of the fundamental differences between Jews and Christians may be traced to the teachings of Jesus Himself. Many of the sayings attributed to Him in the gospels are neither fully authenticated nor free from the prejudices of memory and intention. While there was substance in the denunciation of some Jewish teachers, discrepancies arose with time and the issues taken up by Jesus were largely ignored. Jesus attacked the Pharisees but his greatest predecessor was the Pharisee Hillel. After a study by later day scholars it is clear that there was hardly any difference between the first century Judaism and the picture in the New Testament of the Talmudic teachings a hundred years later. Many of the facts in the New Testament need revalidation with the possibility that the picture of the Jews in the fourth gospel may be a total invention. Jesus denounced not the soul of Judaism but what appeared to Him to be "pessima" since it was "corruptio optimi". But as pointed earlier, it was the fanaticism of the Pharisees and their insistence on details and rituals that kept the Jews going through troubled centuries. This phenomenon is not exclusive to the Jews but will be found in almost all religions. The Pharisees in common with the Jewish teachers everywhere insisted the whole of Israel to know Torah in order to fulfill their mission before God. Though the final authority of Torah is unquestioned there was more democracy in Jewish culture, thought and practice than even with the Greeks. It was not merely a Law or slavish observance of rituals. It was more than that. Torah was to the Jews what Christ is to the Christians. It was a divine ordinance to man to fulfill His will, revealing as it did the life of the Holy community and the Jewish nation and the duty of every individual to fulfill God's purpose on a rational and intellectual basis which was "redemptive" in nature. Torah was not merely a scribe but the soul of Judaism and a covenant and spiritual fulfillment of the Jews. The aversion of Jesus to the Pharisees rose from his views that they obscured the direct relationship between man and God against the tenets of Torah. But Jesus overreached himself when he said that the letter of Torah itself would obscure this relationship, and his followers a century later saw Torah as a dead prescription rejected by Jesus.

Accidentally discovered in 1947 near the Dead Sea some manuscripts dating back to the first century B.C uncannily point to the fact that Jesus and his Christianity were the outcome of an earlier sect, possibly the Essenes of pre-Christian era. The script of these texts is remarkably similar to those preached by Jesus. There was a mention of impending fall of the Sons of Darkness, the Kittim (probably the Romans) at the hands of the leaders of this new sect. The origin of Jesus and John the Baptist is also traced to this sect. The Dead Sea's scrolls have much in common with Christian theology and sources of the New Testament. This Jewish sect possibly was the forebear of the later day Christianity. There is a hot debate going on at present on the synergy between the Old Testament, the Masoretic texts and the theory of the coming of a Messiah. One of the Scrolls was an original version of the Book of Isaiah, depicting the diversity of religious experience in the days of Jesus. Thus on the evidence of these Scrolls, Jesus either belonged to the Essenes, or was the promised Messiah. The rapid spread of Christianity thereafter owes largely to the mighty efforts of Saul of Tarsus re-incarnated as Paul of the New Testament.

Now we skip the centuries of history and come to the new challenge to Judaism through Islam and their Prophet Mohammed. The founder of Islam, born in 570 A.D., did not count for much till in his fortieth year. He started seeing visions of angel Gabriel commanding him to proclaim his faith in his Allah. Not very successful initially with the Meccans, in fact ridiculed by them, he somehow managed to gather about a hundred followers around him. Further, to evade his growing enemies around, he left Mecca for Medina in 622 A.D., the year of the flight called 'Hegira', which became the starting year of the Mohammedan calendar. He found more success there with Khazraj tribe but little response from the Jews. Building his religion on the foundation of the Biblical seers and prophets, he preached his new faith. Proud of his descent from Ishmael through Abraham, he started the practice of turning in prayer towards Jerusalem, respecting Jewish customs and even imitating their hairstyle to identify more closely with them. The Jews however, could not be won over, and scoffed at his pompous and blasphemous pretensions. Without any monetary help from the Jews or the Christians, and to save his starving flock, he turned to plunder, and started looting caravans. He justified his actions as a punishment to the idolators. In fact, he attacked the caravans even during Ramzan, the sacred month when no fighting was permitted, and his ruthlessness and dishonourable actions further frightened the pagans. But for this Mohammed readily produced a justification through his revelations. At the battle of Badr in 624 A.D. with his followers he attacked his former townsmen and won a decisive victory; feeding his followers from the booty and returned to Medina a hero. Mohammed now completely broke away from the hated Jews and inspired by his revelations started reviling the race. Attacking one Jewish tribe after another, he defeated almost all the Jews in battle and would have slaughtered them to a man but for the intervention of Abdullah, a converted Jew. As usual, the booty of the 700 Medina men was distributed among the faithful, thereby sending a strong signal that the rewards of Islam are for this world too. Defeated roundly once again by the Meccans at Uhud he sought to retrieve his fortune by plundering the remaining wealthy Jews of Banu Nadir near Medina. The lack of unity amongst the Jewish tribes led to their rout. Here again, Mohammed broke the sacred practice of the desert by cutting down the date-palms outside the village, an act of vandalism even more shocking than the attack on unarmed caravans during the sacred month. Here again, a convenient revelation to Mohammed justified this outrage.

Leaving here the details of Mohammed's life and the expansion of Islam soon thereafter towards north into the present day Middle East, eastward upto Afghanistan and westward along the Northern coast of Africa right upto the southern part of Spain, we shall now come to a brief development of Jewish history from the tenth century onwards. Persecution of the Jews in England, Europe and eastwards upto Russia is well documented. However, within this period of darkness, the Jews enjoyed a very brief spell of peace and flourished in Southern Spain during the reign of Abd Ar Rahman and his dynasty. Most of the Jews during this period had converted to Islam to avoid persecution, while secretly harbouring their zeal for their own religion. The benevolent statesmanship of Ibn Shaprut and Samuel

Ibn Nagdela, the sublime poetry of Judah Halevi and Ibn Gabirol, works of Ibn Ezra and the philosophy of Maimonides, were the high water-mark of this era. But the situation radically changed from the onset of 14th century and the Jews barley managed to survive, while their genius slowly dried up. Around the sunshine of the Jews in the Moslem areas of Andalusia in Spain, the rest of Christian Europe remained a world of darkness and oppression only partly explained by the barbarity of the times. Exploited by the church, crushed by the nobles, harassed under economic restrictions, and hemmed in by an alien faith, outside the pale of civilization, the Jews held out living at the mercy of their rulers. Except for a brief flicker of Talmudic renaissance in the Rhine area in the eleventh century, there was no respite. They were destroyed by the crusaders in the name of God, while the popes and the princes invented new methods of torture and harassment. The Talmud was condemned and burnt publicly. One by one, every Christian country robbed the Jews, drove them to despair and expelled them to nowhere. Zunz in his famous statement described the horrors of Medieval Jews thus:

> "If there be an ascending scale of suffering, Israel has reached its highest degree. If the duration of afflictions, and the patience with which they are borne ennoble, the Jews may vie with the aristocracy of any land. If a literature which owns a few classical tragedies is deemed rich, what place should be assigned to a tragedy which extends over fifteen centuries in which the poets and actors were also the heroes?"

For a short while, the Jews enjoyed a respite against oppressions, euphemistically described as the Golden Age in Moslem Spain. Although the Jews were totally assimilated in the Moslem Kingdom of Spain for a period of 250 years under the Omayyad dynasty, they still retained their native intelligence and thirst for knowledge. They became high officials in the court of Abd-Ar-Rahim and produced many men of learning; prominent among these are Hasli, Moses and Ben Ened in the 10th century. Samuel Ibn Nagdela became the Vizir in the time of Badrs who succeeded Habus, the other patron of Samuel. Jewish poets of this age were Judah Haloce and Salmon Ibn Gabriel. The genius of their muse flowered to such an extent that the latter was called Dante and Milton of the Jewish literature. Around 1149 A.D. after Moslem conquest of North Africa and Spain, a century earlier the modern kingdom of Cordoba and Andaulausia became centers of Islamic studies, while Toledo become the seat of Jewish life in Spain. Abraham Ibn Ezra, the most talented Jew, was known for his critical approach to the Bible.

A new phenomenon took place at this time in Moslem Spain. A large number of Jews called "Marranos" had converted to Islam to escape persecution but in their hearts they remained Jews and practised Judaism with all possible fervour. That is the reason that many distinguished Jews of this period have a Moslem name. Moses Maimonides was a most influential thinker in the Middle ages and was the author of *Siraj*, a masterly commentary on the Mishnah. His second great work was *Mishnah Torah*, a codification of all fourteen books of all Biblical and Rabbinical law. He was an advocate of conquering flesh, while Nahmanides, his contemporary, believed flesh to be as pure as the soul, both being gifts of God. And then there was Crescas who believed that the path to God lay through love not reason. With him the Golden Age in Spain came to an end.

Chapter 5

The Chosen People

Christian scholars have often questioned the high pedestal that the Jews seem to have arrogated by referring to themselves as the "Chosen People". Even Arnold Toynbee believes that the concept of a Chosen People is indicative of a spiritual arrogance and Jews' exclusivity that should not form part of any high religion worthy of its name. No religion should claim a privileged relationship to God or a special place for its identity. The fact of the matter is that the Bible does speak of God having chosen the Jews, and they did become His "Chosen People". He entered into a covenant and special relationship with them. However, the point to remember is something that most Christians and other Jewish baiters tend to ignore. That these people were "Chosen People" not for conferring any special favour or privilege but for a special service. Chosen for service and not privilege, the Jews were to act as God's instrument to bring all men to his fold, the sheep to the shepherd, so aptly described by Milton in the opening lines of *Paradise Lost*—"The shepherd who first taught the Chosen Seed". They were to be God's instrument or "a light into gentiles". History proves that God did indeed ordain that their destiny was not of privilege but suffering, misunderstanding and death. God says to the children of Israel, "you only have I known of all the nations of the earth" and concluded "therefore I will punish you for all your inequities." That was a heavy responsibility indeed.

Why did God favour the Jew or the Brahmin in the Hindu scriptures? It was not based on the inherent worth of the object but due to the divine grace. This God's grace is central to Judaism and Brahaminism and by extension to those who would be redeemed by them to God's grace.

In the Hindu lore too a similar cross is to be borne by the Brahmin, the chosen one. He is believed to have been born from the head of the creator, Brahma, and was commanded to act as a teacher to the rest of mankind. Not for him the luxury of palaces, but to learn, meditate, acquire knowledge and wisdom and disseminate it to all mankind. He was not to think of himself but others and live for others. To lead and guide men in the ways of God, to prepare them for the ultimate spiritual perfection and salvation, Brahmins were not to earn or store money but were to depend entirely on alms from the laity and other earthly needs and protection from the Kshatriya princes. From womb to tomb a Brahmin had to perform Anusthans (rituals) and *Sanskaras for all varna* or castes, educate the un-initiated, teach the errant princes and even remonstrate and chastise them to bring them back to the narrow path of virtue and "Raj Dharma" (the duties of the king). In brief, their duties lay in teaching the world the rule of Dharma which literally means duty with righteousness and not religion in its current sense which means a sect. Dharma was a very sacred and emotive word during the times of our proto history. One hears of splendour and glory of the kings or Kshatriyas, the material wealth of Vaishya or the treasures of Kuber, the god of wealth, but the Brahmin is always refered to as austere and ascetic. With the passage of time and the coming of priesthood many evils and covetousness entered invisibly into the conduct of Brahmins.

Even in earlier times after the enunciation of the *Chatur Varna* by Manu a man's action decided his caste. No man was born into a caste; this was decided only by his deeds or *karma* not birth. Many Khsatriya kings adopted an ascetic life of meditation in the woods and were called *Rajarishi* such as Rishi

Vishwamitra. There are many more such examples and also cases of Kshtriya princes marrying daughters of Brahmin Rishis and vice-versa. Renuka, wife of Rishi Jamdagni, was a Kshtriya princess. Their son, Parshuram, though brought up in Brahminical tradition was forced to take up arms against the Kshtriya king, Sahasrabahu, who had spread a reign of terror among his subjects, tortured the Brahmins,some time referred to as Bhargava samaj, destroyed their properties, and stopped royal aid to Gurukuls, the places of learning for students from all Varnas. He even killed the parents of Parshuram and waged a relentless war against the Brahmins. In consequence, Parshuram had to cast off his Brahminical duties and take up arms and destroyed Sahasrabahu and his cohorts. It is stated in Vishnu Puran that Parshuram, a devotee of Lord Shiva, cleared the earth of all Kshtriyas twenty-one times to take the revenge of the death of his parents and the misdeeds of Kshtriya king Sahasrabahu.

Coming back to the Jews, and their place as God's Chosen People, Dr. Foerste cites two moving incidents of their immense faith in their religion, their duties and obedience to the Lord's command. In Judaism as in Hinduism, materialism is not a sin, nor spiritualism the sole aim of human life. Both have their importance to man who lives on earth. Coming back to the incidence, the first occurred after Pilate became the Procurator of Judea under Tiberous, the Roman Emperor. He had ordered the installation of pagan images and a statue of the Roman Emperor in Jerusalem which was strongly resented by the Jewish population. Pilate threatened, cajoled and finally used force by surrounding Jerusalem with his armed troops. While Jerusalem was simmering with anger, the country folk streamed into the city. Some hurried to Pilate in Caesarea, beseeching him to remove the offensive images and the statue. Pilate had his orders to carry out but the Jews resisted. There was a stalemate. Ultimately Pilate's patience gave way and he decided to strike down the Jews unless they agreed to tolerate the presence of the images and the Emperor's standards. The soldiers drew out their swords. Immediately, the Jews seemingly acting on a plan threw themselves on the ground and cried out, "Rather would we suffer death than violate the Law." This fidelity to their faith astonished Pilate and forced him to order his soldiers to remove the standards.

The second incident is that of Petronius. He threatened the Jews with death if they opposed his will. He now brought his three legions from Antioch, entered Judaea and prepared to destroy the Jewish resistance. The Jews with their wives and children gathered on the plain of Petronius and requested Petronius not to interfere with their law and punish them for their faith. The legate impressed by the size of the populace and sincerity of their plaint halted his army. He travelled to Galilee and called some of the respected Jewish leaders to the city of Tiberius. He extolled the virtues of the emperor, reminded them of the might of Rome and insisted that the Emperor's image be placed along with the other gods. The Jews stuck to their Law and the custom of their fathers, which forbade the setting up of any image, not only inside the Temple in Jerusalem but anywhere in the land. Petronius replied, "I must obey the orders of my master. If out of regard for you I disobey them, I shall bring ruin upon myself, and then not I but he who sent me and under whose order I stand, will declare war upon you." In reply, the entire crowd shouted, "We are prepared to suffer all things for the Law." After quiet prevailed, Petronius asked, "Do you then wish to fight against the Emperor?" The Jews replied in one voice, "For the Emperor and the people of Rome we bring sacrifices twice a day, but if he wishes to set up the images, he would have to slaughter the whole Jewish people. Gladly would they offer themselves as a sacrifice together with their wives and children. "This unshakable resolve, piety and contempt of death surprised Petronius and he went away without any further action.

Subsequently, he continued his parleys with the Jewish leaders without any results. The stalemate continued for 50 days and the whole people remained idle without even sowing the lands. At last, Petronius relented and said, "Very well I myself will take the risk. If I succeed in softening the Emperor's heart, we will both of us rejoice in common over such deliverance. If I fall into disfavour, I will gladly sacrifice my own life for the sake of so many." With this assurance and the blessings of the multitude, Petronius with his army moved back to Antioch. Later, he sent a despatch to the Emperor describing the events and requesting him to revoke his order. The Emperor was adamant and reprimanded Petronius for his inaction, but by a strange stroke of fate, the messenger bearing the Emperor's orders was caught up in a sea storm and Petronius received the missive threatening his death only 27 days later.

Now Dr. Foerster's words on this incident.

"The following comment can be made, on these two incidents. If the present author were asked to express within the compass of a few words wherein he thought lay the incomparable greatness of the Jewish people, if he were asked to show wherein they had deserved well of mankind for defending its spiritual goods, and in what sense something had irrupted into Jewish history which cannot be found in the history of any other nation, if he were then asked to illustrate the willingness for sacrifice, the courage, and the superb greatness of character that resulted from this –if, I say, he were asked such questions as these, he would immediately recount the two connected incidents which have just been related. They are among the most moving, and most sublime things that have ever happened on this earth, and the spirit that was behind the attitude of the Jewish people in those distant days presents us with a spectacle so splendid that the eternal drama of human worthlessness can only stand beside it in humiliating contrast. Mighty deeds of valour have always been performed by men for their earthly fatherland. In this instance, however, an entire people is ready to sacrifice itself, its youth and its country, so that its fidelity to the unseen God may be preserved."

Chapter 6

The History of Pogroms

The fundamental reason for the genocide of the Jews in various countries and under different dispensations can be attributed to a pervasive propaganda against them in the non-Jewish world. Although it started from the massacre in the land of Palestine itself by the various invaders and tribes, the process continued through Egypt, Babylon, Persia, the Graeco-Roman empires; from the medieval and middle ages in Europe to the beginning of the modern era. Blamed for the crime of crucifixion of Jesus, the Jews were held guilty of shedding Christian blood in different forms and places. Thomas of Monmouth, a monk, invented a story based on the evidence of another monk, Theobald, of Jewish extraction that a child was sacrificed by the Jews in a ritual murder. The incident is said to have happened when the body of a boy was found on Holy Saturday in 1144 A.D. in a wood near Norwich. The boy's uncle, a priest called Stuart, accused the Jews of the murder. Later, a legend was built around this boy and he was anointed St. William crucified by the Jews in a Jesus' like manner. The whole story was based upon hearsay evidence of one monk, who in turn was prompted by Theobald. As a reprisal to this murder a Jew named, Eleazar, was murdered and the Jews' request for justice was rejected on the counter-charge of the murder of William. Theobald was too willing to spread a canard that every year a Christian must be sacrificed by Jews in some part of the world, for without such shedding of blood their dream to return to their fatherland would never be realised. This provided further grist to the mill churning out anti- Jewish propaganda and the edifice of stories of ritual-murders by the Jews. Natural deaths of Christian children started being attributed to Jewish rituals. Lies told in Northampton in the 1370s propagated themselves and multiplied many-fold with time till they became a perfect excuse for hatred of the Jews and the origin of pogroms in its most deadly form. The first pogrom in England started with the coronation of Richard the Lion Heart, when popular fury expelled the Jews from the Westminster Abbey and ransacked and plundered their homes. Then followed the first Crusade and the torture suffered by the Jews has been adequately documented earlier. Milked of all their monies and belongings, the Jews were declared as Crown chattels.Their treatment by the monarchy entirely motivated by money, was a long story of exactions. The extraction of money from the hapless Jews continued as the Jewish community was sold by King Richard to Prince Edward who in turn sold them to the merchants in France and finally arrested and imprisoned the entire Jewish population of about 16000 to compel them to buy-back their freedom. Drained of all their monies the Jews became expendable, their properties taken over by the Crown, and they were finally expelled from the country with almost nothing to subsist on.

It would be difficult to chronicle the mass slaughters of the Jews during the turbulent times of early history around 1000 B.C. through inter-tribal warfare where information is not very authentic and historical dates often muddied a bit.

The large scale murder of Jews has been described in the earlier pages. However, to identify the contours of the process of Jewish slaughter, it would be worthwhile to chronologically record the more prominent among the pogroms,. The first was in Egypt under the Pharoah Ramses from whose subjugation Moses led the Jews out of captivity across the Red Sea to the land of Canaan. The next recorded event of history is the Greek invasion of Judea, which too has been recorded earlier. The Greek invasion was not merely physical but cultural too and had its attraction amongst a part of the Jewish and subsequently the Christian population. So much so that Prof. Frank Sullivan of Loyola University remarked that "though the furniture of our civilisation is Greek, the life of the Judeo- Christian is lived in a house built on Israel." Then came the war with the Romans and the destruction of Jerusalem by Titus, one of the ablest Roman generals, wherein millions of Jews were massacred. And then the crusades, described earlier wherein Richard the Lion Heart was as cruel to the Jews as he was to the infidel. Not far behind came the Black Death which claimed hundreds and thousand of Jewish lives as the scourge of nature against the helpless ones. Torquemada and Spanish inquisition were not long in coming and took a heavy toll of Jewish lives and property, as the Christians rejoiced at the Jews being burnt at the stakes.The story does not end here and King Henry III of England added his might to destroy the persecuted race further. The only light during the dark period of history could be seen in Persia where King Xerses and his wife Esther preferred to look the other way, allowing the Jews to wreak a vengeance on their persecutors. Nearer to our times and before the Second World War Russia obtained the dubious distinction of terming the Jews as enemies of the Proletariat, a natural sequel to the Bolshevik Revolution. And the last and the cruelest among them all was Adolf Hitler who decided to find the final solution to the Jewish problem. He considered them all to be the spies and agents working against the Third Reich. While out of 3,20,000 Jews living in Poland all except 35,000 were killed in gas chambers, a total of six million Jews perished in Europe. Unbelievable but true, and unknown to most historians is the fact that the inmates of Warsaw and other such Jews in German prisons fought determined battles against Hitler's S. S. troops. While the German troops were equipped with the latest weapons, the incarcerated Jews fought with small weapons that they could hide, such as razors and crowbars and even bare hands. Some of these Jews, on a large scale, even took part in partisan war- fare against the Germans in occupied Europe and the Balkans.

There is no dearth of names of the Death prisons for the Jews even in later times. The prominent among these being Bergen, Belsen, Dashan, Auschwitz, Trellinka and Babi-yar. The Memorial at Yad Vashem reads, "The Hand and the Name in remembrance for executed Jews." There is a hall of horrors in Israel where Israelis are taken to listen to prerecorded words of terror and suffering in the concentration camps in German occupied Europe.

Chapter 7

The Genesis of Zionism

Born out of the Judaic trinity of the Earth, Yahweh and His Chosen seed, aimed at establishing through piety and humanism the divine Kingdom in the promised land in and around Mount Zion, the idea of Zionism grew into a mission. Fuelled by centuries of oppressions, sufferings and disabilities imposed by the nations of the world on the suffering Jew, Zionism gradually transformed itself into the ultimate Jewish credo. Each injustice steeled their resolve to realise their God ordained destiny. History heaped one misfortune after another on the hapless Jew. And then one day the worm turned. The meek and the submissive Jew stood up to fight back and the twilight years of 19th and early years of 20th century saw the emergence of a new phenomenon, 'militant Zionism'.

A simple and innocent word which defines the religiosity and destiny of the Jews with patriotic overtones, enjoining upon them to return to their promised homeland, has created considerable apprehensions and hostilities amongst Christian and Islamic countries, particularly those in the Middle East. That word is Zionism. In the same manner, Hindutva that embodies the essence of our ever-evolving culture, anchored on our glorious heritage, inspired by a strong patriotic fervour and rooted in the soil of Bharat has often been berated by the so-called 'secularists' as a rabidly militant Hindu communalism. Zionism too has evoked strong anti-Jewish feelings. Both terms have been misunderstood for reasons based more on prejudices, and facts flying in the face of evidence, rather than sane rationalism. These words have caused more damage to social relationship between communities than any single word in history. We shall first trace the genesis and the content of Zionism before we take up Hindutva later in the chapters dealing with Indian history and culture. The idea of Zionism is a belief shared by a specific people commanded by their Lord God to establish His Kingdom in the specific location of Zion, a mountain once the throne of King David. This spirit of a historic mission, that of establishment of Holiness in a holy place by the God's Chosen People to live under His laws of piety is not exclusivistic like in any other religion. It does not address a nation in the conventional terms of an ethnic identity and geographical borders, but is a God ordained task, wherein the idea of holiness, God and the chosen place does not have any religious basis. It is in fact the association of a people and specific land to achieve a specific purpose as covenanted by their king, the Lord God. All Jewish prayers begin with "offer of the first of his land to Lord God, the giver/ Book (5, 3 f)..." Moses spells out this covenant with God along with the Ten Commandments to his people.

Zionism is synonymous with the free development of the hidden potential of the Jewish nation defining its purpose and direction. It is neither regressive nor deceptive. If Israel confines itself to a lesser goal, its lofty spirit will lose its vigour. Rooted in proto-historical events and their ramifications, it exhorts the "Chosen People" to master the limitations imposed by an unfriendly society to create a new human milieu. The essence of Zionism lies in the communion between God, man and the earth, the sacred soil with all its attendant farming activities which supersedes purely monetary concerns. The soil and the earth is the soul of Judaism, meaning not the same as it does to other primitive people, but is the partner in a God-willed and God-guaranteed association.

Isaiah's Zionistic approach i.e., 'Deutero-Isaiah' begins in the late period of the Exile, and is much more comprehensive and far-reaching, since it declares the time of return of God to Zion to start His Kingdom (52, 7). There is a tacit mutual understanding between wild and tame animals and man where in none hurts or destroys the other on that holy mountain. This moment of the beginning of a God-ruled world from Mount Zion is of world historical significance and a prophecy to Israelis to return to their own land and as the 'Servant of the Lord' bring light to their benighted existence. The 'Chosen People' are called upon to act as the heralds and pioneers of a redeemed world of which Israel is the center and the throne of the King. This thesis, bringing out the unique significance of the inseparable bond between these people and this land reaches its climax in Zionistic thought.

Convictions based on abstract thought and religious zeal bordering on fanaticism do not bring equality between God's people. Christians and Moslems both kill each other in their desire to serve God hoping thereby to obtain entry into paradise. It is axiomatic that both cannot be correct, as one pious conviction confronts the other. Too dogmatic in their own beliefs they forget the freedom granted to man to decide his own life in his own way. Despite God's government of the world, obtained through a dogmatic terminology and practice of these religions, His eternity and spirituality do not come naturally and set the standard for personal life. The Jew regards the doctrines of other faiths as speculative without pointing a possible worldly way to become like the Creator in His Wisdom and Justice. The difference between the promises of other religions to their believers and the teachings of Tora lies in the fact that while the former are promised bliss after death, Tora ordains upon Israel to fulfill God's commandment on earth in a promise that 'Ye shall become my people in Palestine. Ye shall continue in the land that helps you to reach this high level, for it is a holy land. Its fruitfulness or sterility, its good or evil fortune depend, according to your deeds, directly on the Divinity, while all the rest of the world depend on the natural law'. Thus the Biblical-Talmudic view of God's special concern for Israel is synthetic with the Biblical view of the influence of human action on the soil and its history.

Central to Zionistic thought is the idea that Jerusalem is the center of the world. This Haggadic mention presupposes that the work of Creation begins with the heart of the whole world posited at the Holy of Holies at Jerusalem, from where the entire inhabited world is fed. Arising out of Zionistic concept is the beginning of the national idea, 200 years before the French Revolution, which expresses the rights of nations in their unambiguous terms asserting that every people has its own nature and form, stands in its own power and not be subject to any other people. It has a natural dwelling-place and a right to live there and the freedom to choose its own God according to its own view on them. This law is not a human statute but is posited in the order of the world itself against which there should be no trespass. In a truly astonishing way this declaration of the rights of people is the central theme of Zionism.

The theme of primal relationship between Man and Earth recurs in all old lores, as it does in Judaism and Hinduism (Genesis 2,5). "Adama" is a fertile earth and God the potter creates "Adama "out of dust to make man serve it. In Arabic "Adama" means brown or reddish brown denoting both earth and the brown man. In Hebrew "Adama" denotes the unity of man and earth. The Biblical concept that earth has to answer for the sins of man finds its evidence in God's act of initially adding thorns and thistles to the existing fruits in the Garden of Eden. Later as man corrupts himself God wreaks his vengeance by the great flood, leaving Noah as the sole surviving man.

In Vedic lore there is a similar mention of the great flood called "Pralaya" which overwhelms the sinful and destroys the world for man to make a new beginning. Under this belief the first man was 'Manu' who is described variously by different authorities in historiography. In a sense, 'Manu' the man determines the fate of earth by his conduct, a fate which in return becomes his own. The same idea is expressed in Bible thus—"The sinful people brings the land into guilt".

(Deuteronomy 24, 4). "Erets" in Hebrew means earth, and the Mountain of Zion is the seat of God and the heart of Zion. A temple erected there would serve as the meeting place for all the peoples of the world as a community, purified to live in harmony under King God's rule.

A multiplicity of people speaking different tongues that originated in the Tower of Babel shall finally lead mankind again to flock together and stream to Mount Zion, the seat of the divine King, who from His throne shall wipe away the tears of all His people. This was the essence of Isaiah's prophecy. In Vedic thought too, importance of land and its cultivation has been brought out as clearly as in the Jewish thought. Proto-historical man in Bharat and his later generations after considerable intermingling of races settled in the reverine northern alluvial plains. The early inhabitants, initially a pastoral society, also changed to an agrarian mode, just as the wandering Jews settled to cultivate land very early in history.

Chapter 8

Heroes of Israel

The time has come now to briefly run through the facts of history and mention some of the heroes of Israel who have earned a place of honour in the valhalla of national fame. The first such hero was Joshua Bin-Nun who belonged to the tribe of Ephraim, an off shoot of the tribe of Menasha. The land of Canaan denied to Moses, the Promised Land east of river Jordan, was occupied by an attack on the city of Jericho known for its strong and mighty mud walls which surrounded it. Joshua and Caleb destined by Lord to enter the Promised Land had the difficult task of conquering Jericho. The Israelities then consisted of twelve nomad tribes. The siege lasted for six days as Joshua's tribes marched around the town carrying the Arc of Covenant. On the seventh day, The Day of Sabbath, Joshua ordered his tribes to blow trumpets made of ram's horns and the walls came crumbling down, resulting in the capture of the town. After this Joshua made a sacrifice at Mount Ebal above Shechem, today's Nablus. Thereafter, followed the division of land into the tribes of Ruben, Gad and half the tribes of Menasha who were permitted to return to east of Jordan while Levi, the second half and the priestly tribe got six cities, three each, on either side of river Jordan, designated "cities refuge" while the remaining lands conquered in Canaan were divided among the eight and a half remaining tribes.

Deborah, who was a Judge in the 12th century B.C., led the Israelities against Jabin, the Canaanite King of Hazor in North Canaan. Not all the tribes joined together in this effort and the main brunt was borne by the southern tribes of Judah and Simeon. Meticulously planned, the three phase attack resulted in the victory in the Kishon valley. Her name is emblazoned in letters of gold in the annals of Judaic faith.

Next we come to the almost mythical figure of Samson, a genial giant by the end of the 12th century B.C., who destroyed an entire Philistine army single-handed with the jaw bone of an ass. The Philistine King then hired a harlot, Delilah, to find out the secret of his strength. Delilah through cunning, deceit and her charms discovered that this lay in the locks of his hair. She got them sheared as the Philistines blinded him. Later as his hair grew his strength returned and he prayed to his Lord to seek the freedom of his land. Led by a young boy he reached the Hippodrome at Gaza, where the entire Philistine nobility, the King and his cohorts had assembled. With his mighty arms he shook the pillars and brought the building crashing down, killing all inside. No trace was left of the Philistines.

The chronicle leads now to David, founder of Jerusalem and the first united kingdom of the Jews in the land of Judea. Much has been written about David earlier. The excavations at Ophel have brought out the remains of the city of David. Israel's national flag today carries the star of David. We have already dwelt on Solomon, his illustrious son, in some detail earlier.

Judah the Maccabee was the fighter for freedom who conducted the world's first known guerrilla war against the Greek Emperor Antiochus' forces of three armies commanded by Generals Ptolemy, Nicanor and Gorgias supplemented by forces from Idumea and the coastal region. Incidentally, Maccabee is a Greek word meaning 'hammer'. His exploits have also been described in detail.

One of the greatest Jews was Bar-Kokhba, who dared to take on the invincible Roman might during 63 to 73 A.D. in a relentless war against the Roman forces. The story of the Zealots and the epic Jewish war against the Roman Emperor Vespasian and his son, Titus, has been told earlier with the finale of a suicide defence at the fortress of Masada. The rock of Masada is a section of a cliff with a sheer drop to the Dead Sea 1000 feet below and is surrounded by steep ravines on all sides making it an impregnable fortress. This was the last bastion whose destruction would lead to the capture of Jerusalem. The local leader here was Elazar Be-Yair. The Roman Tenth Legion invaded Masada in early 73 A.D. According to a chronicler:

> "Despite the imbalance of forces, capturing Masada was not a simple matter, for the Jewish defenders had more than adequate supplies of food and water. The largest ravine had been dammed, and from it an aqueduct fed a line of cisterns cut into the side of the rock. The Romans destroyed the aqueduct, but there was plenty of water in the cisterns from the winter's rainfall. Herod's storehouses were crammed with grain, oil, dried fruit and vegetables..."
>
> "The Romans set about their siege in a typically methodical fashion, building small forts at every possible point of egress and joining them with a wall circumventing the rock. They then constructed a gigantic ramp of earth and wood in the valley to the west. A remarkable engineering feat for those days, the ramp is still there, pointing like a sword at the fortress. On top of the ramp, the attackers constructed a siege tower under cover of which they battered the defensive walls. They broke through the stonewalls, only to discover that the defenders had constructed an inner wall of wood and earth, which was impervious to their battering rams."

In due course, the Romans set alight this inner wall. The attackers were surprised at the speed with which the fire spread to the whole fortress. The following morning they discovered why. When they entered the charred remains of the stronghold, they found the bodies of the defenders laid out in neat rows. The men had first killed their own families and then drawn lots for a final ten to kill the men, upon which one man had killed the other and then himself". Masada became a place of pilgrimage for modern Israelis and an exploratory archaeological dig was conducted there in the 1950s. In 1963-64, Yigael Yadin, the soldier-archaeologist, led two seasons of spectacular excavations at Masada. Fragments of biblical scrolls and documents of the Dead Sea sect were discovered there, as well as numerous inscriptions, jars with the remains of food preserved in the dry climate for almost two millennia, mosaics and wall paintings.

Masada is rightly a symbol in Israel today, an inspiring monument to heroic ancestors who preferred death to slavery. Young soldiers of the armoured corps swear their oath of allegiance atop the bleak mountain with the vow. "Masada shall not fall again!" According to a chronicler: "Even after Masada fell and Jerusalem and the Temple were no more, the Jews were still not cowed, A series of uprisings and rebellions against the Emperor Trajan surged through the Jewish communities in Egypt, Mesopotamia, Cyrene and Cyprus in 115 A.D., eventually spreading to Judea. Thousands of Jews were killed and order was only restored in 117 A.D. at the start of Hadrian's reign." Recent excavations reveal no indication that Bar-Kokhba intended to fortify Jerusalem or rebuild the Temple. In his constant struggle he had no time for such an activity. The place where Bar-Kokhba rallied his supporters for the final stand is a village named Betar located within the steep-sided valley of Sorek. The location has a spring which flows even today.

Joseph Trumpaldor, another hero, was the Jew who commanded the Zion Mute Corps in the Gallipoli campaign and later the Jewish Legion, fighting alongside the British against the Turks during the First World War. He was also the founder of Hashomer, meaning the "Watchman", i.e., the self-defence forces for protecting the "Yishuv", the Jewish settlement in Palestine. Next on our list is Chaim Herzog, the Prime Minister of Israel, who was a master of military strategy and tactics and a visionary. What a contrast with Nehru who authored two disasters, Kashmir and the war against China. Our narrative of the heroes will not be complete without the mention of Menachem Begin, a born fighter and the father of Jewish revolt prior to the Declaration of Independence. But the tallest of the heroes of the modern era, culminating in the freedom of Israel, is David Ben-Gurion who can rightly be called the 'Father of the modern Jewish State'. We shall highlight his contributions in the making of Israel and shall revert to him again a little later.

PART - 2

From Diaspora to the establishment of a Jewish Home

Chapter 9

Jews in America

Oscar Wilde is reported to have said that America was discovered many times before Columbus, but the fact was always hushed up. Be that as it may, even the man, Columbus himself a Marrano, who discovered America on 12th October, 1492, had five Jewish crew aboard his ship. It has been mentioned earlier that Marranos were the Jews in Spain and Portugal who had converted to Christianity under duress but practised their Jewish rites and rituals secretly. Netherlands, a land of religious tolerance, acted as a beacon of light in the all pervading darkness that shrouded Europe, and a large number of Marranos who were hounded out by the Council of Inquisition found a safe haven here, and later crossed the Atlantic to reach the North-eastern shores of America. Others, forced by the persecution under the same ubiquitous arm of Inquisition, left their homes in Spain and Portugal and headed not only for north-east American shores but also towards Brazil in South America. The 23 Marranos who moved out of Spain for Brazil were again expelled from the port of Pernambuco (Zur Israel) by the Portuguese colonizers in 1654 and set sail for North America. All the ships carrying the Jews belonged to the Dutch West India Company. This motley group of fugitive Jews then boarded a ship "St. Charles" under Capt. De la Morthe and arrived at New Netherlands, (later called New England) and dropped anchor at the port of

New Amsterdam, (later named New York), on the island of Manhattan in September 1654. Simultaneously another batch of Marranos landed at Buenos Aires, the capital city of Argentina.

There were two categories of Jews from Europe who came to America. The first were the Lashkenasim who came from Middle, Northern and Eastern Europe, mainly Germany, Poland and Russia. The second, Sephardim, moved from Southern and Western Europe. The word 'Sephardim' is derived from the word 'Shepard' a place name in the Book of Obadiah in post-Biblical Jewish literature. The Lashkenasims spoke Ladino, a dialect of Hebrew mixed Spanish, while the Jews from East Europe were less educated and sedulously adhered to Talmud and Torah. They were removed from the main communities and forced to live in "Shetl", an all Jewish town or village laid out in the countryside. The Ghetto, on the other hand, was a part of the town, a segregated and sequestered locality where the Jews were permitted to live. It is an interesting but a little known fact of history that the American Indians were thought to be the direct descendants of the ten Lost Tribes of Israel. The Jewish community around Amsterdam was called 'Shearith Israel' while the one which formed the apex platform of Jews solidarity and forum for helping and unifying Jews of all opinions and practices in Latin America was named "B'nai Birth". Some typical Hebrew words in common use in both the continents were "Hechal" meaning Holy Arch 'Sefarim' meaning Scrolls of Law; "Kol Nidre" meant Jews prayer, "Kehilla" meant a religious Jewish congregation; and 'Sholon Aleichem' was the Jewish greeting. The word 'synagogue' is derived from the Greek word "Synagogue" which means a bringing together or an assembly, unlike a church, which means the Lord's house or space for worship. The Jews who landed at New Amsterdam were initially confined to a Ghetto called "Jews Alley" on Manhattan Island. They were helped by the earlier settlers, the Jews of Amsterdam in Holland called "Burghers".

The first leader of American Jewry was Asser Levi Van Swellen, an Ashkenazi Jew, later called simply Asser Levi. He, with the permission of the local Governor, Peter Stuyvesant, was allowed to own one of the six slaughter houses licensed to operate in New York. This was located at the end of the Wall Street known as 'Broadway Shamble'. He was the first Jew to own real estate in America and that too in New York City. Ten years after the arrival of the 23 Jews in New Amsterdam in New Netherlands, Asser Levi was one of the richest traders and citizens of the city. This was the time when the British warship arrived and the Dutch Governor surrendered the colony from the Dutch West Indies Company to His Royal Highness James, Duke of York, who rechristened the city as New York, after his own name. The Christian community in and around New York and New Port, mostly Puritans, respected Jewish emphasis on learning and intellectualism, so much so that they introduced Hebrew as a language in Harvard College which they had founded, a practice which was followed by many Universities later, including Yale.

For the Jews fleeing the persecution in Europe, the United States of America was an ideal destination. A country newly born after a revolution and whose Constitution contained the famous words of Thomas Jefferson, "All men are born equal" was one place where the Jews hoped to find a shelter and a status of equality. But anti-Semitism still persisted amongst the orthodox Christian settlers of Puritanical persuasion. Even an enlightened author like Thomas Paine in his book *The Age of Reason* felt that "While Christians had to be cured of their belief in Bible trash, the Jews had to be cured of their character." Be that as it may, many Jews had fought and helped in the Revolution of 1776. Chief among them were Haym Salomon of Philadelphia, Aaron Lopez of Newport, and Mordecai Sheftall of Savannah. But prejudices die hard. A prominent leader of Jewish community in Philadelphia, Benjamin Nones, who advised Jews to forego some of their rituals and compulsory attendance at the Synagogues, tried his best to fill the cleavage between the Jews and the Christians. The attack on Jews, however, continued here also.

In spite of the tremendous contributions of the Jews in the American War of Independence there had been a long list of cases of attacks on Jews, although the Constitution was profoundly in their favour, despite great stirrings all round. Jews were not quite sure what the new Republic meant to them, nor were the Christians on what they wanted out of Jews. During the American revolution there was a great need for clothing, food, animals, wagons and equipment for Washington's rag-tag army as also for men who knew the financial needs of a war. The new government had no money to pay the troops, but the Jews came forward to advance the cash needed in return for IOUs whose redemption was doubtful. Some Jewish merchants, particularly Gratz brothers of Philadelphia, volunteered to purchase British goods badly needed by the troops, while some Jew traders like Isaac Moses and Aaron Lopez fitted cannons to their vessels to prey on British shipping. Benjamin Nones, a French Jew about whom much will come later, offered to enlist in the Continental Army. He fought so gallantly in many battles such as the siege of Savannah that he was promoted to the rank of major commanding "the Jews' Company". Haym Salomon also mentioned later, who fled in 1772 from Poland to America and played a leading role in the revolution, was a member of the Sons of Liberty, and along with young revolutionaries Kosciusko and Pulaski, worked behind locked doors for the oncoming war. One of the longest highways in America is named after Pulaski. He carried out many acts of sabotage against the British and was captured by them. He escaped and acted as Paymaster-General for the French forces fighting with the Colonials against the British. Rightly called "freedom's financier", Salomon was as generous as could be with his money to the nation, and financed the Continental Congress at Philadelphia. He was the founding member of the Congregation Mikveh Israel and Philadelphia's first synagogue which he opened in 1783 after providing more than one-third of the building cost. He died at the age of forty-five from a chronic lung disease, a direct result of his war exertions. He left a huge legacy for charitable causes, and fittingly on the 150th anniversary of the Bill of Rights, during a dedication ceremony, his statue was erected in Chicago where he is shown joining hands with George Washington and Robert Morris, symbolizing the founding of a nation of freedom. Even before the formal declaration of independence on 4th July, 1776, during the early part of the year when preliminary operations against the British had started, Ethan Allen, a giant of a Jew, led his green Ahomitani Boys and captured the fort of Ticonderoga on May 10, 1775.

Antipathy to the Jews took many forms, ranging from verbal diatribe to physical assaults. *The Gazette of the United States* came out with the scathing attack on Benjamin Nones for being a Jew and a Republican, a supporter of what is today called the Democratic party. Nones' anguished reply to the attack was as follows:

> "I am a Jew. I glory in belonging to that persuasion, which even its opponents, whether Christian, or Mahomedan, allow to be of divine origin–of that persuasion on which Christianity itself was originally founded and must ultimately rest, which has preserved its faith secure and undefiled, for near three thousand years–whose votaries have never murdered each other in religious wars, or cherished the theological hatred so general, so unextinguishable among those who revile them....
>
> "But I am a Jew I am so– and so were Abraham, and Isaac, and Moses and the prophets, and so too were Christ and his apostles. I feel no disgrace in ranking with such society, however it may be subject to the illiberal buffoonery of such men as your correspondents....
>
> "I am a Republican! ...Among the nations of Europe we are inhabitants everywhere – but citizens of nowhere unless in Republics. Here, in France and in the Batavia Republic alone, we are treated as men and as brethren. In monarchies we live but to experience wrongs..."
>
> "How then can a Jew but be a Republican? In America particularly, unfeeling and ungrateful would he be, if he were callous to the glorious and benevolent cause of the difference between his situation in this land of freedom, and among the proud and privileged law-givers of Europe."

But the contribution of immigrant Jews to the well being of America continued with even greater vigour.

The following five Jews, despite all the disabilities heaped upon them in their adopted homeland, did America proud. The first was Isaac Toure, who took part at New Orleans in the 1812 war against France. A patriarch, prophet and a philanthropist, he gave out innumerable charities to synagogues in every nook and corner of the new country. The second was Solomon Etting of Maryland, a friend of President Jefferson, who helped in the drafting of the Bill for Equality of Rights. His brother, Reuben who was appointed Marshall for Maryland, also helped his brother in his philanthropic work and the two spared no pains in helping the Jewish community and even the Christians no end. The third was Uriah Phillips Levy, the first Jew to join the US Navy, who retired as a Commodore, the highest rank in the Navy at the time. He abolished the flogging of sailors and faced a Court of Inquiry in 1857 on false charges and defended himself with success. An escort vessel to a destroyer of US Navy, was named after him as *USS Levy*. The fourth Jew, Simon Simson founded the first Jewish hospital named Mount Sinai Hospital in 1852 for benevolent, charitable and scientific purposes. The last, Mordecai Manuel Noah was a versatile journalist, politician, playwright, diplomat, author, philanthropist, sheriff, surveyor of the Port of New York, lawyer, judge and many things rolled into one. He was appointed Ambassador to Tunis and founded a colony for the Jews near Niagara and Buffalo, "Avarat" named after the place where Noah's ark settled in Turkey.

The immigrant Jews helped each other after the arrival of the German Jews in 1840s and 1850s. A dozen youngmen applied in 1843 to the Odd Fellows Lodge but they were refused membership. These young Jews then met together and organised a comparable body of their own, the independent "Order of B'Nai B'Rith". In the preamble of their constitution the founders proposed to do everything possible from uniting Israelites in the work of promoting their highest causes and those of humanity, to visiting the sick and providing for widows and orphans. The emphasis on "humanity" by the founders of "Order of B'Nai

B'Rith" was a way of saying that they, the Jews who had been forced into an organisation of their own, were truer representatives of the cause of a united mankind than Gentiles of the Odd Fellows who had excluded them. This assertion would recur over and over again for the next century or so, as the quintessential response by the Jews to anti-Semitism. Many more such organisations and higher membership followed. By 1849, some 50 Jewish organisations, charitable, social and fraternal in New York with a membership far greater than that of the Synagogues, sprang into existence. These societies gradually became the major homes of organised Jewish life. The Jews, under the leadership of Isaac Mayer Wise, a Jewish resident of Bohemia and a teacher and religious functionary in Radnitz, struggled to become equal, and later surpassed even the Americans in wealth and position. The life of Wise is the central story of the "German Jews" in America from their arrival until around 1900, as the year of his death. By 1880s, three quarters of all clothing business of all kinds in America was controlled by the Jews. Even the rich Jews were later segregated due to their success and wealth and consigned to their 'gilded ghettos'. The German Jews who formed the back-bone of the economic strength and rich enterprise and tried to Americanise themselves were rebuffed initially, but by sheer perseverance later succeeded to a degree. With the arrival of East European and Russian Jews these rich Germans helped them to establish and prevented them from returning home, where they were a burden on the country and thus indirectly encouraged anti-Semitism. They were taught English in place of their earlier German and Yiddish language and helped to settle in non-conventional jobs, since there was already unfounded resentment against the Jews dominating the Wall Street. The new Jews were thus kept away from New York.

Of about thirty-five million immigrants arriving in the United States in the 50 years after the Civil War, more than two millions were the Jews which comprised 15 percent of all European Jewry, and nearly eight percent of all immigrants to the United States. The main cause of this immigration was over-population in Europe and later the hope, the "push factor" and an even stronger "pull factor", i.e., attraction for America where land for farmers and industrialisation in cities was creating millions of jobs. And lastly, the "push factor" from anti-Semitism. These Jews were poor people, the peddlers and tailors and largely uneducated, but rose in less than two generations to the very apex of American life. They brought socialism and revolutionary zeal, but soon got transformed into capitalists and moderates. 'More attached to their relatives, left behind and conscious of anti-Semitism, as opposed to the "German Jews" who were partially absorbed, the "Russian Jews" were intensely involved in maintaining their separateness. The "German Jews" had been few and they had defined themselves in an open expanding America and to a very great degree on its frontier. It was easy for them to think of themselves as different from other Americans only by religion. The "Russian Jews" on the other hand came to the city when America needed hands for the factories and they came in large numbers. These Jews and their children would have far more trouble finding their way into America.

Serious anti-Semitism in America appeared only on the arrival of the "Russian Jews". Though apparently targeted at them, it was also equally affecting the "German Jews" who were also under direct fire. The "German Jews" posing to Gentiles as superior and more American than the "Russian Jews", nevertheless, felt responsible for and looked after them. The German and Russian Jews remained separate communities, the Germans hoping that the Russians would, like them, become "Americans of Jewish religious persuasion." The Russians, however, did not fall in line and remained trapped in their prejudices and had to find their way out of this Ghetto. They saw no profit or balm in respectability. A peculiar phenomenon existed in the poor families of Jewish immigrants in America. The fathers of low class large families, unable to fend for themselves, deserted their duties and the mothers took over not only as the bread-winners but also as keepers of the Jewish faith. Thus came the invention of the concept of 'Jewish mother.'

Between 1914 and 1918, the "German Jews" lost out to "Russian Jews" who rebelled and won in the name of Zionism. Instead of playing the game the American way and force the majority for legitimacy and social justice, they pressed forthright for Jewish interest. Louis Dembidz Brandeis, a friend of President Wilson, heading the Zionist organisation, gave it respectability and transformed the purely Russian movement into a public force. Before 1914, Zionism in America differed from Zionism in Europe, where it meant the Ghetto to live in and move out to Palestine as a national home. In America it existed only to take pride in and to help the country but not change itself by moving out to Palestine, thereby conveying that they had made a mistake in coming to America for a home and re-pack again to leave for Palestine.

The second generation Jews were not content to simply disappear amongst the hoi polloi of America. These idealists wished to make a difference as Jews. And they answered anti-Semitism by striving to remake America. They knew in their bones that they had special responsibilities because they were Jews. These men and women were not "adjusting" to the existing America, and, least of all, to the life of their own enclave of rich, respectable Jews. The classic doctrine of Jewish theology, "chosen-ness" had reappeared among American jews, in the guise of their special vocation to fight for social justice. The "Russian Jews" about which we have talked earlier, did not take very kindly to the patronage of the "German Jews" or Gentiles. And this was the root cause of the birth of modern Zionism. To quote Arthur Hertzberg, "By acting as Zionists, these immigrants ceased being silent protégés of the "German Jews." By demanding power in the American Jewish community, and by refusing to let the "German Jews" speak for them to the Gentiles, the immigrants had taken the first major step towards refusing to remain "on approval" in America."

After 1920 due to the Russian Revolution, the suspicion of "Communist Jews" and their Bolshevic leanings was an adverse factor in the assimilation of Jews. However, the Russian pogroms brought out the evil aspects of Bolshevism and the Jews obtained some sympathy from American society as victims of their arch-enemy, Communism. Nevertheless Immigration Laws for the Jews were tightened further, and the gates to the land of liberty were partially closed. On the other hand, the children of Ghetto had no alternative but to flee Russia, Poland and Romania and their torture chambers to the safety of the United States. Jews needed acceptance in America more than any minority and their morale reached its nadir in l930, which coincided with the depression and anti-Semitism. However, redemption was close at hand. And the benevolent king of Jews in the person of Frederick Delano Roosevelt (FDR for short), emerged on the scene as the President of America. His place in the American history is unique as one who offered the New Deal, brought in State Reforms and applied correctives to unbridled capitalism that put America back on it's path to prosperity. In this gigantic effort the Jews occupied the largest number of positions in the Administration. Benjamin V. Cohen and Samuel Rasenmen were his most trusted bureaucrats while Henry Margentham Jr., his friend and neighbour in Duchess County, was the Secretary of Treasury. Felix Frank Furtler, the famous Professor of Law at Harvard University, regulated the Economic Committees at the White House. The Jews were visible, almost definably so, in the upper reaches of Roosevelt Administration. Though always consultants to the President, their very presence was a signal of hope to the Jewish masses, endangered by Nazis abroad and anti-Semitism at home. Civil services were open to the Jews through competitive examinations and many Jews entered the Government as many white collared jobs were created benefiting the Jews. From the large pool of unemployed graduates, the Jews entered almost all professions. The Work Progress Administration (WPA), put people to work at Government expense. Yiddish, the language of the ghetto, was encouraged and was pronounced a part of the American life. Though the WPA's Yiddish writer project was a small recompense for the discrimination of the Jews in the Immigration Laws, this beneficent image of FDR was etched in the Jewish psyche. It was as much a product of fantasy as substance. In spite of his active assistance to the Jews, the public opinion forestalled many of his progressive measures for the Jews. Some of his own party-men rose against him. There was this tragic case of the ship *St. Louis* carrying 700 valid Jews for entry into the United States via Cuba which was sent back for the travellers to be gassed by the Nazis as Roosevelt stood helpless. The British blockade of Europe was as much directed against Hitler's Fortress Europa as against the Jews trying to move out to their home land. At last, America did act and its two years of neutrality ended in 1941 after Pearl Harbour, as fresh news of the murder of 700,000 Jews in Poland alone reached the State Department. This acquiesing in the holocaust till 1943, by the US Administration and even some Jews is a riddle which has not been fully explained till today. The reason could have been FDR's not being sure of an Allied victory and he waited for the tide to turn against the Nazis. This indecision proved fatal and six million Jews perished in Europe. The insensitivity of the Americans contributed in no small measure, to the failure of American Jewry's attempt to finesse the difference between Jews and other Americans while insisting that there was no difference. Though the "German Jews" did not appreciate the depth of anti-Semitism feeling in America, the Jews remained a "sui generis" minority.

The self enforced amnesia of the American people to Jewish sufferings did create problems in their assimilations in American body politic... To quote Arthur Hertzberg:

> "Perforce, American Jews looked at the death camps which had been discovered by the Allies in 1945, but they preferred to bury the issues raised by the newsreels of bodies attached like cordwood in Bergen-Belsen, or of the ashes in the ovens of Auschwitz. American Jews did not want to stand aside from the rest of America. In their deepest souls, the sight of the death camps had suddenly made them very lonely in the world. As "cobelligerents", the Jewish people had lost their war. But American Jews needed to feel that they were part of America, that they were among the victors. Possible American complicity, by inaction, in the murder of the Jews of Europe could not be discussed. If such an accusation

were true, America's Jews would have had to continue to think of themselves as deeply alien. In the midst of the euphoria of the spring of 1943, American Jews would have been left to imagine themselves as stepchildren, more of a nuisance than a source of pride, to America as a whole, and even to the "gracious king" Franklin Delano Roosevelt."

The Jews also took active interest in the emancipation of the blacks. Otto Klineberg declared "that the charge of inherent racial inferiority is utterly without warrant", and further that "the Jewish intellectual, steeped in the prophetic tradition of his people, is necessarily a defender of democracy, a champion of justice for all people". Arthur Hertzberg again:

> "To be sure, the involvement of Jews in the cause of blacks did not come cheap. Jews paid an outsize share of the financial bill for the black organisations. Few statistics are available, but it is a fair guess that at least a third of the money that financed the NAACP and the Urban League in the 1950s came from Jewish contributors. Thousands of Jews helped organise and participated in the protest marches in the South and in the North. These men and women were most often passionately convinced idealists—but their efforts for the black revolution served Jews in a very deep way. The era after the Second World War was the time when Jews were on the march, with the intention of arriving at the very top of American society. By the mid-1950s, they had made base camp, through their rapid economic rise, for the final assault on the Mount Everest of elite status in America. Now, through their role in the black revolution, Jews were making their first overt bid for a major place in the American elite. They were announcing themselves as a major force for solving America's worst problem, racial tension. The Jews were the only white community in America that was very nearly united - in support of blacks. The great and passionate participation of Jews in the battle for blacks was the very first time, in all of American history, when Jews were not pleading for themselves. They were leaders at the very cutting edge of social change - and thus they had "arrived" at the centre of American life."

To say that the Black American was grateful to the Jews for the espousal of his cause would amount to being economic with the truth. In fact, he took this noble gesture as a condescension from another white community and a token of hypocrisy to the underdog. Black nationalism took various forms and these movements were essentially similar in their Negro chauvinism and in their 'anti-Whiteism.' The Negro Muslim movement is also anti-Christian and anti-Jewish.

The creation of Israel offered the Jews of America a place they could call their homeland, and in which they could take pride and achieve a normal status in America. Again Arthur Hertzberg:

> "It was inevitable that American Jews would conceive of their old-new homeland as uniquely heroic. This nation had arisen again after a hiatus of two thousand years. This "miracle" had more than a hint of "chosenness" about it. Those who identified with the new State of Israel could feel very special as Jews, even as they were becoming Americans with roots in a homeland of their own, just like all other Americans."

In the fall of 1947, Abba Hillel Silver, the elected leader of the American Zionists, took a seat in the United Nations along with Moshe Shertok, the political secretary of the World Zionist Organisation. A reformed rabbi from Eastern Europe, who arrived in the United States as a child, Silver was possessed of enormous demagogic power as he took the cause of Zionism in ringing tones with an American accent before the United Nations. He swayed the Assembly to the approval of the ultimate dream of his generation. This son of the immigrants to America was speaking for all the Jews of the world, as an equal to princes and prime ministers.

The American Jews were sure that the involvement in Israel guaranteed the survival of their Jewishness. The faith in their homeland informed the rhetoric and the actions of the American Jewry. It was more evident in the 1950s and 1960s that their support for Israel would also guarantee the Jewishness of the next generation of American Jews. Funds were raised for Israel to remind all Jewish children and grand-children that they shall remember that they are Jews. They also now formed a solid vote bank for any aspiring Presidential candidate. Increasingly, and ever more overtly, Jews were making the support of Israel into an American political issue, and they were rising to the heights of American politics precisely because of their involvement in Israel.

American interference in the Suez canal crisis where the Israeli forces along with the British and French troops occupied the Suez Canal consequent to its nationalisation by Nasser of Egypt in 1956, was a temporary damper to the Jewish enthusiasm. Americans had their own reasons for what they did. But Israel had equally valid reason to capture Suez as a reprisal to the constant raids by the Egyptians into Israel's territory. But for all that the Jews in America were now convinced that they could no longer exist merely on American goodwill but will have to be in a commanding position in the country of their adoption, to be not merely heard but respected and satisfied.

With President John F. Kennedy dawned another era of the resurgence of Jewish influence in America. The Jewish "otherness" needed a positive juxtaposition as American Jews had to convince their children for its need and rationale. To be "proud to be Jew" and not merely to be angered with their enemies. A "useable past" had to be constructed and editing of memories had begun as soon as the Jews started arriving after the World War II. The Rosenberg affair, where a Jewish couple Ethel and Julius Rosenberg were convicted of spying for Russia on "atomic secret", had "corrected" the notion that many Jews were pro- Communist. The Jews insisted that they had always been the most respected American citizens. It would not be improper to state here that the biggest event of history known to the Western world is the mass migration of the scientific communities of the Jews from Germany to America carrying with them the secrets of the atom bomb. Hitler's loss was America's gain and the result was the bombing of Hiroshima and Nagasaki which brought the end of the Second World War. The new generation was not overtly keen to exhibit its separateness. Nathan Glazier and Senator Daniel Patrick Moynihom in their book *Beyond the Melting Pot* wrote:

> "Neither the Synagogues and Temples nor the charitable and philanthropic work, nor the fund raising for Israel and defence, seems sufficiently vital and relevant for the most coveted and young people who are emerging from the community. Nor it is that other community that was scarcely less Jewish, that of the radical movement and trade unions engaged them much."

"The events of 1967 answered some questions that administration of the community had been asking for several years before, how to define Jewishness in America's open society. In June 1967, the Jews of America were "saved" from having to think about the issues of meaning and value that the intellectuals and ultra orthodox had posed. They did not have to face the question that Phillip Roth had asked; "What is Jewishness to the unbelieving Jews?" There was a ready answer; "It is glory in Israel."

This high drama did not last very long. American Jews thought they had solved their problems as American and Jews but they had not. They were in fact, even more comfortable with their place in the jostle of American society and ever less-secure within themselves. This is also true of the Indians settled in America. But there is a difference. Today, the Jews are in the driving seat of almost all intellectual activity in America just as the Indians occupy key positions in scientific research, computer software, business management, medical profession, engineering and other white collar jobs.

Reverting to the golden era of President John F. Kennedy, the Jews rose to positions of eminence. These included not only such figures as Arthur Schlesinger, Jr., who had Jewish immigrants in his immediate family tree, but also McGeorge Bundy, who was descended from the oldest Puritan families. Kennedy's "Camelot" was, thus, not an unvarnished overturn of the older America by an ethnic "pol" who transferred to Washington the machine politis of his grandfather, the first Irish mayor of Boston, John F. Fitzgerald. The minorities were not now simply being given their turn to stuff themselves at the political trough. Kennedy's "Camelot" thought of itself as a meritocracy, as a national leadership of the ablest mandarins, who were recruited regardless of their origins. This theory of merit was satisfying to the Jews, for they had been pushing for two centuries for the concept of "careers based on talent."

During my visit to Amsterdam, from 28 to 30 May, 2001, on my way to the USA, I was pleasantly surprised when my Dutch car-driver, who showed me around the city, informed me that the Jews formed twenty-five percent of the total population of Holland. But he added that these simple hard working people posed no problem to his country. They had merged so well with the local population that they were in-distinguishable from the majority Christian population. They not only achieved remarkable success in their professions and occupied commanding heights of economy, but also in the process left no rancour in the heart of the majority community. It was almost impossible to single out a Jew from the rest. Though Dutch liberalism and a great spirit of accommodation like that of a Hindu has much to do with this painless assimilation of a minority, the Jewish genius is equally responsible for this process. This appears to be in sharp contrast with the Muslim population in our country which forms only fifteen percent of one billion of our total population. Undoubtedly there are mitigating facts in their favour, such as their obscurantist religious leaders, Mullahs, Maulvees and many self professed leaders of the community not least among them the Imam of Delhi Jama Masjid. Syed Shahbuddin, a retired I.F.S. Officer and a self-styled leader of Muslim community, once mentioned on a T.V. channel. "I am a Muslim first and an Indian later." Recently in a similar outburst on a T.V. show, "The Big Fight" Mr. Banatwala, Chairman of the Indian Muslim League, also said that the Muslim response to any national or international issue has to be circumscribed by the teachings of Koran and the laws of Shariat.

There is no Pope, bishop or priest in Islam. Likewise, there is no hierarchy, religious or social in the tenets of Koran. One is reminded of the lines of great poet Iqbal, *"Ek hi saf me khare ho gaye Mahmud-o-Ayuz* (the King and the slave pray together)". But the stranglehold of the Muslim clerics on laity is so strong that they can justify any action, and order the faithful to go to any limit of cruelty and barbarism, all in the name of Allah and the cry of 'Jehad'. One can see even today the sharp polarisation of Muslims all over the world against the legitimate punitive actions against terrorism. Terrorism knows no religion, and the murder of innocent civilians by acts of terror cannot be justified by any logic or religious exhortation. But this is precisely what is happening, when the simple issue of combating terrorism had been hijacked by the religious fundamentalists and given the name of a fight between the Western infidel and Islam. All this has the blessings of Mullahs and Maulavis all over the world, who are acting as cheer leaders to infuriate the mobs against the West. The Muslims in many countries enlisted in the ranks of the Talibans and proceeded to Afghanistan to fight the so-called scourge of the Western colonialism. The Indian Muslims should not forget that in 1920s they during the Khilafat Movement were ordered for 'Hijrat' (migration) to Afghanistan. Their self styled leaders and divines were enjoying sumptuous meals in their cosy homes while their followers were serving in the cold and ragged mountains of Afghanistan. Some of these fighters were even jailed in Afghanistan and some sent back to India. Muslims, like Jews, should act as respectable citizens of the countries where they live and which have given them shelter and respect.

Chapter 10

Judaism and Justice

Judaism is a religion based on law and divine commandments. The Jewish laws contain 24,529 words of rules and regulations in the Book of Leviticus and form the edifice founded on the 'Lord's Commandments' at Mount Sinai. The origins of the Jewish laws are found in the Torah consisting of five books of Moses whose interpretations and analyses are spread over two dozen volumes called Talmud. A considerable corpus of discussions, debates and opinions of rabbinical scholars forms the great moral foundation of the democratic Hebraic commonwealth. Judaism is the only religion in the world which is founded on law, though there are striking similarities in this regard with the Hindu religion. Like Manusmriti in Vedic lore, Mosaic laws lay down the paradigm of moral and political principles. There is a saying that every Jew is a lawyer. While Christianity focuses on the hereafter, Judaism concerns itself mainly with the present and immediate future. While the Christian preoccupation is the saving of souls through faith, Judaism is concerned with saving mankind through acts of justice. While Christianity emphasises relationship between God and man, Judaism stresses the relationship between man and man. For a Jew belief transmutes into social action and hence the importance of law and the need for justice. Although Mosaic Law and Talmud prescribe for humanity only general principles, the details of a man's daily routine unlike Quranik teachings and Fatwas are left subject to evolution, review, intelligent interpretation and reform. Even though every Jew spends much of his time studying and memorising not only the Ten major Commandments but hundreds of regulations that rule his life, his day-to-day conduct is rational, practical and forward looking, and not fossilised in a time warp. 'No man is a stranger, and God belongs to all human beings', is the credo of Judaism. With the march of history, particularly after the seventeenth century, the effect of Biblical and rabbinical writings can be seen in the development of secular justice all over the world. Therefore, it is no wonder that even in their adopted home in America the principal contribution of the Jews has been in the field of law and justice. The movement for prison reform, abolition of capital punishment and rehabilitation of criminals is entirely a Jewish contribution derived by repealing the ancient Mosaic law by independent interpretation of the same with a mix of reason and humanity.

A powerful rabbinical figure between two world wars, Abba Hillel Silver, a Lithuanian migrant to Cleaveland State in America, led the largest Reform congregation in America known as "The Temple". A great orator, writer and a courageous liberal, he helped introduce the first child labour laws and Unemployment Insurance Act into the statute books. Along with his other accomplishments such as head of the Zionist Organisation of America, the United Jewish Appeal, the American Section of the Jewish Agency, the Central Conference of American Rabbis, and the American Zionist Emergency Council, he contributed substantially to the 1947 Palestine Partition Plan. In his provocative book *How Judaism Differed* he stressed the "different-ness" of the Judaic faith and questioned the so-called egalitarian approach of labelling up all religions under a common denominator. Judaism has five unique features not shared by other religions, except Hinduism. It never contends that:

(i) Man was born of an original sin from which he has to be redeemed;

(ii) Man should not enjoy life and remain austere;

(iii) Men are not equal; this resonates with the Hindu view of 'Vasudhaiv Kutumbakam', i.e., fraternity and equality of men.

(iv) Men are not free.

(v) Death is better than life.

Thus he remonstrated with the heads of other religions against placing Judaism in the same mould.

Judaism attaches great value to the worth of man, just as Rabbi Akiba observed that "Precious is man, since he is created in God's image." Judaic laws ordain that everyone has the right to express his individuality and develop his uniqueness. He is free to express or subsume the thoughts of his mind and the dictates of his soul. This is surprisingly similar to Hinduism where the worth of man is considered even more than that of gods. The gods are immortal but unlike the mortal man, they have no freedom for action or "Karma". Judaism is unique in that it has prescribed punishment for wrong conduct but never for wrong opinion. In the history of Judaism there have been no burnings at stakes or Councils of Inquisition. Hundred years before Jesus declared in his Sermon on the Mount, "Therefore on things whatsoever ye would that men should do to you, do ye even to them." Hillel the Elder had put forward a different proposition, "What is hateful to yourself do not do to your neighbour." The two disparate wordings of the Golden Rule bring out the fundamental difference between Christianity and Judaism. Hillel's version guarantees more freedom and privacy than the words of Jesus. In other words, Judaism ordains that the neighbour should neither be proselytized, nor punished for his beliefs.

Judaism has been called a religion of social idealism and surprisingly no righteous causes anywhere seem alien to the liberal rabbis of America. Humanitarian causes of other faiths come naturally to them. Corruption and special privilege is repugnant to Judaic ethics. Movement for fair wages for labour, better working conditions, ending child exploitation, better housing, social security, prison reforms, international peace and foundation of the League of Nations and subsequently the United Nations had the unwavering and unstinted support of the Jews and Israel. The first Director of the Peace Corps, Shriver, asked David Ben-Gurion in 1967 during his visit to the United States, "How do you account for the fact that 40 percent of those in the Peace Corps are Jews and some 70 percent of those involved in civil rights and social justice causes are Jews?" With a twinkle in his eyes Ben-Gurion replied, "Because they are Jews!"

In the old world as well as New England, earlier known as New Netherlands due to its first settlers being Dutch Jews who also named present day New York as New Amsterdam, the Church was the lynchpin of any State. This concept, however, was repugnant to the Jews who separated the State from the religion. Henry Wordsworth Longfellow described this Jewish character in his poem written in 1852 questioning the logic of Jewish presence in the colonies around Newport, Rhode Island, and supplied the answer himself—religious freedom and inherent right of the people. Roger Williams, an outspoken Jew immigrant who championed the right of all minorities and fought for justice and rights of all people, bitterly opposed the idea of a church state and forced conversions. A rebel against all the stupidities that interposed a barrier betwixt men and the fellowship of their dreams, Roger Williams proclaimed: "That cannot be a true religion which needs carnal weapons". While a Roman Catholic spends half an hour in a church, counting his beads, reciting Ave Marias, genuflecting before a crucifix and lights a candle in adoration of Virgin Mary, while a Quaker sits for half an hour in silent meditation at a Friends Meeting House, while other Protestants from Holy Rollers in High Church Episcopalians conduct their prayers and rituals, an Orthodox European Jew goes to his synagogue which he fondly calls 'schul', the Yiddish word for school; thereby implying that synagogue is not merely a place for prayer and worship but for study too. Judaism's primary command is study, similar to what Lord Krishna enjoins in Geeta as 'Gyan Yog' for attainment of the Supreme. Mark Twain, the famous American author, in an article written in 1898 mentioned that the Egyptians, the Persians, the Greeks and the Romans came and went, yet the Jews, less that one percent of human race "who properly ought never to have been heard of' have kept their culture and civilisation alive through millennia. "Why?" Perhaps it is because while others were observing religious rituals, the Jews kept thinking and studying and sharpening their brains, not forgetting the words of Isiah - "My people are gone into captivity for want of knowledge". the Russian intellectual Ahad Ha'am, writing to Rabbi Judah Magnes, said: "Learing-learing-learning, that is the secret of Jewish survival." Claude G. Montefiore, British scholar, put it a little differently : " It is the intellectual element in Judaism which enabled the Jews to go through unheard of degradations and persecutions, and yet never to suffer degradation of the soul", while Sigmund Freud, himself a Jew, mentioned that "it was the Holy Book and the study of it that kept the scattered people together." Emma Lazarus in one of her best poems, 'Gifts', mentions that the Egyptians wanted wealth, received it and vanished from history; the Greeks wanted beauty and after being granted the same also disappeared; the Romans wanted power, got it and then they too were gone; the Jews asked for truth and nothing else and they live from centuries to centuries, age to age, proving the saying that "Synagogues and houses of study are Israel's towers." Hillel had long before told the impatient pagan: "Go forth and learn!" Gems such as these abound in Talmud: "The prayer for knowledge is first among the Benedictions." "No mercy for him who is without knowledge."

During the Civil War the Jews suffered discrimination of various kinds. In an order by General Grant dated December 17, 1862, the Jews were accused of violating the regulation of trade established by the Treasury Department and were singled out for punishment for illegal smuggling, a charge which was not true. Some were arrested and held in confinement. The American Jewry reacted strongly against this anti-Semitic outburst and led a delegation to President Lincoln himself to get the order repealed. It is said that one of the members, Caesar Kaskel, personally explained the case to Lincoln, after examining which the President said: "And so the children of Israel were driven from the happy land of Canaan?" "Yes," replied Kaskel, "and that is why we have come unto Father Abraham's bosom, asking protection". "And this protection they shall have at once," the President promised. Though the General Order No. 11 was rescinded, the damage to the Jewish prestige had been done. Sparks of bigotry were fanned and spread to many colonies. While some Jews were indeed guilty of illegal practices and were duly punished, the majority of the Jewry stood solidly behind the Federal North. The Christian media, particularly the Confederate press, was as vituperative as the one in the North. In the slave states Jews were held responsible for many crimes, real or imaginary, such as illegal trade with the enemy, price inflation, creating artificial shortage of goods, counterfeiting Confederate money, avoiding military responsibilities and many more. The Jews of the South reacted with anger and one Jew even challenged a Richmond editor to a duel. Rabbi Wise spoke further for the entire American Jewry in the following terms:

> "Our sons enlisted in the Army, our daughters sew and knit for the wounded soldiers and their poor families, our capitalists spend freely, our hospitals are thrown open to the sick soldiers of all creeds, our merchants represented at every benevolent association contribute largely to the wealth and prosperity of the cities, give bread and employment to thousands; we keep away from politics, gambling houses, public offices, penitentiaries, and newspaper publications- what else must we do to heal these petty scribblers from their mad prejudice?"

In 1965, Rabbi Maurice N. Eisendrath, the President of the 48th General Biennial Assembly of the Union of American Hebrew Congregations, replied to the charge of 'Communistic leanings' hurled at the American Jewry, that it was not a crime to criticise the foreign policy of the Administration. To seek a test ban treaty, was once considered unpatriotic in America. But it was finally adopted due to pressure of public opinion, was that to be a Communist? To oppose Multilateral Force, considered indispensable earlier, and now all but abandoned, is that being a 'Communist'? The right of dissent, he emphasised, even in inconsequentials as also in the church was a prominent distinction between dictatorship and democracy. As a religious Jewish community, seeking justice, the Jews could not still their conscience or muffle their voice, on issues they felt so strongly about. And so he went on.

During this time, the owner of Hilton hotel refused permission to a Jewish leader, Seligman, on the plea that he did not like the Jews as a class and he did not mind losing his custom on that count. The controversy aroused wide scale interest in America, leading to publication of innumerable articles and editorials from both sides. As the controversy was about to be dying down Austin Corbin, the President of Long Island Rail Road, the leading Company, sparked off another conflagration by his statement that he hated Jews and could do without their custom. The fire of enmity between Jews and Christians was flamed again with the boycott of the Company's business. However, during this turmoil, Revered Henry Ward Beeches, a famous Protestant minister of the times, whose sister wrote the novel *Uncle Tom's Cabin*, became an outstanding champion of the Jewish cause and advised the Jews to ignore petty insults hurled at them. His famous statement, " A hero may be annoyed by a mosquito; but to put on his whole armour and call on his followers to join him in making war on an insect would be beneath his dignity," calmed the temper somewhat. Ten years after the Seligman-Hilton controversy the anti-Semitic impulse of the time forced President Grover Cleveland to retract from appointing a Jew as a U.S. Minister to Turkey. Beecher again pleaded with the President to take the right course for the Jewish cause. He lauded the American way of life, their human values, concern for Jews' freedom and love for equality. He exhorted, "Why should we not make a crowning testimony to the genius of our people by sending a Hebrew to Turkey? The ignorance and superstition of medieval Europe may account for the prejudices of that dark age. But how a Christian in our day can turn from a Jew I cannot imagine. Christianity itself sucked at the bosom of Judaism, our roots are in the Old Testament. We are Jews ourselves gone to blossom, and fruit. Christianity is

Judaism in Evolution, and it would be strange for the seed to turn against the stock on which it was grown." Oscar Straus, the first Jewish cabinet member under President Theodore Roosevelt, was an ardent supporter of President Wilson's ideas of peace after war, which resulted in the covenant of the League of Nations. As the Senate hesitated to permit the U.S. to join the League, Salmon Levinson, a Jewish lawyer in Chicago, made out a case in his publication *The Outlawry of War* which became the basis of Kellogg-Briand Pact signed by fifteen nations at Paris in 1928. After the arrival of Hitler when oppressions on Jews reached unacceptable levels, the American Jewry petitioned the Government to increase the quota of Jewish migrants from Europe much higher than the earlier figure of 168,000. These were not ordinary Jews, the poor huddled masses or wretched refuse but the greatest flight of talent the world had ever seen. These were scientists, musicians, artists, university professors and twelve future Nobel Laureates.Then came the great World War. Never in any American war had the Jews played such prominent role. Sixteen of them reached the rank of admirals or generals. Ten thousand of a total of 600,000 who fought the war were decorated for bravery. Major General Maurice Rose, son of a synagogue official in Denver, Colorado, led the 3rd Armoured Division in Belgium and was the first army commander since Napoleon to invade the German Reich from the west, the first one to breach the Siegfried Line, and the first to capture a German town. There were many other Jewish officers and nurses who helped in the American war effort. Hadassah, the Women's Zionist Organisation of America, was founded in New York by thirty-eight American Jewish women and its many branches all over the world helped in humanitarian causes on every call. Hospitals and nurses from this organization went out all over the world to care and heal. Mount Scopus near Jerusalem is home to the most ultra-modern hospital in the world, financed entirely by the American Jewish women and is located alongside a new medical center of 300-acre site in the Judean Hills. It is significant that these 318,000 American Jewish women who recognised their religion's emphasis on social justice devoted so much of their time, money and energy to serve all mankind.

Nevertheless the story of the Jews in America is one of constant fight against inequality, injustice, discrimination and denial of equal rights to all communities. This sentiment was re-echoed by 721,000 Jews, half of all the Jews in the world outside Israel who lived in America in 1968.

Chapter 11

The Struggle and The Homecoming

There are three pioneers who conceived the idea of a Jewish State in the Land of Israel. Dr. Leo Pinkin in his book *Auto Emancipation*, Theodore Herzl in his work *Jewish State and their Precursor*, Moses Hess, spelt out his ideas in his work *Rome and Jerusalem*. In effect, while Moses Hess can be considered as the founder of the modern Zionist system of thought, it was, Herzl, the Chairman of the Ist Zionist Congress in 1897 and the High Priest of Zionism, and Baron Edmond de Rothschild, the father of Yishuv, who laid the foundations of the formation of the new Jewish State.

The conference at Vienna, the Dryfuss's trial and the events preceding these, had convinced the European Jewry that Jews can expect no justice from any quarter unless they have a land of their own. While Dr. Chaim Weizman, with his personal charm, proceeded on the diplomatic course, Rothschild, the richest man of his time, opened his coffers for the resettlement of Jews in their homeland. We shall skip over the earlier political and diplomatic efforts to the formation of the Jewish State and arrive at the momentous year of 1917 when the British Prime Minister, Balfour, made his famous declaration of providing a national homeland for the Jews in Palestine. However, the actual struggle for Palestine began when the British drove out the Turks from the fertile crescent, whereafter began three decades of British mandate under the sanction of the League of Nations in 1921. The conflict with the Arabs, who were the existing residents, was inevitable. The Israeli historian Yehoshua Porath states that "In 1891 the leaders of the Muslim and Christian communities in Jerusalem petitioned the sultanate to prohibit Jewish immigration to Palestine and the purchase of land by the Jews. Before the Turks withdrew they had warned the Palestinians and the general Arab public that the British conquest meant Jewish rule."

Ahad Ha- Am, a cultural Zionist, wrote a warning in 1891:

> "We abroad have a way of thinking that Palestine today is almost desert, uncultivated wilderness, and that anyone who wishes to buy land there can do so to his heart's content. But that is not in fact the case. It is difficult to find any uncultivated land anywhere in the country... We abroad have a way of thinking that the Arabs are all savages, on a level with the animals, and blind to what goes on around them. But that is quite mistaken. The Arabs, specially the townsmen, see through our activities in their country, and our aims, but they keep silent and make no sign, because for the present they anticipate no danger to their own future from what we are about. But if the time should ever come when our people have so far developed their life in Palestine that the indigenous population should feel more or less cramped, then they will not readily make way for us...." How prophetic!

The British policies from 1917 which had sown the seeds of Arab-Jewish conflict bore its bitter fruit in 1948 when the State of Israel came into being. While the ambivalent policies were responsible to a certain extent, the real cause of their conflict was a refusal of the Arabs to accept the existence of a Zionist led Jewish nation on their soil. While the Zionists admitted to settling into Palestine as many Jews as possible, Jerusalem was totally devastated during World War I, with famine and disease, shortage of clean water, useable roads, and electrical breakdowns.

Even though the military Government did carry out essential repairs and improvement works, foreign investment was the main instrument for the reconstruction of the town. Tourism and pilgrim trade revitalised the economy of Jerusalem as new schools and libraries were opened along with the centres for learning. Many churches were constructed. Hadassah Hospital came up on Mount Scopus along with the Jewish National Library and later the Hebrew University in 1925. The posh King David Hotel was built in 1930 and the flurry of construction activity continued with the construction of the American colony and Sheikh Jarrah east of Jerusalem. The new Jewish developments came up in the western part of the city: Romemah (1921), Talpiyot (1922), Rahavia (1924), Bayit Vagan (1925), Kiryat Shmuel (1928), Geula (1929), and Tel Arza (1931). Beit Hakerem was the first suburban settlement constructed in 1923 on the western edge of Jerusalem. The British tilt towards the Arabs resulted in the construction of large number of Arab churches, mostly of Anglican adherents. There were also churches of different countries. By the end of it all the British Administration left a reasonable, liveable and well-developed Jerusalem. The British ambivalence and contradictory promises to Arabs and Jews made their positions in the Middle East in 1917 untenable. France and Britain divided the spoils of the lands vacated by the Turks into their areas of influence; France opting for Lebanon and Syria and the British for Egypt and Palestine. As a result of the Sykes-Picot Agreement of May 1916, the map of Middle East was redrawn as stated above with Russia having some areas of influence. It was this secret agreement that allowed Britain to be given its mandatory power over Palestine by the League of Nations. As Syria was cheated of its dreams of expansion and a Greater Syria, King Hussein of Jordan too was short-changed in Transjordan and western Palestine. It was a no-win situation for the British as the creation of an Emirate in Transjordan in 1920 infuriated the Zionists, who considered this action as a betrayal to the cause of their national home in the whole of Palestine, which to them included Transjordan and western Palestine as well. The Balfour declaration of November 2,1917 read:

"His Majesty's Government view with favour the establishment in Palestine of a national home for the Jewish people, and will use their best endeavours to facilitate the achievement of this object, it being clearly understood that nothing shall be done which may prejudice the civil and religious rights of existing non-Jewish communities in Palestine or the rights and political status enjoyed by Jews in any other country."

This Declaration was not entirely philanthropic in content, since there was a political percentage attached to it as explained by Eugene Bovis in the following words:

".....Some British statesmen came to believe that, if given a chance, many Jews would flock to Palestine after the war to settle and that if Great Britain supported the idea of a Jewish national home in Palestine, it might be able to establish a British protectorate over the country, thus assuring exclusive British control rather than international control. The Balfour Declaration would thus give moral weight to a British claim to be the protecting power, just as the military conquest then in progress would give the British claim a material basis."

There had been many waves of immigration into Eretz Israel called 'Aliyas.' Mention has been made of the First Aliya consisting of the founding fathers who on arrival bought land and settled in various parts of Palestine. The second wave or Aliya was a result of the abortive Russian revolution of 1905 and the bloody pogroms that followed. The dislocations caused by the Ist World War and the conclusion of the Russian revolution as also the Balfour Declaration of 1917, turned the earlier trickle into a tide which formed the core of the Third Aliya. The immigrants of the third wave came mostly from eastern Europe and Russia, totaling about 35,000, mostly men and women in their early 20s, passionately inspired by an anti-authoritarian idealism to which formal Government was an anathema. The new settlements called "chalutzim" were to be voluntary establishments for communes of the like-minded democratic enthusiasts. These ideas of the young minds soon evaporated into hard realities due to the need for discipline and cooperation. The credo of these young enthusiasts was defined in 1923 in a statement that:

> "Chalutzim" is not sacrifice but fulfillment; the "chalutz" is an "Individualist" and driven by man's own desire; the "chalutz" is the socialist (commune-man) par excellence, and finally that individualism and collectivism emerge in an ideological impulse that harmonizes the polarity of Body and Spirit, Being and Value."

Joseph Trumpeldor, a veteran of the Russo-Japanese War who settled in Palestine in 1912, was the most articulate votary of all that "chalutzim" stood for. He established a Labour Brigade in the early twenties including a group of "chalutizists" aiming to convert the entire country into one great 'Kibbutz' for agriculture and industry, operated by its members. The idea, however, underwent a change as a central authority was established in Israel and the labours and the enthusiasm of these zealots turned into making a new nation state. Karl Marx and socialists including even David Ben Gurion modified the model of Russian socialism into a practical patriotic central national authority, representing the State. There were many strands of idealism among the early pioneers and they differed violently on the matters of state, personal property, commune labour and physical time. But they had one thing in common—love of the land and to make a home for themselves with physical work. The utopian dream of these commune enthusiasts midwifed many settlements; one of them Bittania boasted of the most open society, called communators. Weizmann, one of the founding fathers mentioned earlier, was fascinated by these communards and once remarked that, "To be a Zionist it is not necessary to be mad, but it helps." In Bittania as in other communes the life was hard and often primitive. Arthur Koestler, a profound writer of his times, left his studies in 1926 at the University of Vienna and joined the commune at Hepbzibah. He was shocked at the ramshackled conditions of the commune which resembled those of the poorest in Europe. In spite of differing views, the foundation of the Jewish ideology was laid by the First Aliya in the following terms: (1) the party system- its unique centrality in political life; (2) strong belief in equality; (3) continuing informality and simplicity in manners, dress, and language; (4) agrarian ritual; (5) belief in voluntary action; (6) the notion of an official (Zionist) "state ideology."

Although the Jewish society is widely split in its views on almost everything, from temporal to spiritual and this diversity has given rise to many political parties from extreme left to left-of-center, centre, right and extreme right, the fusion of these parties in 1965 guaranteed that what began in 1930 will characterise Israel's political life for many many years. The political machine set up by the founding fathers has proved so powerful and self-actuated that all the differences sink in the overall national interest. Today Histadrut Labour Union is the most powerful instrument of social activities and social justice in Israel, comprising 80 percent of its population. The public transport system is controlled by a Drivers' Cooperative under the Histadrut. So also are the other social sectors of economy including a vast array of different industries. Construction and investment companies, mines, banks, credit finance, and foreign trade comprising 40 percent of the total economy are owned by the"Commonwealth of Labour" represented by Histadrut under the benevolent gaze of government. Government controlled Kibbutz and the cooperative moshavs represent two-thirds of the total farm population as well as an increasing share of the country's manufactured products and cybernetics based industries.

Ideology forms the life-breath of the Israeli social life. A shrewd observer once remarked: "removing ideology from Israeli polities would be more than depriving the traveller of his roadmap, it would mean divesting him of most of the landscape and much of his vehicle as well.... Higher living standards and well-trained technocrats are not likely to alter characteristics which are such a basic part of modern Israel's heritage." A basic thought that permeates all sections of Jews in Israel is that during the Second World War when the greatest calamities had befallen the Jewish people in their long and arduous history, very few non-Jews and not a single sovereign state actively came to their rescue or showed any intention to save them. It is thus not easy to completely understand the implications of this on the evolving national temper. Jewish sense of isolation, therefore, is not unfounded.The terrifying consequences of this feeling against the background of the holocaust has generated a pessimism of encirclement and utter loneliness in the world, so aptly described below:

> "When our children under the gallows wept,
>
> The world its silence Kept..."

This loneliness is the root cause of Israeli's attitude which seems unduly stubborn to the outside world. Pious admonishments from outside onlookers have very little meaning, and they further drive even the most tolerant Israeli into a quarantine against foreign criticism. A harassed people under the logic of convulsive circumstances at last came into their own. A planned orderly exodus turned into a desperate bid for escape. Always and ever running away from their historic fate, a total dependence upon the shifting shades of tolerance of others, Israelis knew no calm and rest. With conflict staring them in the face there was no light at the end of the tunnel. Fight for survival seemed to be the fate that their God had ordained for them. The return of the Jews to their ancient patrimony is aptly described in the following three lines, a saying from Talmud, a song of the pioneers, and a statement by Herzl:

> *"If I am not for myself, who then is for me?*
>
> *We came to build the land to be rebuilt by it....*
>
> *If you will it, it is no fairy tale."*

Be that as it may, the saga of immigration into Eretz Israel "The land of Israel" reads like a Greek epic and holds a candle to the rest of the world as to how a miniscule society of Jews coming from different lands all over the world converged on to their promised land in search of shelter and home. They came from all sides and by all possible means, openly and under cover, through small craft boats, merchant vessels, even liners but mostly stealthily landing at night on inhospitable seashores, policed and patrolled by the officials of the British Mandate. Many died in the way, many were sunk in the sea and many starved to death. But those who made it to their land had the burning zeal to make Palestine their home. There is no example in the world history where people in driblets from all corners of the world undertook long sea voyages to reach their distant home. They came from America, and they came from Germany, Poland, Central Europe and Russia. The first Jew settler in the Eretz Israel was Ahron David Gordon, who formed the vanguard of the first Aliya. Most of these early immigrants spoke Yiddish, a German Jewish dialect spoken in Russia and East Europe, i.e., Poland, Latavia, Estonia, Lithuania, and Bukhara. Along with these were also the Sephardic Jews coming from Spain, and distant lands. Wave after wave of this immigration (Aliya) in three distinct phases, i.e., First, Second and Third Aliya moved into Israel and this Aliya was not completed till the end of the 30s.

One of the important features of the Jewish migration to Palestine is the help rendered by Hagannah, the Jewish Self-Defense Organisation which conducted rescue operations for the European Jews and smuggled arms inside the ghettos. There were one million such Jews in Hungary, Romania and Czechoslovakia. One Hanah Szenes, a daring Jewish paratrooper in Hungary, paid the price for his endeavours to smuggle out the Jews. He was caught and summarily shot. Hagannah's assault force called Palamach, the youth wing was commanded by Yigal Allon. Every member of Palamach had to take the following oath:

> "That this weapon which has been entrusted to me by the Hagannah in the land of Israel. I shall fight with for my country against enemies of my people without surrrender, without flinching and with complete dedication."

Though the Jewish immigration in Palestine before 1917 was resented by the Arabs, they did not actively oppose it till the inflow increased after 1920s and became a torrent in 1930s, which made them feel hedged in. The Jewish population in Palestine before 1840 was a mere 24,000 most of whom were very poor and lived in small ghettos of Safed, Tiberius, Hebron and Jerusalem. They subsisted mainly on charitable gifts from abroad and led a pious and dedicated life. The pogroms in Russia and East Europe in the late 19th century doubled the Jewish immigration to 50,000, their favoured place being Jerusalem. Increasing with each successive Aliya, the Jewish population in Jerusalem city alone rose to 100,000 while Muslims stood at 40,000 and the remaining 25,000 being Christians of Arab and European origin. Thereafter, the Jewish population increased steadily by about 10,000 each year to 174,000 in 1932. However, this was too meager for the consummation of the Jewish state, since the Jews represented only 23 percent of the total estimated population of Palestine at 760,000. However, the flood gates were opened due to mass migration of the Jews from Europe under the holocaust of Hitler's anti-Semetic laws and oppression in Russia. As a result, from 1933 to 1936 the Jewish population doubled to 370,000 forming 28 percent of the total. In the next 13 years, the flood gates opened wider and the Jewish population doubled to 600,000 or 32 percent of the total population in 1947. While the Jewish population did increase between 1917 to 1947, the Arab population during the same period practically doubled from 620,000 to 1,300,000.

After the First World War and the establishment of the British Mandate, there were three Arab organisations of political significance in the State of Palestine. The most important was the Muslim Christian Association (MCA), which stands for Al-Jamiyya al-Islamiyya al-Musihiyya. They had more than 200 members in 1919 and aimed at firmly opposing Jewish immigration into Palestine, the idea of Zionism and the creation of a Jewish National Home on their soil. They demanded unconditional independence for Greater Syria and internal self-government for Palestine as part of the broader Syrian State. The other two organisations were Muntada meaning a literary society, exclusively Muslim with 600 members. The third being al- Basduak- Arabi (the Arab Club) also exclusively Muslim and Arab with 500 members, demanded self-goverenment of Palestine under Greater Syria with minor changes from the demands of M.C.A. Then there was the Supreme Muslim Council (S.M.C.) which prevented any land purchase by the Jews by bringing them under Waqf's jurisdiction.

Arabs strongly resisted the Jewish influx by force. They had already rejected the United Nations' Resolution of 1947 for the partition of Palestine which was logical and fair to both the parties. However, the Arabs refused to accept it. In the U.N. resolution both Arabs and Jewish States were to be part of Palestine while Jerusalem was designated as a "corpus separatum" to be governed by an international administration. This satisfied neither the Jews nor the Arabs. While disliking this geographic split and award of fertile lands to the Arabs, David Ben-Gurion was prepared to accept the plan as a price for international support. The Arabs, however, refused to concede even an inch of territory and the five surrounding Arab nations prepared for war. The British did their best to control the events. But the nationalistic rivalry of the two combatants drained their resources and they had to leave the country.

British policy in Palestine was born out of their war aim to defeat the Turkish empire in the Middle East with the help of the Arabs. While Gen. Allenby was in overall command, a diversionary attack by the famous Lawrence of Arabia with his Arab contingent occupied the Gulf of Aquaba. This was the background of the traditional friendship between the British and the Arabs to oppose Jewish migration during the period of the mandate. Arab attacks on Jewish settlements, or Kibbitzun as they were called, continued under the benevolent gaze of the Mandate authorities. In all propriety, Courts of Inquiry were held to investigate and punish the guilty But this was a mere eyewash. The sufferers were always the Jews. While Arab hostility and active British connivance was aiming to shut the gates for the immigrant Jews, the pressure from Hitler's butchery was too strong to deter the immigrants. To quote Begin:

> "Soon any dormant belief that the sealed frontiers of Europe would prevent their escape was shattered. The Irgun Zvai Leumi, which in association with the Zionist-Revisionist Party and the Betar youth organisation, had brought many thousands of "illegal" immigrants into the country, never halted its activities. The British authorities exerted themselves to horrify the world by gruesome descriptions of the

> conditions aboard the refugees ships, the "coffin-ships," which old and dilapidated, were crowded to the gunwales." The aim was to discourage immigration."

All efforts by the East European countries to prevent the exodus of the Jews failed miserably. The ships carrying these unfortunates were deliberately sunk, sending many to their watery graves. But they reckoned without Haganaah and the Irgun and the resources of the Jewish Agency. The British people most hypocritically claimed to be helping the victims of "Gas Chambers" by making pious statements. However, they also warned that many "German spies" in the garb of Jewish settlers were also migrating to Palestine. This was the excuse to prevent mass exodus of the Jews from Europe. Then there was the case of 'Struma' the ship which arrived off the coast of Eretz Israel and was returned by the blocade authorities to its point of departure in Romania. The ship sunk and all on board were drowned. The cause was never discovered. There were also "The Milos", "The Pacific" and the "The Patria." They too were returned to their points of sail while "The Patria" never sailed again. Begin again:

> "Dark night, the darkest of all nights, descended on the Jewish people in Europe. One million five hundred thousand Jewish children were transported in the death trains to the gas-chambers. Millions of men and women were shot, or drowned, or burned, or gassed or buried alive. When man becomes a beast, the Jew ceases to be regarded as a human being. There is no room here for self-delusion. It was not only the Nazis and their friends who regarded the Jews as germs to be destroyed. The whole world which calls itself "enlightened" began to get used to the idea that perhaps the Jew is not as other human beings. Just as "the world" does not pity the thousands of cattle led to the slaughter-pens in the Chicago abattoirs, equally it did not pity- or else it got used to the tens of thousands of human beings taken like sheep to the slaughter in Treblinki. The world does not pity the slaughtered. It only respects those who fight. For better or for worse, that is the truth.

All the peoples of the world knew this grim truth except the Jews. That is why our enemies were able to trap us and shed our blood at will.

Britain enforced an economic blockade against the territories occupied by the Germans: that was her war against Nazism. But she also enforced a political blockade against the Jews in German occupied territories, which was an aid to Nazism."

The Jews too, mainly the Irgun and the Stern group, used terrorist method to frighten the Arabs and the British to the state where they could not effectively resist their entry into Eretz Israel. While all this was happening on the high seas and the shores of Palestine, the Arab attacks continued. The chronicle goes.

"The historical facts of the Arab attacks are known: the pogrom in the Old City of Jerusalem in 1920, the murderous attack in Jaffa in 1921, the blood-bath of 1929, the incessant campaign of violence from 1936 to 1939. The psychological consequences of these one-sided attacks were as disastrous as their political aftermath."

As a result of Jewish aggressiveness, the Arabs began to take the Jews seriously as a *walad-al-maut* –a child of death- and to look forward to the great festival of "bathel yahud". or general slaughter. Slowly and steadily the initiative passed from the hands of the Mandate authorities and the Arabs to the Jewish immigrants. The Irgun mounted triple attacks on the Police Headquarters in Jerusalem, Haifa and Jaffa which had far reaching consequences. Thus terror was met with terror. Talking of high intentions without action to follow, breeds contempt in the minds of the adversaries. As Begin says:

"But great as may have been the influence of our literature, it is certain that deeds had a greater effect. The fact that the mighty British Government not only failed to put an end to our struggle but, on the contrary, continued to be subjected to blows of ever-increasing severity, exercised a very healthy influence on the Arabs.Their imagination did the rest."

The Jewish underground' borrowed' and looted T.N.T., other explosives and weapons in an even-handed manner both from the Arabs and the British. This legend of the Jewish strength created by the underground operations of the Hebrew revolt had a far-reaching effect both on the British before they left, and the Arabs before and after the birth of the new state. Undoubtedly, Hagannah played its historical role against the Arab invaders along with the regular Israel army. The memory of Hagannah dating back to the "havlagah", could hardly encourage the Arabs for their new fight. To quote Begin again on the open hostilities of the British:

> "Reliance, or undue reliance, on the moral restraints of an enemy, is no part of strategy. So, we did not depend on the Government's 'humanity.' We had witnessed the wanton behavior of the airborne troops in our towns and villages and kibbutzim. We had read the internal literature distributed among the British soldiers. Characteristic of the attitude of some of the troops was the threat scribbled on a copy of our underground newspaper *Herut*: "Oh Gee, oh Gee, Hitler killed 6,000,000 Jews. The Sixth Airborne will kill 60,000,000 if you don't bloody well behave yourselves."

Since the firing incident at Amritsar in Jallianwala Bagh on an unarmed crowd the British became more careful about the effect of their actions on international opinion. Reprisal killings of the British by the Jews was one thing the British dreaded most. They did not want to be killed. This was confirmed by Colonel Patterson, Commander of the Jewish legion formed by Vladimir Jabotinsky in the First World War, a British officer of Irish extraction who went into exile and denounced the British Government's betrayal of the Jewish people. The British now realised that Tel Aviv was not Amritsar nor Eretz Israel, Punjab. The world could ignore happenings in distant British colony but Eretz Israel was the center of world interest and the cockpit of the Middle East.

The Arab opposition to Zionism, despite its intensity, was fragmented due to their inter-tribal rivalries. However, there was a consistency in the Muslim opposition to the Jews in the formation of Jerusalem Municipal Council, where alternatively Jews and Arabs boycotted the Council meetings on the plea of growing numerical strength of the rival parties. The flash point of riots in Jerusalem after 1920 was the Jewish practice of making seating arrangements by bringing chairs and benches for their prayers at the Western wall of the Temple Mount. To the Arabs these were "offending objects" and an indirect way of claiming squatter's rights on the place where Mohammed's famous horse, al-Burq, took him on his heavenly journey. The Supreme Muslim Council under Mufti Haj Amin al- Husseine prevented the Jews from bringing the "offending objects" to the site of their prayers in 1922, 1923 and 1925, starting a world-wide propaganda that the Jews were keen to rebuild their third Temple at the same location. Thereafter, broke Arab-Jewish riots with casualties on both sides till in April 1936, a royal Commission (the Peel Commission) arrived to investigate the situation and suggest corrective measures. The Peel Commission recommended the partition of the country into two separate Arab and Jewish states, setting aside the area of Jerusalem, Bethlehem and Nazareth to be kept under mandate administration.

Understandably, the Peel Commission report created a mixed reaction. While some Jews, headed by Dr. Chaim Weizmann favoured the proposal of the Royal Commission for a Jewish state, with the power to control its immigration policies in spite of the fact that Peel Commission recommended restrictions on Jewish immigration during the period of the mandate. The majority of the Jews, headed by the Jewish Agency, were of the view that the Jewish Palestine without Jerusalem would be a body without a soul. This connection between Jerusalem and the Jewish people was to be emphasized with a consequence of internationalisation of the Holy City. The dispute still continues. The report was also resented by the Arab states of the Middle East. It later took the form of Palestine Liberation Organisation (PLO). Events overtook the Peel Commission as the World War II broke out, distracting their attention. However, by May 1939, a White Paper was issued imposing restrictions both on the Jewish immigration and land purchased by them; in fact permitting only 75,000 Jewish immigrants in a five-year period before its final termination. As mentioned earlier, the Jews opposed the White Paper, treating it as a betrayal of the Balfour Declaration, the sore point being restrictions on immigration. Hounded out from a Hitler dominated Europe, the Jews had nowhere to go. Despite the Jewish support to the British against Hitler during the war—30,000 Palestinian Jews had enlisted in the British Army up to 1942—the Jews decided to oppose the White Paper and as brought out earlier, David Ben-Gurion, the Head of the Jewish Agency, solved the dilemma by announcing that "we shall fight Hitler as though there were no white paper and fight the white paper as if there is no war".

After a period of calm, during the World War II, the Jews carried out their guerrilla operations to assist Jewish immigration and fight the Mandate authorities. The rival claims over Palestine by the Jews and Arabs have been analysed in fairly great detail by Mark Tessler in his book *Arab Israel Conflicts*. The author has given the following sound arguments for Jewish claim:

> "The burden of much, if not most, of the grievance of the Arab states which I've read or listened to against the State of Israel, or Zionism, or, at its most forthright, against the settlement of any Jews at all in this region, seems to rest on the conviction that the Jews have been absent so many hundreds of years that they have become foreigners in what was once their land. The Arabs who were in the majority from the seventh until the twentieth century except for the brief Crusader Kingdom are seen as having established themselves over a period so long that any other people, any other government, is the vilest injustice.
>
> "I suppose it is unfair to attempt to introduce logic or the historical facts of life into what is essentially a violent exercise in propaganda, but aside from the fact that the Jews founded their State with the blessings of the United Nations, when this was contested by force, they established themselves by right of conquest, as had been done before them by the Turks, the Crusaders, the Arabs, the Romans, the Greeks, the Egyptians, the Hebrews, the Canaanites, the Syrians, the

Babylonians and the others going back to the dawn of history and probably before."

"With all of the migrations, the conquests and the colonies which have accompanied them, there are as many pockets of people, different races, religions and varieties of origin very much alive in Israel today as one could possibly imagine. Even with the departure of the Bosnians there are some twenty-six hundred Circassians, a handsome people from the Caucasus once famous in the Middle eastern slave markets, who remain in Israel and ten thousand of whose fellows live across the valley in Jordan, serving as the traditional bodyguard for King Hussein as they did for his grandfather King Abdullah.

"Jews have lived uninterruptedly in Israel since they returned from Egypt to the Promised Land more than two thousand years ago, in spite of the wars and dispersion, sometimes many, sometimes few, sometimes banned from Jerusalem, sometimes masters there, but always living in this land. There are Catholic and Protestant sects without reckoning, and there are some schismatic Moslem sects, too, like the six hundred Ahmadia in Galilee. There are two hundred members of the Bahai faith, a universalist religion which was founded in Persia and with many members living in the United States and England, but whose center is in Haifa. There are Turcoman villages, settled by Uzbek and Kazakh Moslems from what is now Soviet Central Asia, and in the south of Israel there are Negro Bedouin, descendants of the Africans, brought from Nubia and East Africa by Arab slave traders."

"There are many differences in the difficulties faced by the two minorities, but just as the frustration and resentment of the American Negro has become real bitterness and anger no longer masked, and with an increasing readiness to lash out against the barriers which confine him, or even at that which he sees as symbolic of his second-class state, so the Israeli Arab may feel many of these same inequities of schooling and housing and the chance to earn a decent living. The Israeli Arab, no doubt, has many imaginary woes, or at least distorted out of all perspective and fanned by hostile propaganda from the surrounding Arab states. But many of the problems faced by Israeli Arabs are real enough, particularly land tenure. The government is certainly aware of this, and has consistently maintained its position ever since the founding of the country that without peace between Israel and her neighbors there can be no satisfactory solution to persistent problems such as repatriation or compensation for the Arab refugees who fled Palestine and, generally, the establishment of a modus vivendi between Israel and the Arab lands. It's curious that, with all the agitation calling for immediate reparation to Arab refugees without considering other allied issues at stake, few people have mentioned the property of which about a million Jewish refugees were relieved before being permitted to leave their Arab homelands, before they came to Israel."

As the process of nation making starts, certain 'landmark' events of the past stand out. Again Mark Tessler:

"Chaim Weizmann, who was to become the first President of Israel and who was for many years president of the World Zionist Organization and the Jewsh Agency for Israel, was very likely the most influential of that disparate collection of extraordinary talents known as Zionists. Deeply influenced by Asher Ginzberg whose pen name was Ahad Ha'am, a Russian-born philosopher and major writer in modern Hebrew who taught that jewish culture rather than economic, political or military power was the base of the unprecedented survival of this people. Weizmann agreed with this conclusion, adding science to the humanities as part of this Jewish cultural inheritance".

"Arguing at the Eleventh Zionist Congress in Vienna in 1913 for his dream of a Hebrew University, Weizmann said: "Although we have at present an ardent desire to see our people plow the fields and to make it faithful to its soil, we know that we are and shall always be the people of the Book. Our strongest weapon is the spirit, and it is our duty

> to cultivate this spirit, to sharpen the weapons with which we must fight for a better existence. The university will be our spiritual dreadnought; it will be of greater value to us than armies and navies are to other nations."

Isaiah Berlin, Chichele Professor of Social and Political Theory and Fellow of All Souls College at Oxford, has said in his brief beautifully written biographical essay 'Chaim Weizmann:'

> "As he reflected on the poverty of the land and its lack of natural resources, he placed his hope upon turning the one kind of capital that the Jews did seem to possess technical skills, ingenuity, energy, desperation—to the production of miracles in scientific technology."

> "In all of Weizmann's long and single-minded struggle to establish a Jewish State, education was central to his plans. With his friend Martin Buber he published a pamphlet in 1903 which said plainly that to make cultural Zionism a reality would call for a Hebrew University in the Holy Land. In 1918, with Turkish troops retreating in the distance and British artillery pounding away from the outskirts of Jerusalem, Weizmann laid the foundation stone of the Hebrew Univesity on Mount Scopus. Now, the new Hebrew University at Givat Ram in Jerusalem works together with its medical faculty at the Hadssah University Medical Centre at the Jerusalem suburb of Ein Kerem and the original Mount Scopus campus recovered in 1967,which is the site of the Harry S. Truman Peace Memorial. The university also maintains branch institutes in Haifa and Beersheba as well as the agricultural faculty at Rehovot."

The Jews despaired of their never-ending captivity underestimated the innate resources of the human spirit. Menachem Begin describes the metaphysics of Jewish rebellion in the following way:

> "The revolt sprang from the earth. The ancient Greek story of Antaeus and the strength he drew from contact with mother Earth is a legend. The officials of the British Foreign Office had no conception of this when they made their

plans. What could they foresee of those hidden forces which Herzl used to speak of as the 'imponderables'; their error was not mathematical; they were not wrong about the number of Jews wanting to come to Eretz Israel. They assumed that in Eretz Israel, too, the Jews would continue to be timid supplicants for protection. The conduct of the Jews-or rather the attitude of their official leaders, expressed in the well-known policy of self restraint (Havlaga)—seemed to justify and confirm this assumption. But those unseen forces, which have ever saved the Jewish people from obliteration, demolished the British assumption....A new generation grew up which turned its back on fear. It began to fight instead of to plead. For nearly two thousand years, the Jews, as Jews, had not borne arms, and it was on this complete disarmament, as much psychological as physical, that our oppressors calculated. They did not realize that the two phenomena were interdependent; we gave up our arms when we were exiled from our country. With our return to the land of our fathers our strength was restored...

"When Descartes said: 'I think, therefore I am', he uttered a very profound thought. But there are times in the history of peoples when thought alone does not prove their existence. A people may 'think' and yet its sons, with their thoughts and in spite of them, may be turned into a herd of slaves-or into soap. There are times when everything in you cries out: your very self respect as a human being lies in your resistance to evil.

We fight, therefore we are."

Between Irgun and some moderates of Hagannah, the over-arching organisation for the struggle of freedom, there were serious differences on tactics of punitive measures to be undertaken against the British. Irgun wanted to retaliate for the kidnapping of their men while Hagannah advised restraint. It is a measure of common unity among these groups that ultimately the writ of Hagannah ran. It avoided dissensions among their ranks, despite strong provocations from the British authorities. The Jews held their hand and did not persecute their persecutors.

However, one of the daring actions of the Irgun was the attack on the Ramat Gan police strongpost. The Irgun fighters dressed as 'Arab prisoners' and guarded by the British officers, raided the armoury of the police station and robbed it of all its weapons and ammunition. Soon after the dacoity was discovered, heavy fighting took place between the two forces and Irgun lost three of their men and some others were wounded. Their undergound newspaper *Af—al—pi*, described this daring operation in some details as a protest against the complacency of the Hagannah authorities, towards this sacrifice of the Irgun, which stirred their conscience to take a more proactive stance. The Irgun also openly declared their policy to the British authorities that for every Jew prisoner hanged there will be retaliatory hanging of a British national. And they stood by their words. A typical example of this policy is given in the biographical book of Menachin Begin *The Revolt*:

> "There followed the heroic drama of this wounded prisoner, unique not only in our annals but in human history, the via dolorosa of suffering and ultimate sacrifice along which he went despite all our efforts to save him. We wanted to prevent the execution of the men who were sent to the gallows; we had the gravest repugnance to hanging British captives. Not only Joshua at the Sarafand camp ordered his British prisoners to run for their lives before he lit the fuse, many a time we took British prisoners, scores of them, but once they had raised their hands in surrender they became a sacred trust and safe against all harm. At the exhibition grounds in Tel Aviv we raided a British camp for arms. Over forty British soldiers were taken prisoner. But they were not hanged."

But the British did not reciprocate this gesture. One Irgun fighter, Dov Gruner, fell into their hands and he was sentenced to be hanged. He happily climbed the gallows singing 'Hatikvah.' The Irgun again warned that " Execution of prisoners of war is a premeditated murder. We warn the British regime of blood against the commission of this crime." As a sequel a British officer was hanged. Constant repetition of such retaliatory, hangings of the British ultimately had the desired result, and there were no more hanging of the Irgun underground fighters by the British Authorities.

The Jewish Secret Service, Shim Bet, and it's intelligence was extremely effective. They got information both from the British and the Arab sources, through bribes, intimidation or temptation. British intelligence on the other side based on the same tenets of acquisition of intelligence, utterly failed in Eretz Israel. Some of the Jewish well-wishers like Arthur Koestler advised them to use drinks as a lubricant for diplomacy. But the Jews did not buy the argument and obtained all their intelligence through abstinence. While the British underestimated the single-mindedness of the underground Jewish organisations, the Jews obtained whatever information they wanted. The British intelligence never succeeded in breaking through the counter intelligence cordon of the underground Jewish fighters.

Despite serious differences between the various forces operating under Hagannah, no serious surface cracks developed and the strategy of joint struggle agreed upon by the Hagannah, Irgun and the freedom fighters for Israel (FFI) worked very satisfactorily. However, there were moderates who sometimes went to extremes to restrain the radical Irgun by adopting a countervailing peaceful course. But the supreme fighting spirit continued. As Menachem Begin states:

> "They went to concentration camps, were thrown into dark cellars, starved, beaten, and maligned yet not one ever broke his solemn undertaking not to retaliate on his tormentors. I saw them in their anguish and I was tormented with them. But I also saw them in their greatness and I was proud of them. Discipline? What is military discipline, discipline in action, compared with this discipline of inaction, when your whole soul cries out for retaliation and retribution. A human "order" would have been of no avail here. The order came from "somewhere," from the depths of Jewish history; and it was obeyed. We were spared the catastrophe of catastrophes. And before many months went by the revolt embraced the whole people. The persecutors and persecuted

> of yesterday went out to battle together, to a common battle for our people and our country...."

There were two factors affecting the Jews during the Second World War. First the extermination of millions of Jews by Hitler in occupied Europe and the British cussedness in keeping the gates of the Jewish "National Home" tightly shut against the migrants. Menachin Begin comments on the indifference of the world community towards the extermination of the Jews thus:

> "Indifference-that is the danger. Humanity might claim that it was at least progressive when it could be aroused on account of injustice to a single Dreyfus in Paris to a Sacco and Vanzetti in America, to a Dimitrov in Berlin. Humanity will retrogress into the darkness of savagery if it remains unconcerned about the fate of millions of 'Dreyfuses' or if it fails to produce- as it has failed during these terrible years- a single Emile Zola. And if humanity at large is threatened by the enemy called indifference, how much greater is this threat to the Jewish people? That is why the most solemn warning for Jews as for Gentiles, speaks to us in Kipling's immortal words, "Lest we forget!"

The Indian people, on the other hand, have a propensity for forgetting historic wrongs.

One thing which emerges out clearly from the records is that the British attitude towards the Jews in Palestine was not merely indifferent but also aimed to achieve the maximum reduction in the number of Jews wishing to enter the land of Israel. The Balfour Declaration left more questions unanswered than it sought to answer. While the mandate lasted, theoretically the Jews were free to immigrate, though restricted in numbers, thanks to British generosity. But those who did so would be forever aliens to the land and open to rebellion by the Arabs as if fighting a foreign invasion. Thus the Jews would be forever a threatened minority and each side to be protected by the British bayonets.

True to their form, the British followed a similar policy in India when they abetted and incited Moslems to call for a separate homeland based on religion. While our 'secularists' continued opposing this two-nation theory. Islam prevailed, and the British and the Moslems got what they wanted. The result, a partition of the country on religious lines, riots and blood-bath and crores of bruised national feelings in India. Here, as in Palestine, the British left a legacy of two nations permanently hostile to each other with no possibility of reconciliation.

Irgun repeated their warnings on subsequent Days of Atonement to the British that any violent action against the Jews would be met with violence. Although moderates under Hagannah counselled restrained, Irgun continued their operations unhindered without breaking the unity of the resistance movement. The warning to the British on the Wailing Wall was followed by an attack on police strong posts at Haifa, Beit-Dajan, Kalkiliah and Katara. The British had learnt their lesson and on the Day of Atonement stood passively by. Extensive campaign of enlightenment by the Hebrew Committee of National Liberation in the United States also played an important role in awakening world opinion towards the happenings in Eretz Israel. Nevertheless, the Irgun and other terrorist organisations had their moments of worry. The one truth that emerged from the struggle was that the "idealists" and the "materialists had to work in tandem. To quote Begin again:

> "Which is cause and which effect? Do men make events or do unavoidable events make the men? In our underground cellar we did not find the answer to this weighty question. But we did learn that an idea, after it has taken shape, mysteriously gives birth to the men who bring it to fruition.Recognizing this truth, I assert that if at any stage of the revolt all of us in the Irgun had been captured or killed, others would have taken our places and fought the oppressor until he was beaten. We learnt that the aim makes heroes of the weak, turns privates into officers, quite ordinary people into swayers of minds and hearts, theoreticians into men of action, students into strategists. I have read somewhere a denial of the old theory that nature abhors a vacuum. What is certain is that an idea will not tolerate a vacuum in the ranks of those who are to bring it to fruition."

The apple of discord between the Arabs and the Jews as pointed out earlier, was the Wailing Wall of the Old City of Jerusalem. The British authorities adjudicated in the matter and issued an "Order-in-Council 1929" stating that "Jews are forbidden to blow the Shofar at the Wailing Wall and declared their resolve to enforce this edict forcefully. But subsequent events showed how ineffective the British judgement was. To quote Begin again on the supreme importance of the Wailing Wall:

> "These stones are not silent. They do not cry out. They whisper. They speak softly of the house that once stood here, of kings who knelt here once in prayer, of prophets and seers who here declaimed their message, of heroes who fell here, dying; and of how the great flame, at once destructive and illuminating, was here kindled. This was the house, and this the country which, with its seers and kings and fighters, was ours before the British were a nation. The testimony of these stones, sends out their light across the generations."

Forbidding the blowing of the Shofar at the Wailing Wall, the British underestimated the Jewish sentiments who ignored the ban for almost 13 years under the leadership of Jabotinsky and till as late as the Day of Atonement in 1943, the ritual continued. Everytime the British tried to disburse the mob the crowd gathered again. Describing that memorable evening of the Day of Atonement in 1943, Begin has this to say:

> "That night as, more heart-sore than injured, we stood by the Wailing Wall, we said to each other: 'This is the real slavery. What the Roman proconsuls did not dare do, Britain's Commissioners are doing.' What our ancestors refused to tolerate from their ancient oppressors, even at the cost of their lives and freedom, is tolerated by the generation of Jews which describes itself as the last of oppression and the first of redemption. A people that does not defend its holy places that does not even try to defend them is not free, however much it may babble about freedom. People that permit the holiest spot in their country and their most sacred feelings to be trampled underfoot are slaves in spirit. And

we determined there and then that when the time came we would cleanse our people of this shame, and if we should have the strength we would not permit the oppressor's myrmidons to violate our Holy place, disturb our prayers and desecrate our Festival."

As juxtaposed to this sentiment is the sad story of Indian history where successive invaders, conquerors and Moslem rulers destroyed hundreds of temples without even a whimper of protest from the local populace. Our fatalism and spirit of tolerance had more often than not verged on cowardice. We forgot the teachings of our sages and Lord Krishna that injustice should not be tolerated. To submit to tyranny is a bigger crime than committing tyranny itself. The recent case of Ayodhya has shaken the conscience of our people. The holiest of our shrines, the Ram temple, the birth place of Lord Rama, was destroyed by Babar and a non-mosque structure erected in its place. This misdeed has been crying loud for retributive justice. The sentiments of the people were so aroused that a mob did what our weak-kneed leaders failed to do. The structure was destroyed. But the furore which followed from the so-called 'secularists' defies comprehension. Instead of calling 6th December,1992, a Day of Deliverance and Restoration of National Honour, these secularists have been calling it a Day of National Shame. What a difference between the attitude of Jews and our 'secularists' who claim to be the opinion makers of our nation.

The Floggings

Certain sections of the British Government seemed to have a fatal attraction for the whip. In fact, flogging by the whip became the visible symbol of British rule in their colonies. A cane or a little whip was enough to scare the natives as some one described the whip as the "scepter of gentle peace". But this bestial punishment was not acceptable to the proud Jews and they decided to retaliate. While floggings of the Jews were common in Hitler's occupied Europe, Eretz Israel stood apart. The Irgun decided that if the British Army whipped their boys they would whip British officers in return. This warning was published prominently in their underground newspaper and pasted on the walls of Jerusalem. Prompted by the incredulity of the rank and file of the British occupation forces that their officers may be flogged the hierarchy refused to believe this "preposterous" threat. As it happened, British took a young Jew, Kimche, out of the Jerusalem jail and gave him 18 lashes in public, as per their law. Soon after *Herut,* the underground newspaper, issued a second warning to the Government:

> "For hundreds of years, you have been whipping 'natives' in your colonies-without retaliation. In your foolish pride you regard the Jews in Eretz Israel as natives too. You are mistaken. Zion is not Exile. Jews are not Zulus. You will not whip Jews in their Homeland. And if British Authorities whip them British officers will be whipped publicly in return."

The news spread like wildfire. The Irgun warned that if "whip-education" was good for Hebrew soldiers it was good for British officers as well. And retribution followed. In Nathanya, Tel Aviv, and Rishon-le-Zion British officers were caught and given eighteen lashes each. The British were quick to learn the lesson and the flogging stopped. Jewish warning went:

> "If the oppressors dare in the future to abuse the bodies and the human and national honour of Jewish youths, we shall no longer reply with the whip. We shall reply with fire."

The whole world laughed at the discomfiture of the British authorities. While the Irgun was kind to British captives, the gesture was not always reciprocated by the British authorities. Dovgruner was one of the brave Hebrew boys who was captured and sentenced to death. So was his comrade Meir Nakar. The third such martyr was Yaacov Weiss who had valiantly saved the lives of hundreds of Jews from the Nazis. While Dovgruner was hanged alone, the two Jewish boys and the third one Haviv were to be hanged together. As the British officer in charge of the execution said to Haviv, Nakar and Weiss "You will be hanged by the neck until you are dead." In reply all the three sang Hatikvah just as our revolutionary freedom fighters sang 'Vande Mataram' before taking the noose, The hangings were avenged

The fighting spirit of the Irgun could not be suppressed. They carried out an assault on Acre prison and released Jewish prisoners; they blew up King David Hospital; they looted armouries at Sarafana and Ramat-Gen as described earlier. During the war they carried out acts of sabotage against the Mandate authorities, revenged floggings and hangings and they carried out the conquest of Jaffa.

Chapter 12

Making of a Nation State

David Ben-Gurion declared the independence of Israel on 14 May, 1948, and the British Government decided to terminate its mandate on May 15, 1948. Anticipating a chaos and an inevitable Arab offensive, the Jews prepared for a war along with guerrilla operations to protect their homeland. Truly enough, within hours of the British withdrawal armed forces of Egypt, Syria, Iraq, Lebanon and Transjordan attacked Israel from all sides to destroy the nascent state. We need not go into the details of the war where the Jews fought with exceptional valour and military expertise, coupled with guerrilla tactics and worsted their opponents. The siege of Jerusalem lasted about two months ending on June 11, 1948, as the first truce began. But during the intense fighting, particularly in the Jewish quarter, the Jews bore the brunt of the battle, where 2000 devout Jews huddled in closed dwellings surrendered to the victorious Arabs, and the city passed into Arab hands. Some Jews were taken prisoners and the others moved out to Katamon area of west Jerusalem. On their departure, in keeping with the historical precedence, the Arabs looted synagogues, schools and homes of Jews and put to fire everything they could find. In all, twenty-seven synagogues and thirty schools were damaged or destroyed. The area of east Jerusalem under Jordan rule for almost 19 years, which contained the famous Jewish cemetery on the Mount of Olives, was vandalized. According to a historian:

> "Graves had been ripped open and bones scattered; thousands of tombstones had been smashed or removed by the Jordanian Army to build fortifications, footpaths, army camps, and latrines. The Arab Jerusalem Municipality had granted concessions to merchants who destroyed graves and sold the gravestones to building contractors."

The remains of the Jewish quarter bore the look of Stalingrad or Berlin after the World War II. Appeals of the Jews to the United Nations of Jordánian's destructions fell on deaf years. While the Jews complained of the breach of the truce agreement and the safety of shrines and holy sites, Jordan replied by citing desecration of some so called Muslim graves in west Jerusalem. Jerusalem thus divided into two halves by a barbed wire fence, virtually became two states with the Jews dominating the west and the Arabs dominating the eastern part. This caused avoidable clashes in both the communities visiting their holy places on either side of the fence.

Despite their losses, Israel and Jordan emerged as the gainers in the 1948 war. Syria and Lebanon lost most of their claimed territories as in May 1949, King Abdullah signed an armistice agreement with Israel dividing Palestine into two parts, with Transjordan boundary lying along the river Jordan and claiming east part of Jerusalem. In spite of the world reaction and Arab protestations to the contrary, Jordan and Israel stood their grounds and undertook the task of governing the partitioned territory of their respective halves of Jerusalem. The Israelis carried out heavy construction works, including University Campus, hospital complexes, hill side suburb of Ein-kerem and moved their Foreign Ministry's office from Tel Aviv to Jerusalem.

Before we start narrating the growth of the new state of Israel after its inception on 14th May, 1948, a few important facts have to be kept in mind. The Jews arriving from different parts of the world spoke different dialects. Mention has been made earlier of Yiddish. The local dialect of the indigenous Palestinian Jews called "Sabra" was part Arabic and part Hebrew. In 1951, four-fifths of the Israeli soldiers corresponded in foreign languages. But in an achievement of linguistic coherence five years later, just as many wrote their letters in Hebrew. The leader of the immigrants David Ben-Gurion carried a socialist baggage due to his birth in Bolshevik territory, as was the case with other East European Jews. However, intense nationalism and devotion to their homeland tempered these ideological differences across the spectrum from capitalism to socialism. The construction of 'Moshav' was one off-shoot of the Russian collective farming. Thanks to David Ben-Gurion's sense of pragmatism and his personal charisma, divergent political ideologies and varying dialects merged themselves into a Jewish theme and Hebrew was declared a common national language. This is reminiscent of Mahatma Gandhi uniting contradictory political ideologies on one common platform for the struggle for national freedom. This general confederation of Hebrew workers called 'Histadrut' was on the lines of our Indian National Congress. David Ben-Gurion turned the Labour Zionist movement into the main instrument of national renaissance. There were many other constituents under this umbrella organization. The Jews also raised a demand of one billion dollars for the Jewish properties usurped by the Germans under the Nazi regime which was accepted by Chancellor Konrad Adenaur as a starting point in the Jewish reparation.

On termination of the War of Independence in 1948, as pointed out earlier, while David Ben-Gurion accepted the U. N. recommendations, the Arabs refused. Ben-Gurion spelt out the future policy of the new state. Firstly, there shall be no return of the refugees who had left Israel. Being the "aggressors" they forfeited that right. However, David Ben-Gurion invited the Arabs in the task of building of the new state. The Arab exodus, he stressed, was not of Israel's making. His argument was:

> "We did not want the war. Tel Aviv did not attack Jaffa. It was Jaffa which attacked Tel Aviv and this should not occur again. Jaffa will be a Jewish town. The repatriation of the Arabs to Jaffa is not justice, but folly. Those who declared war on us have to bear the result after they have been defeated."

By 1st August, Israel Government was faced on the one hand with the problem of reintegration of the returning Arabs, a humungous task by any measure, on the other there was a question of rehabilitating streams of Zionist emissaries and the victims of Diaspora, some willing, others not so willing to return to their home. Secondly, there was to be no return of territory, a principle clearly enunciated by the first cease-fire, "all that we have taken we shall hold." And that became Israel's policy in its dealings with its neighbours and any third party. Security was the supreme aim. "Israel would not participate in its own destruction." All that Israel asked of the Arabs was to accept it: as we are, with our territory, our population and our unrestricted sovereignty. As for the UN Partition Plan, that recommendation, pronounced 'unassailable' on 15 May, was dead and buried.

The implacable logic of Zionism held in check by the Mandate now came into action. There was to be no response to the whining of the international community. The Arabs had rejected the earlier plan. Now they had to accept an enlarged Israel as it now existed. While the Palestinian Arabs vowed to "liberate" their land, the Zionist's impulse to fight back hardened.

Before the declaration of freedom on 14th May, 1948, David Ben-Gurion had a vision of the shape of his nation state. His vision was not unaccompanied with realism, ground realities and the capabilities of his people. Unlike Nehru whose head was in the clouds and feet nowhere, Ben-Gurion knew that a vision without pragmatism and practical sense becomes a hallucination. He exhorted his people that the new state was bound to be home to a small people. Had not Moses said, "For ye were the fewest of all peoples." He thus demanded that the children of Israel behave as a Chosen people, keeping their spiritual ascendancy alive as the basis of survival of a small people. He knew that neither the material and spiritual nor the political and cultural changes of thousands of years of Jewish existence had diluted the vitality of his people nor the twists and turns of history undermined the unique national character of the Jews. It was the strength of Bible, a secret resource which safeguarded their existence and their uniqueness in spite of continued threats to their national sovereignty. Empires like Egypt, Babylon, Rome and Greece, rose and fell, but tried as they did, they could not wipe out the Jews from the face of the earth. They survived the onslaught of the other Semitic religion Islam and excesses of Christianity which ironically was born out of their own religion. The emancipation of the Jews did not lead to assimilation but resulted in a new expression of their national uniqueness and Messianic longings. They no longer saw that the promised land was a mystic dream, but was a fusion of vision with realities, in the formation of the land of Israel, which his people had to build with their skill and creativity. The biggest blow to Israelites after the struggle between Bar Kochba and Hadrian of ancient Rome was a life and death battle between Bolsheviks and the Jews in Russia. From the days of the first Aliya, the Jews saw nothing but struggle to settle in their own home till this very day of May 14, 1948. The Jews could never compete in physical power with their neighbours who even questioned their right to exist. But thousands of years of their history of oppression and struggle taught them to survive and endure and act as a beacon to the nations of the world. Their land was the melting pot of the Jews returning from Diaspora.

The more the Arabs threatened to "liberate" Palestine, the more the Israelis, surrounded by enemies on all sides were forced to fall on a strategy of offensive survival. To ensure their national security, the Jews resorted to military exploits which further deepened the Arab hatred which in turn needed a stronger military response from Israel, and the vicious circle continued. Israel's military prowess, the competence, and daring spirit of its commanders and the courage of its soldiers was an invaluable asset for a nation perpetually at war. It fought a number of "little wars" as punitive expeditions in retaliation to trans-border raids which in some cases resulted in the 'big wars'. After independence in 1948, Israelis fought three 'big wars' against its Arab neighbours. The first in October 1956, a '100 hours war' with French and British allies was a five-day "blitzkrieg" against Nasser's Egypt, where Israeli's forces occupied the whole of Sinai and the Suez Canal. The second war on 4th June, 1967, was almost a 'virtuoso' performance by its generals and military artists. Most prominent among these was General Aerial Sharon, the present day Prime Minister of Israel. His breath-taking manoeuvers, earlier at Mitla Pass in 1956, and later at El Agheila with a series of daring night maneuvers, tightly controlled, and against conventional military wisdom, succeeded in breaking the Egyptian defenses and proved a decisive point in the victory. More of this later. During the Yom Kippur war in October 1973, the Egyptians gained initial surprises against Israeli's defences who while observing the National Festival were unprepared for war. However, Israeli resilience reasserted itself and Sharon, the intrepid "Rommel" of the Israeli army, found a gap in the Egyptian defences along the Suez Canal. He poured his army of fast moving armour into the breach and encircled the Third Egyptian Army, thereby leveling off the initial Egyptian advantage. Purely on military prowess he could also be counted amongst the heroes of Israel.

Despite its offensive posture and the semblance of a militarist society, the core of Israel has always been spiritualistic. However, there should be no doubt about its belief that 'the army is the people.' Their armed might is not merely the instrument of their preservation but the means to carry out Zionism's unfinished agenda. It is not merely punitive but also purposive. The biggest exponent of this creed is another great soldier and politician Moshe Dayan. Like all great civilizations destined to endure, Israel does not intend to stand still. Now a retrospect

The nascent state even before it was born was attacked by the surrounding Arab countries. Mention has been made earlier of the war of Independence and its sequel, resulting in an uneasy peace. But the Jews had arrived and prevailed in their Promised Land. Israel was the rectification of two millennia of historical shame. A desert became garden, 7800 sq. miles of energetic virtue in a world all gone over, complicated and boundless. The land rich Arabs were struggling for unity while the homogeneous Jews were defending a dream of land come true. Eight years after the cease-fire and six years after the tripartite declaration of 1950, Egypt became openly hostile and started sending its guerrillas called the 'fedayun' into the Gaza strip. The incursions increased in severity and gunfire causing heavy casualties to Israeli civilians and settlements. The Egyptians under President Nasser started making blood curdling noises against the Jews and threatened their very existence. War seemed imminent. David Ben-Gurion warned his people that they had learnt their hard lesson that if they themselves had strength, they would have peace, if they lacked it, no one would support them. In the meantime, Western nations particularly, France, America and Czechoslovakia started arming the Egyptians. Ben-Gurion quoted to the Western powers the Armistice Agreement under which the Jews were to have free access to their holy places and the cemetery on the Mount of Olives, as also a free passage to the Suez Canal. But the United Nations did nothing. Then Ben-Gurion roared back that they cannot be expected to sit with folded hands while the Egyptian marauders ravaged their country and intruded into their sovereign territory. Egyptian suicide commandos and cut-throats were sent into Israel to kill and mains the Israelites and mine their transportation system. David Ben-Gurion was fully aware that for the Jews it is not easy to win friends. Others who have, do so through a common religion or language, like the Arabs and Latin Americans. Others form an alliance against the common enemy or object of fear. Israel had neither wealth nor power nor territory, neither did they have a commonality of language or religion with any other state except the Arabs who were their sworn enemy. To a counsel of restraint from America, David Ben-Gurion mentioned that the United States Government had sent troops into Mexico in March 1916, after having failed to stop marauders on their frontier and these were withdrawn only in early 1917. Repeated representations to the United Nations and America brought no result. Egyptians continued their attacks in increasing proportion and the barometer started falling. Finally Ben-Gurion was forced to declare, "If our rights and our people's lives were assailed by acts of violence, we reserved freedom of action to take such measures as we thought fit to safeguard those rights and lives." He again warned, "Our right to self-defense was not only a natural right, it was expressly stated in the U N Charter in Article 51." Some of the United Nations personnel denied them this right. They stigmatized as "reprisals" the defensive measures the Isralis took against the murders organised by Egypt and Jordan. All the United Nations observers and representatives knew as well that the 'fedayun' worked under orders from the Arab Governments, with Egypt taking the central position. Captured 'fedayun' had admitted these things in Israeli courts, and the Egyptian Minister of Religious Endowments, Hassan al-Bakuri, said the same thing in a broadcast from a Cairo radio station under Nasser's control: "There is no reason why the 'fedayun', who hate their enemies, should not penetrate deep into Israel, and make the lives of her people a hell." Ben-Gurion knew that the first duty of a Government is to protect the integrity of the state and the lives of its people. Any Government which failed to do so, is not worthy of its name. And so on October 27, the Sinai war erupted on the cockpit of the Middle East and in a lightening campaign, codenamed 'Operation Sinai,' "A Hundred Hours War" Israel swept the Egyptian army back beyond the Suez Canal and the world including Nehru's India, forced the Israelis to relinquish their gains and return to their pre-war boundaries.

Despite all it's wars, Israel never sought aggression nor believed in a constant state of war against its neighbours. The abiding philosophy of the Israelis can be summed up in the following lines of chapter 85 from the Book of Psalms,

> "Mercy and truth are not together: righteousness and peace have kissed each other."

President Eisenhower had once mentioned that peace and justice are indivisible but David Ben-Gurion believed that there can be no peace without justice. A country that could not protect its sovereignty, its security and rights, could not preserve either peace or justice.

Even after the termination of the Sinai war Israel knew no rest. While its people were involved in nation building and sweating to convert the desert into a bloom, Arabs were planning once again to destroy the nascent state. Barely eleven years after the last conflict war drums started beating again in Cairo. President Nasser paranoid on the strength of aided Russian weaponry and his self-appointed leadership of the Arab world was once again trying to challenge the Israeli might. The first step in this belligerency was the closure of Sharm-et-Sheikh, the town controlling Tiran Straites, the entrance to the Gulf of Aqaba, and choke Eilat, the only southern Israeli port with access to the Red Sea and South Asian waters. To the western observers there was an incessant flow of heady propaganda, a call to Jehad and for the destruction of Israel. The Arabs were drunk upon their own rhetoric and language. Arabs, Arabic and Islam are inseparable, each recreating the other in an undefined process of cross-pollination, till the words are exalted to the level of reality. The Arab emotions took control over their logic and the ground realities. Islam is a religion devoid of theology. It means submission to the will of God and a total surrender to what He wills or ordains. Though it is difficult to interpret the will of God, Muslim leaders down the ages have conferred legitimacy to their cause from worship to slaughter, all in the name of God's will. The Suras of Quran have a rhythm and a nuance all their own. They proclaim, implore, chant, croon, weep and laugh and the torrential flow of Arabic creates an image that charms. This repetitiveness in Islam overwhelms imagination and calcifies reason. The holy language intoxicates and sanitises the brain in a manner that only the language counts and not its substance. In such an atmosphere, it is easy to understand that the Arabs, who for fourteen hundred years had turned inwards upon the spoken words, and numbed their senses to the heat and poverty of the desert, lapped every word of the Mullah, the Cairo Radio broadcast and the exhortations of Nasser. The stage was, therefore, set for a Jehad, a word often misused for any form of offensive action as willed by God. Egypt plunged into war not knowing the battlefield or the Israeli army.

As the 4th June of 1967 neared the land of Israel prepared for the impending war to break off from the stranglehold of its maritime blockade of the Arabian sea. There was no doubt about Israeli's military capability, but it will be useful to look into the mind of the Israeli soldier. The Israelis at war did not succumb to rage or arrogance. After planning with an unending passion for detail, they fought with dedication and drive. In spite of this decisive advantage they were never unduly conceited nor over confident. The psyche of Diaspora and the element of anxiety permeates into their subconscious. A subliminal anxiety underlines the soldier's personal awareness and exerts on him a primordial and strong pressure, since his victory only means continuation of status quo, may be, slightly better than before, while on the other hand, looms the risk of extinction of his land. This inner vision of Armageddon impels the Jewish soldier in war. While the Arabs, in spite of their defeats, are intoxicated with a notion of what victory brings, the jews, fight for survival is pitted against the Arab pride of victory. If the Jews were to lose Israel for the third time, history becomes meaningless to them. And the fourth return to the land or Aliya, is unthinkable. To quote a personal observer of June 4-9, 1967, Israeli blitzkrieg, "In every people the power tobe great is resident, but not every people fulfills this potentiality for glory; some die, some stop before the summit is attained, some turn upon themselves and crush the ephemeral capacity in rages of self-destruction. But if greatness is ever achieved, it is never forgotten. The memory of it persists and the subsequent history of the people who once achieved themselves is dictated by how they use the memory of their greatness. In the centuries between return to the northern fertile crescent and the death of King David, the Hebrews became Jews and fulfilled their capacity to be great."

The Jews won a resounding and absolute victory. They extended their territorial boundaries to include the areas of the West Bank of River Jordan, the whole of Sinai peninsula, and the Golan Heights in Syria, thus achieving 'lebensraum' and strategic depth. Today Eretz Israel stretches about 470 kms in length and 135 kms in width at its widest point, and covers an area of about 20,700 sq. kms, with an additional 7,477 sq. kms, of occupied territories of West Bank, Gaza strip, East Jerusalem and Golan Heights. But the jewel in the crown of this victory was Jerusalem. They captured the whole of Jerusalem and restored their national pride. Did they not offer their prayers, "If I forget thee, O Jerusalem, let my right hand forget its cunning." It is the right hand that steers the plow and kills.

Though we have skipped the details of this war, but as an ex-soldier I cannot resist the temptation to label this conflict as the most perfect example of a swift and decisive war involving an ideal combination of diplomatic skill, the higher direction of war and strategy and tactics; the perfect use of the lightning power of air to smother enemy air capability and subsequent unleashing of armour, coupled with infantry in encircling movements, resulting in a breath- taking velocity of operations. This five-day campaign of far-reaching military consequences is taught in various schools of military Instructions all over the world and I too have written some detailed accounts and references of this war in my various military writings.

The six-year interregnum between this victory and October 1973, were a period of twilight for the land of Israel when its leaders and soldiers were basking in the glory of battles won and smugly looked to the future with confidence. But this sense of complacency was soon to be shattered, and a militant Egypt under Anwar Sadat, in a surprise move, broke through the Israeli defences on the Suez Canal and forced them to fight during their holiest period of 'Yom Kippur'. A new chapter now opened in the Middle East history and Anwar Sadat became a hero of the Arab world.

Chapter 13

Intifada and After

After October 1973 "Yom Kippur"(the Jewish day of atonement) war there was a marked change in the Arab attitude towards Israel. Even though for a short time, the Egyptian army had prevailed against the Israeli military might, to the Arab mind it meant that Israel was not invincible. To the 1.7 million Palestinians in the West Bank and Gaza strip, this was heavenly elixir and revelation. History has its ways of influencing nations and events. This very same year, Arabs found out that Islamic nations were sitting on 67 percent of the world's known reserves of oil of which 2/3rd lay in Saudi Arabia alone. This was a tremendous earthly power granted to Islam and the Arabs intended to make full use of it. The Crown Prince of Saudi Arabia, brandishing his sword, proclaimed that henceforth the Arabs shall use their oil power for diplomacy and war. This event caused a civilizational catharsis among the Arabs who were now looking at the world as future conquerors. No longer were they poor and subservient to the West, but they could be their masters. Then followed a spree of direct take-overs of all oil wealth resources, refining activities, transportation and sale of oil to the world. Foreign operators and engineers working at the oil rigs were suddenly reduced from owners and operators to hired employees. The oil rich Middle Eastern Arab states, started buying everything in the West ranging from real estate, hotels, tourism, industry, oil companies and even those companies trading in alternate fuel. Their secret accounts spawned the entire western world. The balance of power in the Middle East shifted from Israel to the oil rich Arabs, and the American policy yoked to its commercial interests changed course by befriending as many Arab countries as possible. This resource victory for Islam was an important factor in the power balance between the Judeo Christian and Islamic civilizations.

This new-found confidence of oil power amongst the Arabs in general and Palestinians in particular, gave a boost to their hostilities towards Israel. Palestinians living on the West Bank and the Gaza strip somnolent so far, suddenly woke up to their God-sent power and the fact of Israel's vulnerability. There indeed existed some disaffection amongst the Palestinians living in the Israeli occupied territories after 1967, but it was still latent. It is pertinent to point out here that inspite of the vast spaces in Sinai and Jordan and even those bordering Syria, these Arab countries did not help the Palestinians to seek new homes in these places. Their sympathy was confined to the typical Arab rhetoric. In stead of assimilating these displaced Palestinians, their coreligionists, in their territories, they preferred to keep them in Israeli occupied lands in a permanent state of anger and despair, an easy enough instrument to destabilise Israel and ultimately destroy the nation. Certainly, there were hardships, inequities and disabilities that the Palestinians in the West Bank and Gaza strip had to suffer under the Israeli rule. But by and large, Israeli rule was sympathetic and fair. After all David Ben-Gurion had said that everytime it was not Israel who went out to attack the encircling Arabs, but the Arabs who invaded the Israelis. Thus the Israeli logic was very simple. You came to destroy us and were defeated. We thus need to have enough safeguard in strategic depth by retaining the occupied territory. We have given you a benevolent occupation and that should be enough. Defeated invaders cannot ask the victors to follow their dictates. Be that as it may, Palestinians did not accept this logic and discontent kept simmering fueled further by their new found confidence and rhetoric. The surrounding Arab countries not only gave sanctuaries to the Palestinian terrorists but actively provoked them to acts of violence against Israel. The pot kept boiling for two decades; discontent grew, right down to the grassroots level, and a mass upsurge was about to break out even without any leadership. According to the Arab view, what Israel had refused to see thus far was now splashed on the horizon. And on 8th December, 1987, the Arab discontent and rage long suppressed, ignored, shelved, quashed, pushed aside and swept under the carpet, burst out as 'Intifada'.

The perceived fears, frustrations and grievances of the Palestinian Arabs took the form of Islamic Jihad. There was looting, burning, attack and destruction of Israeli property and civilians, everywhere in the occupied territories. The critical mass, so to say, of the bomb of discontent was reached and the explosion took place not at one ground zero but every- where in the occupied territories. Israeli Defence Forces (IDF), their reservists and para-military organisations did their best to cope up with the situation and succeeded to a degree. The Palestinian predators declared that "If military action in a well known guerrilla war concentrated on the armed forces of the enemy, then those who shared the belief of those whom the revolution wants to fight, the Palestinian revolution owing to the nature of Zionist society does not recognise the distinction between enemy's armed forces and people. The colonialist Zionist society is a military society, root and branch, and there can be no distinction between military and civilians." The same is happening in Kashmir today. But the Israeli response to the Intifada has been much more effective and salutary. The garrisoning of conquered territories of West Bank and Gaza strip was indeed a strain on the Israeli Defence Forces, its administrative organs, and interior civil administration. This was not their normal task. In the initial stages there was a confusion in the division of responsibilities between various organs of defence of the state. But this was soon rectified. The situation was not dissimilar to that prevailing in Kashmir. West Bank and Gaza are still aflame and there are periodic breaches of peace and ceasefire agreements between the Government of Israel and the Palestine Liberation

Organisation. While Ariel Sharon is in total control of his forces, the same is not true of Yassar Arafat, the Chairman of the P.L.O. His writ does not run down to the level of foot soldiers and many splinter groups, are still perpetuating mayhem, terror and suicide attacks amongst Israeli settlements in occupied territories as also within Israel itself. As of now, there is an uneasy peace between the Palestinians and Israelis. Though the Israelis can be restrained to an extent by American pressure, there is no such countervailing force against the Palestinians exerted by any Arab country or countries.

It is a point worth noting that every single clash in the occupied territories starts by a provocative attack from the Palestinians which naturally invites swift and strong retribution. The world around, and many reporters from Middle East and the West often criticise Israel for its harsh treatment of the Palestinians. Prime Minister Yitzhak Shamir similarly questioned once lashed out with a reply typical of King Lear: "We are not allowed to kill; we are not allowed to expel; we are not allowed to beat. You ask yourself, what are we allowed to do? Only to be killed, only to be wounded, only to be defeated." Shamir later added, "We have plenty of 'friends' in the world who would like to see us dead, wounded, trampled, and suppressed, and then it is possible to pity the wretched Jew. When Jews are killed in this country, does the United Nations discuss it? It has never yet happened. But we do not want to be deserving pity, we want to fight for our lives."

Faced with the recurring and indiscriminate assault of the Palestinians and the murder of innocent civilians, Israeli armed forces have evolved a new doctrine; "assassinate the assassin and accept the collateral damage as incidental and unavoidable.' In pursuance of this new policy Israeli Defence forces recently killed a leading Hama terrorist who was responsible for the murder of a Cabinet minister and a large number of civilians. On 23rd November, 2001, a helicopter gunship fired missiles on the car in which the terrorist Mohmoud Abu Hamoud was traveling and destroyed the car and its occupants.

The foot soldiers of the Intifada believe in the following maxim. 'Normally wars are not won by dying for one's country. They are won by making the enemy die for us.' Unfortunately, the holy wars are not waged under this harsh but rational precept. The Palestinian terrorists had perfected the art of assassinating Israeli leaders and their prominent citizens, even if it involved a suicide attack. The word assassination has originated from a Shia sect, the "Hashishin" whose members carried out suicide attacks on and raided both Christians and Sunni Muslims. They had a hiding place in a mountain in Iran. The intoxicant "hashish" was also given to young killers before they set out on their missions. Their leader in 1090 A.D, Hasan-al-Sabah lived in a hilly fortress at Alamiet in Iran, and was called the "old man of the mountain". Another word in the vocabulary of the Palestinian marauders was "Jehad", so commonly heard these days. The "Jehad" in Arabic means 'effort', a rallying cry for the masses to advance the world's newest monotheistic religion under the threat of sword, against non-believers. With the passage of time, the word came to stand for a "righteous war". As per the thesis of Muslim clerics, 70 Muslim nations put together constitute the "*Dar-ul-Islam*" The remaining infidels are cursed to live in '*Dar-ul-Harab.*' "Sunna" in Arabic means tradition and those who follow the traditional values are called "Sunnis", which form the majority of the Muslim population. Those who wanted the Prophet's first cousin and son-in-law Ali to succeed him to the Caliphate, and followed the Iranian tradition of divine light of kings were called 'partisans' of Ali for which the Arabic word is 'Shia', the community which forms the principal segment of the Iranian population.

Beyond the miasma of imagined hurt, atrocities and suppression lies the principal impulse of Intifada, the Islamic hurt. Islam should only conquer but never be subjugated. Islam and Arab are indivisible. Since Islam threatens both Hinduism and Judaism, both historically and geographically, it is necessary to understand the Muslim mindset. To understand Islamic and Middle East politics, one has to enter into the mind of the primitive Arab Bedouin. In the wilderness of Arabian deserts with few sources of water and sustenance, the Arab develops the lone wolf mentality, more to be feared than to be loved. Love can be bestowed or withdrawn, but fear does not leave so easily. As such the Arab prefers to be feared rather than loved. This subliminal impulse makes him obedient and respect a power centre Thus in Islam, monarchy, comes naturally and forms the focus of a nation's power and authority going from the tribal leader upwards and power is respected even if it is barbarous or vicious. Thus the Muslims are not unduly attached to collective authority or equality. Even the Koran ordains subservience to the will of Allah, which over the ages has come to mean unquestioning obedience to temporal authority, liberal or despotic. In consequence, the history of Islam is full of bloodshed, through the acts of tyrants. The first brutal authoritarian in the Islamic history was the founder of the Abbasid dynasty in Baghdad, Abul-Abbas al-Saffah who ruled from 750 to 754 A.D. His name itself meant "Abul Abbas the Bloodletter". Authoritarianism sits lightly on Islam's shoulders and the Middle East kingdoms are full of such dispensations. The primordial tribal loyalties get coalesced into submission to the authority of the state, governed mostly by kings, despots or dictators.

We now return to the Intifada and the Palestinian Jehad against Israel. Most of the suicide groups or human bombs which have been sent to kill Israeli leaders or innocent civilians come from the ranks of Al Fatah, DFLP (Democratic Front for the Liberation of Palestine), its splinter group PFLP (Popular Front for Liberation of Palestine), another small group APF (Alliance of Palestinian Forces); the Hamas and Hizbollah (Party of God), or the Islamic Jehad. Finding it impossible to directly challenge the enormous military might of Israel, the Palestinians and the PLO (Palestinian Liberation Organisation), encouraged, supported and actively assisted through propaganda, arms and even safe sanctuaries by three highly vocal Arab States including even Iran, have tried to pin down IDF (Israeli Defence Forces) and their reservists in warding off terrorism. They have the tactical advantage of striking at their chosen place, time and target. Any student of elementary military tactics would realise that this is a different form of war; a low cost war of terror stretching the enemy forces to the full and keeping them in a permanent state of alert thus tiring them down and leading them to death through a thousand cuts. A similar form of low cost proxy war is being waged by Pakistan against India to achieve its aim of grabbing Kashmir and bleed India. But the response of Israelis and Indians to the same threat is not similar. While Israel hands out swift retributive justice and avenges its human loss by well aimed retaliatory attacks, India dithers and confines itself to diplomatic whining and only in rare cases to defensive and reactive operations.

Let there be no mistakes, four times since the birth of Israel the combined forces of Arab countries have attacked it to wipe out its existence. Each time they failed ignominiously. Israel, has occupied enough space on the West Bank and Gaza to secure its borders, ensure strategic depth, and prevent further such attempts for its dismemberment and destruction. What moral right do the Arabs now have to claim back their lost territories? India was foolish enough to return its war gains to Pakistan under external pressure in two wars it fought against it in 1965 and 1971, and even its own integral territory recaptured from Pak invaders in Kashmir in 1949. Israel is not obliged to make the same mistakes.

It is the Arab countries fired by their own heady Islamic rhetoric who attacked Israel and lost, thereby creating refugees in the West Bank and Gaza. It is they who made them suffer without fulfilling the promises they had made and the victories they promised to the Palestinians within Israel and even in occupied territories. These hapless souls would have continued to live as peaceful citizens in their own homes if their 'fair weather" Arab friends had not betrayed them. Now that the loaded dice has fallen the wrong way and Arabs have failed, it is incumbent on them to grant some living space to their own brethren, in stead of allowing them to remain as refugees in a state of so-called squalor and deprivation. You cannot have your cake & eat it too. Some Arab countries want precisely that. Israel did not come out to fight the Arabs. The Arabs did. They lost. Now they have to help their Islamic brethren for whom there is such an exhibition of concern, breast-beating and shedding of crocodile tears. Hypocrisy has its limits.

Yasser Arafat and his PLO terror machine was hounded out of Lebanon and Jordan by his co-religionists. Now he has been granted quarters at Ramallah, but his terror machine is still working over-time. Repeatedly, by his silent connivance and tacit support, he has failed to restrain his suicide bombers from killing innocent civilians. Thus, far from solving the problem of suicide attacks and bombings he is part of the problem himself. Not unjustifiably Aerial Sharon, Israeli Prime Minister, has called him 'the enemy of Israel'. The final solution can come only if the Palestinians demonstrate a sincere desire to co-exist peacefully with the people of Israel. They cannot fight geography which has placed them so close to their avowed enemies. It takes two to do a tango. It will not be in Paris. It has to be on the streets of Rafah and Ramallah

The same problem of cross-border terrorism plagues the Indian State. Pakistan is waging a low cost proxy war by recruiting Talibans and Jehadis from its Madarasas and the killing fields of Afghanistan to send them on a 'glorious mission' of "freedom fighters" or Jehadis to spread terror and death in the saffron fields of Kashmir and the hills of Jammu. American policy aimed at containing, fighting and wiping out terrorism has, due to geographical compulsions, to use Pakistan as a front-line state. But Pakistan itself is a nursery of terrorism and like Yasser Arafat part of the problem. It may make friendly gestures to the USA in its attempt to get the much-needed financial bail-out, and put Kashmir on the international map by allowing the US troops a base on its soil. General Musharraf's promises and body language to the Western audience has only one aim, to forestall any military retaliation from India in its reply to Pakistan's terrorists' campaign in Kashmir and the rest of India. Pak's ostensible support to the US in its war against Al Quaeda and Talibans, a Frankenstein midwifed by them both, has a hidden agenda to reinforce its cross-border terrorism against India by redirecting the now unemployed Talibans and other terrorists into Kashmir.

India will have to fight its own battle against terrorism without the US help or sympathy or support from Washington, just as Israel has to fight its battle of survival against Palestinian terror machine despite countervailing pulls from it's 'friends'!

The foreign policy aims of America just do not gel with those of India and Israel. In an effort to befriend oil rich Middle East Arabs in their war against Iraq, the foremost visible member of George Bush's "axis of evil", America will have no compunctions in abandoning Israel, just as in their effort to engage Pakistan they had no moral qualms in sidelining India. America is still quite far away from its aim of dismantling the structure of international terrorism. It is a humongous task. What has been achieved in Afghanistan is merely a few ground victories collateral aerial damage and depietion in the ranks of Al Quaeda and Talibans, with changes of guard in Kabul. The internecine tribal and ethnic strife continues unabated, and a large part of Al-Quaeda and Talibans have quietly sneaked into Pakistan to continue their good work. General Mushrraf's duplicity is well-known. He has perfected the art of running with the hares and hunting with the hounds. Only recently in a carefully mounted FBI Operation in many cities of Pakistan on 10th April, 2002, including 13 saids in Faislabad itself, his known shelter, Osama bin Laden escaped the dragnet. Pakistan's intentions to fight terrorism need to be taken with considerable scepticism. It is almost certain that America would soon realise the futility of using a thief to catch another thief. Meanwhile, it would be naive for India and Israel to expect too much of American sympathy or support in their fight against terrorism.

Chapter 14

Archaeology, Science and Thought

Interestingly, in the land of Israel Bible is used as a guide in all matters archaeological as well as military, by the Jews as was true in all their wars since 1948. Prof. Yigael Yadin, Commander-in-Chief of Israeli forces during their war of independence, was a great archaeologist and obtained a Ph.D. degree in the subject before the war dragged him from his cherished occupation. He wrote a monogram on the discovery of Dead Sea Scrolls. Moshe Dayan and David Ben-Gurion were scholars of Bible and great linguists with a command over many languages and religions. Even now Israel lives on Bible from day to day. No archaeological evidence unearthed till today has controverted the places and occurrences given in the Old Testament. Archaeology along with the Bible is the lifeblood of Israeli scholars and soldiers. The search for the soul of their nation and validation of its existence through texts in Bible is the staple of all Israelis.

The following historical landmarks of the Jewish history mentioned in Bible have been validated by the recent discoveries and intensive research:

(a) The well of Abraham. The 'Tree' near the well still survives being the only tree that could withstand adverse weather and an unhabitable terrain for a period of almost three and a half millennia.

(b) Mount Sinai located in South Sinai, the place where the Lord of the Jews, Yahweh, gave his Ten Commandments to Moses.

(c) The town of Jericho. Its ruins are still visible and remind the reader of its capture by Joshua who circled the town beating drums and carrying torches and by sheer noise of the drums and trumpets the walls of the town came tumbling down.

(d) The ruins of the town of Hebron.

(e) The ruins of the towns of Tabor and Safed in the province of Gallilee.

(f) Solomon's mines located near the Port of Eilat on the Gulf of Aqaba. These mines are still being used to extract minerals such as copper and tin with smelting plants in existence, close by.

(g) The town of Jerusalem still exists and is the hub center of Jewish history having been invaded and destroyed 40 times in three millennia. Almost every place of historical importance is still intact and revered by the Jews.

(h) Archaeological evidence points to a settlement of four structures in Jericho built with strong fortification and extended circular watch towers surrounded by moats dating back to 7000 B.C.

The four cities holy to the Jews were Tiberius and Safed, both in Galilee, Jerusalem and Hebron, the last located 200 miles south of Galilee. Tiberius has a sub-tropical and warm climate, situated as it is on the shores of the sea of Galilee, which used to be the center of Jewish faith. Safed is located on the top of an extinct volcano near Mount Tabor, Mount Meiron and Mount Hermon.

Masada has been discussed earlier. The rock of Masada at the eastern edge of the Judean desert is a sheer drop of more than 1300ft to the western shores of the Dead Sea. Attacked by the Romans in the Ist century A.D. with the overthrow of the Jewish Maccabeans in the middle of the previous century, there had been periodic rebellions in the country. But in 66 A.D., a Jewish revolt flared up into a full scale countrywide war which raged for four years. Ultimately, the Roman General Titus conquered and sacked Jerusalem in 70 A.D., destroyed the Temple and expelled the bulk of the survivors from the country. One outpost was held till 73 A.D. and that was Masada. During the two archaeological excavations led by Yigal Yadin from October 1963 to March 1964 and November 1964 to April 1965, consisting mainly of volunteers from different countries they discovered the remains of Masada. In the siege of spring of 73 A.D., 960 men and children had killed themselves here rather than surrender and be taken prisoners by the Romans, preferring death to loss of liberty. The excavations found a number of small artifices of the poor defenders, such as ovens and charred children's sandals in addition to all the remains of King Herod's palace, garrisons, store house, armouries, aqueducts and all the relics of the battle, fought to the end.

In present day Israel archaeology is as sacred as the Bible. Archaeologists have learnt how men used to live in Israel in the late Mesolithic Natufian cave on Mount Carmel, and their ancestors had already tamed the dog ten thousand years ago, learnt to harvest seed grasses as their relatives west of Lake Hula had perfected the art of buring decapitated bodies in a walled pit. The present day discovery stretches from far back to Chalocolithic civilization, which was destroyed in the thirty-second century B.C. ushering the Bronze Age of walled cities in Canaan, down to the age of Abraham. This search is not futile, offering as it does, lessons in conservation, irrigation and cultivation from the rich past. Scientists at the Negev Institute of Research at Beersheba are engaged in finding solutions to conquer the desert. Around sixty to eighty engineers, physiologists, physicians, biologists, agronomists, architects, meteorologists, climatologists, geologists and experts on soil and desalination are working over time to turn Negev green. All this research, Israel claims, will not only help Israel but enable the transfer of technical assistance to neighbouring countries in the Middle East and similar other areas. In a project launched by the United Nations Educational, Scientific and Cultural Organization (UNESCO) in 1956 at Beersheba for arid-zone research and experimental work in India, Pakistan, Israel and Egypt, considerable progress has been made. Beersheba today can boast of a sixteen-acre Ecological Desert Garden where a large number of agro-desert researches are being carried out on plants from Australian Out Back, the American prairie, the Soviet steppes and Central Asian deserts, the South African veldt, Negev, and other arid zones whose flora has proved to have economic potential and can supply food, fodder, fibers, oils and medicines, as also a cover for the increasing number of dunes and deserts in cut-over lands. Also grown here are ornamental and shade plants for desert towns to meet aesthetic demands.

Most of the guidance for the research work at Beersheba comes from Bible. The first tree which Abraham planted in the soil of Beersheba was a tamarisk. Following this lead, Israelis have planted two million such plants in this area, extending this activity even to arid south expecting another success. The Institute at Beersheba works in close cooperation with the Hebrew University's Agricultural Research Station at Rehovot to evolve the right agricultural techniques that can be used with the existing meager supply of water in Negev which is highly brackish or saline. The answers were not long in coming. Groves of date palms highly resistant to salinity have been planted around each salty spring or well in places like the Wadi Arabah as a good economic investment. Another flora reed Juncus is used in the manufacture of paper. In Israel even saline water is harvested to irrigate sugarbeets and other commercial crops. Science and technology is the staple of the present generation of Israelis. They have perfected the technique of anchoring the roving sand dunes, which had earlier laid waste a quarter of a million acres of cultivable soils and threatened much more. It was in these areas that tamarisks, eucalyptii and acacia were planted along with pulses, hay and vegetables. With sufficient irrigation and a little fertilizer, the dunes became productive in three or four years, even the sea water was used to irrigate the dunes, passing through and around them and flushing out sediments of all concentrated poisonous salt which had deposited there over the passage of time.

To Ben-Gurion's call to "harness the sun and sweeten the sea", the scientists rose to act in unison. Along with the U.S., Russia and France, Israel is the fourth country where harvesting of the sun is the major project. Two thousand kilowatt of heat scorching yearly, every square mile of Israel has tantalizing possibilities. The sunshine in Negev alone produces as much heat as the total annual fuel imports of Israel. The blazing curse of the deserts is God's gift to Israel, where solar energy is being used to operate refrigerators and air conditioners, in addition to meeting other power demands. In fact, Israel can boast of the world's first sun-operated industry at Beersheba.

Thus from their primitive nomadic origin the wandering children of Israel have not only found their home in the Promised Land but have made it according to their Lord's Covenant a nation that acts as a light unto other nations of the world. From every index of human progress, Israel is and shall remain a leader for centuries to come.

There are many under-currents that go together to form the main stream of Israeli psyche. The main amongst these is one that conjures up collective memories from the history of the Jewish past; the Czar's pogroms, centuries of holocaust and persecutions, and the mass graves inNazi' death camps in 1945. The subject of holocaust is one of the essential elements in the high school education and the Israel Army officers' course. They do not go to the first Kibbutz Degania, but rather visit Yad Vashem, the massive hilltop memorial in Jerusalem that honours six million Jews killed in Hitler's war. Today, all Israeli youngsters are not only conducted to Yad Yashem but also sent in hundreds on field trips to Poland to see the death camps of Auschwitz, Majdanek, and Treblinka—thus conveying the subliminal message that these camps are a vital part of Israel.

The Israelis view history as a linear process of moral advancement through divine laws and a steady improvement of self in this world, in order to bring about a messianic reign of absolute peace and harmony. Human history and politics, they feel can do much better; the slaves can be set free, the exodus from Egypt is possible and Promised Land lies at the end of the desert. There is a marked similarity in this thought with the sublime Hindu thought. The sense of loneliness is all-pervasive. The entire Middle East rejected them. The Jews had to make a state where their people were not present, and they were not a majority in their country. They had to literally seize the ears of the world, since juridical arguments were of no avail. They had to make and prove themselves exceptional, and so Israel tried to be an exceptional people, both in terms of their historical and spiritual lineage. They were showcasing the country mainly to the west, to whom the Bible was both familiar and attractive. In the process of their rhapsodic defence and rhapsodic rhetoric they became both its victims as also the torchbearers of ancient Jewish morality. No wonder, the world judges Israel not by the standard of other people but by those set by Israelis themselves. When Syria murders thousands of the people no one cares, they do not expect the Syrian Hamas to do any better, but the killing of a few Palestinians causes accusing fingers from all directions. At the same time, Israel needs world attention for its own security. Two thousand years of rejection by the world, and an existence on the margins of society has burnt deep into Israeli' consciousness. This is one reason why Israelis are so sensitive to the world opinion.

Israel like many other countries of the world has many historical and religious schools of thought. The first one consists of secular and nonobservant men like Shimon Peres and Yizhak Shamir who really built the new state of Israel. Without overdoing the Jewish rituals, these secular Zionists are more concerned with building up a modern society and army and other organs of the state. To them the defining feature of Israel is not Torah but science, technology and turning the desert green. Looking more to the future than to past, as Orthodox Jews do, they use their past as a strong foundation to future achievements. The second school consists of religious Zionists, the traditional or modern Orthodox Jews who while supporting a secular state, emphasize that it is not a substitute for the synagogue. They find the state, the synagogue and the Torah as compatible. They mainly serve in the army, celebrate Israel's Independence Day as a religious holiday and send their children to state-run religious schools. The third school also composed of religious Zionists has a more messianic bent. To these messianic Zionists, the rebirth of the Jewish state is not merely a religious event but the coming of the Messiah, the state being merely a material instrument to bring this about. Politics, defence and foreign policies all should subserve this end and the children of Israel must settle in every inch of the land of Israel.

Lastly, there are the ultra-Orthodox, non-Zionist Jews known as Haredim which means "those filled with the awe of God". They put the highest emphasis on the Messiah, and politics and the state do not really matter. These Haredims, descendants to the great eighteenth, nineteenth and twentieth century Yeshivas and Rabbinic dynasties in the Jewish towns and ghettos of Eastern Europe, though a small percentage of the local population, are a strong influence in Israel's polity with high accent on religion rather than politics. They have taken upon themselves the role of the conscience keepers of the state of Israel. Despite superficial differences between all the four groups, they all believe in the words of the prophets, the letter of the Bible, the innate spirituality of Judaism, concede the importance of Torah and the commandments which kept the Jews together in Israel, and believe in the eternal truth that only when they return to their Promised Land, can they play the role assigned by God.

The Jews are in Israel today to fulfill the commandments of their Lord to settle in the land of Israel, which means complete Biblical territory of Judea and Samaria, the heart of Israel, and the lands mentioned in the Bible, so they can be redeemed. The sages of Israel have always distinguished between this mitzvah of settling in Israel from the other mitzvot. The mitzvah in the land of Israel is weighed against all the other seven mitzvot, since a majority of the 613 commandments can only be performed in the independent land of Israel by an independent Jewish people. Only a minority of mitzvot can be performed outside Israel. These mizvot relate to family, private, individual lives, religious rituals, as also to the national life and the Temple. It is not possible to complete the Torah society without the mitzvot which in turn, as the sages say, are only possible in the land of Israel where the individual can reach the highest spiritual level of achievement. The most progressive Jews like the Hindus believe in their history, family roots and the religion, but just as Sinai is not a closed book and Torah has to live in constant dialogue with the world so also Hinduism constantly reinvents itself into new forms and is a religion in perpetual evolution. The modern Jew learns from everywhere. To the Jews Israel and Judea is the foundation from which they can absorb the best values of the world without losing their individuality. So also the Hindus have an open mind where everything new and progressive has a place. One cannot forget the past living in Israel. It comes to haunt you from every state corner. That is why if the Jew does not reclaim his past or interpret it in terms compatible with the modern world, the past will overwhelm the future.

To those who wish India and Israel well, and their natural friendship get deeper, the following observation of an Indian news reporter who recently visited Israel would be heart-warming. Israel's deputy Prime Minister and Foreign Minister, Shimon Peres, summed up the interest India generates in their country. "India is not a business; it's a culture. If we were to write the Bible again, Gandhi would be our prophet". This interest manifests itself in the fact that almost 20,000 Israelis visit India every year, the same way as the so-called "hippies' in the 60s visited our land seeking 'nirvan'. Mr. Peres further stresses that, "in the eyes of the youngsters India is a soul, a sense, a feeling", and in consequence the Israeli youth, like the hippies of the 60s era, are reaching out to India for spiritual salvation.

According to Prof. Yohanan Grinspon, Professor of Indian Studies at Jerusalem's Hebrew University, "Young Israelis are overwhelmed by the sense of freedom in India. They feel a certain acceptance. After three-and-a-half years of army service it is an exhilarating moment to stay in and feel India, to look for the self. Out of every 100 Israeli students who visit India, 98 stayed on for at least six months and even longer." Prof. David Shulman, Head of the Department of Comparative Religion and a Vedas expert at the University, has this to say, "There is a certain sense of familiarity with India among those who have travelled to India. These are people whose lives India has touched. And, enough numbers return to take serious interest in India as a country". The Israeli youths' interest in India is forcing the parents to turn eastward. Yossi Klein Halevi, the Jerusalem correspondent of The New Republic whose 16-year old daughter is already packing for her India's visit, stated, "It is not simply youthful romanticism, it is something deeper. In both Israel and India, there is a continuity of memory with the mythic past. Both nations are struggling to figure out the relationship between myth and modernity." The biggest tribute to our culture comes from the fact that Israelis have named their youth festivals 'Boomba Mela' to emulate the spirit of the 'Kumbha Mela' which is held every 3-4 months with around 50,000 youth participating to celebrate the spirit of India.

Israeli's interest in India is not of the Maharaja, rope trick or elephant ride vintage, but has gone much too far. At the Hebrew University's Department of Indian Studies, extensive research is going on to explore the "mysterious bond between the Vedas and the Bible". Indian studies are flourishing much to the surprise of many Indians here. Prof. Liat, who is studying Sanskrit at the Hebrew University, explains, "India is different and exciting in a unique way. It is a good mirror for me, to understand myself better. The Israeli youth is deeply influenced by India, by Indian food, Indian philosophy, elements of which have been introduced into Jewish tradition." And finally Prof. Grinshpon made a point that, "We are trying to understand Gandhi's peaceful attitude to events because the main aim for Israel in the current situation is peace. We are trying to promote openness in this regard." It is ironic that the prophet and his philosophy is derided in his own homeland.

Victor Hugo once remarked, "No power on earth can stop an idea whose time has come". Idea is stronger than weapon. A nation draws its strength and longevity from an idea that permeates its people. This idea when in tune with the national ethos turns into belief. Belief turns into faith and faith can move mountains. John Stuart Mill has said, "A man with belief is equal to ten thousand who have only interests". This motive power of idea, faith and belief is the force multiplier that makes even a nation of few people challenge the most populous nation in the world. In war, Napoleon once remarked, "The moral is to physical as three is to one". Large armies have been routed by a small band of inspired fighters that changed the course of history and redrew the political map of the world. Large land mass, population, material resources do not a nation make. The few with faith can enlarge the living space, sweeten the sea, make the desert bloom and supersede more populous and naturally endowed countries. India and Israel with their roots embedded in their oldest civilization and faith in their destiny can overcome any challenge. While both have the strongest civilizations to support and sustain, Israel has faith, India needs one. It is the man who matters, he creates wealth and plenty, moves the plough and turns the wheel. It is he who harvests nature, discovers and invents and makes a better world. He is God's best gift to our planet. Israel already has that gift. India has the potential. The human resource of both the civilizations is invaluable and that is what counts.

PART - III

India - Past and Present

Chapter 15

A Critique of Indian History

The history of India, known to our forefathers and imbibed by them in our culture, is diametrically opposed to what was imposed later under the British rule. The pioneers in this regard were Christian missionaries under the benevolent protection of Lord William Bentinck. The Governor General, advised by Macaulay and Max Muller, embarked on a strategy to de-Hinduise their Indian subjects by striking at the very roots of our culture. The strategy, well thoughtout and meticulously planned, was three-pronged—physical subjugation, academic distortion of culture through dis-information after a deep study of Sanskrit texts and finally conversion by the missionaries, all three working in tandem.

Thomas Babington Macaulay was a member of the Governor General's Council. In his minutes of 1835 A.D., he advocated the use of English amongst the Indians to create a class of clerical staff in order to sub-serve the interest of the British Empire. This became the official policy on 7th March, 1835. Another member of the council was Chales Edward Trevelyan. Born in 1807, he served East India Company at Bombay, Madras, Calcutta and Delhi, and was an Assistant of Sir Edward Colebrooke, an old India hand. He was promoted as Secretary of General Committee of Public Instructions. This intrepid man gave further boost to Macaulay's plan through his book *Christianity and Hinduism*

Contrasted. According to his thesis the religion closest to Christianity was Islam followed by Buddhism, which too was to be in the same league due to its benevolence. The Hinduism, however, was considered as inferior, being an old system of idolatry. Another luminary in this coterie was Sir Richard Temple, a civil servant, who became the Head of Political Department in the Council of Governor General and assisted in this effort of denigrating Hinduism. For these services, Philip Mason heaped praises on him in his book titled, *The Man Who Ruled India.* Armed with such support from the Governor General and Member of his Council, it is no wonder that the attempt to de-Hinduise Indian culture succeeded beyond expectation. For further study on the subject the reader is referred to the books highlighted in the Bibliography.

Though due credit must be given to the British for the abolition of *Sati* and liquidation of *Thugi,* these two measures were basically the olive branch meant to attract the Hindus to follow blindly the so-called reforms originated by the Governor General and the transformation of Indian history by the British scholars, to which even the progressives in West Bengal like Raja Rammohun Roy fell a victim. Roy founded the Brahmo Samaj, but the material sheen and the shallowness of the renaissance of Hindu culture originating in Bengal had to bow down to our ancient culture and soon became a thing of the past. The writings of Bankim Chandra Chatterjee, Sarat Chandra Chatterjee deeply rooted in our ancient culture soon made Brahmo Samaj irrelevant to the Bengali society in particular and India at large in general. Thus, Sanatan Dharma triumphed over this gratuitous effort to graft alien values on Indian culture.

Indian history has also suffered grievously at the hands of the so-called 'colonial Marxists', who instead of contributing hard facts by getting to the original source, have merely provided recycled material containing excerpts from the English translations of the last century. Such historians like Niharranjan Ray, B.D. Chattopadhyaya, Ranbir Chakravarti and V.R. Mani, belonging to ICHR in their book titled *Sourcebook of Indian Civilization* have gone nowhere near the true source of Indian history.

Another book under the aegis of ICHR written by these worthies, *The Vedic People* and authored by Rajesh Kochhar, points to Afghanistan as the seat of Rigveda, Ramayana and Mahabharata. There are numerous references in Rigveda to oceans and ships. The Vedic poetry is replete with prayers for the safety of ships and passengers undertaking long ocean voyages – most famous among such hymns being the Nasadiya Sukta. With such imagery of oceans, "Darkness concealed in darkness, the whole universe was like an ocean without light", to place these people in a landlocked country like Afghanistan is almost tantamount to declaring Nepal a naval power.

People who really endeavoured to find facts about our ancient history such as K.D. Sethna, David Frawley, A Seidenberg and Shrikant Talageri have drawn from authentic original sources of Vedic texts to resurrect our ancient history. The latest findings of relics of Hindu temples in the excavations at Fatehpur Sikri raises a question mark on the secular credentials of Akbar, who has been espoused as the great Mughal by our so-called 'secularist' historians, including the great Nehru.

Just to illustrate the Iconolastic fervour of Aurangzeb, the cruelest among the Mughals, it is enough to read a few pages of the book *Mathura, A District Memoir* written 125 years ago by F.S. Growse, District Collector of Mathura. That a European of his mould could write with such candour and feeling about the Hindu humiliation should open the eyes of our today's secularists.

"There is not a single building of any antiquity either in the city itself or its environs. Its most famous temple–that is dedicated to Kesava Deva—was destroyed in 1669, the eleventh year of the reign of the iconoclastic Aurangzeb. The mosque erected on its ruins is a building of little architectural value."

And on this land was raised Idgaah all around. In a small corner of this Idgaah in a dingy room the statue of Kesava Deva can be seen today, visited by Hindu devotees. The author further writes:

> "Beyond all doubt this was the last of famous shrines of Kesava Deva and its demolition was regarded as a death blow to Hinduism."

The author continues:

> "In a short time, with the help of numerous workmen, this seat of error was utterly broken down. Glory is to God that so difficult an undertaking has been successfully accomplished in the present suspicious region, wherein so many dens of heathenism and idolatry have been destroyed. Seeing the power of Islam and the efficacy of true religion, the proud Rajas felt their breath burning in their throats and became as dumb as a picture on a wall. The idols, large and small alike, all adorned with costly jewels were carried away from the shrine and taken to Agra, where they were buried under the steps of Nawab Kudesia Begum's mosque, so that people might trample upon them forever. It was from this event that Mathura was called Islamabad."

After the destruction of Kesava Deva temple, Aurangzeb began to complete his unfinished agenda in the right earnest. Temples were broken and ripped inside, and all jewels and precious materials were used to construct steps to newly raised mosques so that the feet of the faithful could tread on the shrines of the Kafir.

It is time every right thinking Indian studies such scars of humiliation on the Hindu psyche in our national history. For further details the reader is referred to the book titled *What Happened to the Temples in India* by Ram Gopal.

The leftist historians and our great 'secularists' would do well to study the following facts of history based on the evidence given by the Muslim writers themselves.

In a period of 1200 years according to the accounts given by Al-Biladhuri in Arabic written in the second half of the ninth century and by Syed Mahmudul Hasan in English written in the fourth decade of the twentieth century culled out from eighty historical documents, contain vivid accounts of sixty-one kings, sixty-three military commanders and fourteen Sufis, who were the zealots of the vandalisation of Hindu temples at one hundred and fifty-four places stretching from Transoxiana in the north to Tamil Nadu in the south and from Khurasan in the west to

Tripura in the east. This gigantic effort took almost eleven hundred years and as per their religious customs, new mosques, madarasas and khanqahs were erected on each site of destruction, using temple material. This was indeed a service to the Prophet Mohammed.

The records maintained by the British rulers tell another sad story of desecration of a temple. At Vidisha in Madhya Pradesh 40km from Bhopal, there used to exist a Hindu temple called Vijay Mandir, which was first destroyed by Sultan Shamsuddin Iltutmish, succeeded by Sultan Alauddin Khilji as recorded in *Mirah-I-Sikandry.* Another iconoclast, who followed 200 years later, Sultan Bahadur Shah of Gujrat, repeated the noble performance of his predecessors by desecrating the Vijay Mandir further in the service of Islam. And finally the greatest iconoclast of them all, Aurangzeb or Almgir as he used to call himself, the protector of Islam, dealt the final death blow to the temple in 1682, destroyed what was left of the temple completely and raised the Bijamandal mosque on its ruins. By a sheer act of providence, in 1991, heavy rains washed away the wall on the façade of this mosque and the remains of the temple became visible. Soon after Archaeological Survey of India (ASI) was compelled to excavate further to discover the remains buried under the platform which was used as the hall of prayers by the Muslims, specially on Id. A rich haul of temple material was recovered including spectacular statues upto 8ft. high. However, the work was abruptly stopped under the order of Mr. Arjun Singh, the HRD Minister of the Congress Government during 1991-94, and the so-called 'secularist' par excellence. In spite of the pressure from the local population and the officers of the ASI, the Government stood firm on its stand. Incidentally, Vijay Mandir has striking similarities to the famous Sun Temple at Konark. But this architectural treasure-trove remains sealed till date with no attempt to retrieve the remains of the temple. While the ASI has been leashed to inaction, the agitation for the excavation of the Vijay Temple continued in Vidisha. This struggle lasting 50 years is vividly remembered by Shri Niranjan Verma, a former M.P., who recollects how Nehru reluctantly ordered a fact finding delegation, where in the Union Education Minister, Maulana Abul Kalam Azad, deputed Prof. Hùmayun Kabir, his Secretary, to conduct an on the spot inquiry. To be fair to Prof. Kabir, he accepted the presence of the temple and the need for further excavation by the ASI. However, being a mere bureaucrat he could do very little under Nehru's veto. See-saw struggle between the Bijamandal Mosque and the Vijay Mandir continued. Later, Chief Minister Mandleo agreed to the ASI's request, but fearing the wrath of Nehru, he decided that discretion was the better part of valour. However, Shri D.P. Mishra, who became the Chief Minister of Madhya Pradesh, was sympathetic to the Hindu cause and donated Rs. 40,000/- for separating the Idgaah from the temple site. Lal Bahadur Shastri, who succeeded Nehru, was sympathetic to the cause, but did not live long enough to see the work completed. Thus, a Hindu heritage of great artistic value and religious sentiment remains buried under the eloquent silence of the secularist forces in the country.

The Leftist historians have highlighted the antipathy of the Brahmin class to Ashoka for his declaration of Buddhism as the State religion. The main reason ascribed to this was the prohibition of animal sacrifice, an edict disseminated in the largest empire ever established in the Indian subcontinent. But the evidence for the above assumption is totally lacking. First, the historians have not made clear as to what percentage of income of the Brahmins came from the offerings during these sacrifices. Secondly, was it possible for such a large kingdom with difficult communications to enforce these edicts in all parts of the country, and thirdly, what percentage of the Brahmins was really involved in living on these sacrificial offerings. These are big gaps in their arguments but the canard has been spread that the 'Brahmins', read 'Hindus', were the destroyers of Buddhism and their properties.

The Secondary Board of the West Bengal Government issued a circular on 28th April, 1989, issuing large scale amendments to the History books taught thus far in Bengali script in schools of the State. Sample the following:

In the original sentences "In Sindhudesh the Arabs did not describe Hindu as Qafir. They had banned cow-slaughter", "they had banned cow-slaughter" was to be deleted.

The original sentences "using force to destroy Hindu temples was also an expression of aggression and "forcibly marrying Hindu women and converting them to Islam before, was another way to propagate the fundamentalism of the Ulema" were to be totally "deleted".

Similarly, in the original passage " the logical, philosophical, materialist Mutazilla disappeared. On the one hand, the fundamentalist thinking based on the Quran and the Hadis...", it was directed to delete "on the one hand, the fundamentalist thinking based on the Quran and the Hadis...".

"Sultan Mahmud used force for widespread murder, loot, destruction and conversion" was to be replaced by the innocuous statement that "there was widespread loot and destruction by Mahmud". No reference of the killing or forcible conversion.

Mahmud's plunder of 2 crore Dirhams from the Somnath temple and the use of Shivling on the steps in a masjid in Ghazni was to be changed to imply that Shivling was used on the steps of the above masjid. There is no mention of the plunder. While the original text admitted that the relations between Hindus and Muslims were a sensitive issue and the non-believers i.e. Kafirs had only two choices –death or conversion. All these have been deleted. Even the instructions to Hindu women to remain indoors to avoid being seen by the Muslims were deleted. Extensive corrections have been applied on the chapter dealing with Aurangzeb's policy on religion, and the Mughal rule had been shown to be tolerant and benign. Even the invasion of Chittor by Alauddin Khijli to marry the beautiful queen Padmini, wife of Raja Ratan Singh, was to be deleted. S.N. Jha's book "*Society, State and Government*" written for Class XI, and published by NCERT is full of such pearls of wisdom.

R.S. Sharma in his book *"Ancient India"* published by NCERT, glosses over the religious fundamentalist zeal of the Turks to destroy Buddhism, which they considered at par with idolatry, inspite of Buddha's teachings and describes this misdeed to merely an economic motive. Bracketing the Turk with Brahmins in their zeal, the author gives enormous coverage to the persecution of Buddhists by Hindu rulers, while ignoring the contributions of the Turks in this regard. While the motive of the Hindu rulers was religious, that of the Turks was really economic. Like the distortions in Christianity and Islam owing their origins in some evils of the Hindu religion such as caste system, the degeneration in Buddhism is also attributed to the evils of Brahaminism. Thus, the original sin has been committed by the Brahmins and guilelessly followed by the other three major religions. The same theme is peddled by Mr. Sharma's comrade, Satish Chandra. The carnage and destruction meted out by the Muslim rulers is mellowed down and attributed to extraneous economic factors and the need to ensure a trouble free governance.

Satish Chandra glides over the cruelty of Sultans of Delhi, their persecution of the Hindus, and vandalizing of their shrines by conceding that "Despite the pressure of a section of the orthodox theologians, this policy of broad toleration was maintained during the Sultanate". A vivid description of the persecution and slow torture to death in the royal court, of a Brahmin who refused to embrace Islam is given by Shams-ud-Din bin Siraj-ud-Din in his *Tarikhi-Firuz Shahi*, but Satish Chandra exonerates the Sultan by saying that conversion to Islam was not through the power of sword but due to persuasion. The fact of the matter is that the Hindu heads far out numbered the swords of Islam and exhausted the strength of their wielders. Thus, due to the sheer enormity of the task the conversion was confined mainly to big cities and power centers and the Hindus in the countryside by and large remained unaffected. Baruni also corroborates this fact. Now the reverse charge of Hindus destroying the places of worship is peddled by these Marxists. Sita Ram Goel asked these worthies to give any example of a Hindu text, which ordains such an act as the tenets of Islam do. He even challenged them to single out a person, who has been honoured by the Hindus for his idol breaking efforts. A deafening silence was the only answer.

Even during and after the reign of Harsh Vardhan in the 7th century A.D., India was subjected to barbaric raids from the north west; Huns, Sakas and Mongols, the latter only touching the fringes of north-west India, perpetrated untold atrocities on the helpless Hindu. And then came Islam from 10th century onwards. Hordes of nomads given a generic name Turks from Afghanistan, Gazni, Uzbekistan and Iran continued to pour into the north west rich lands of our country. Alien kingdoms rose and fell ending with the death of Aurangzeb in 1707 A.D. The actual Muslim period really lasted from the establishment of Sultanate at Delhi, in early 14th century till the end of Mughal Empire in 1707. The vast land of India was divided into principalities and small kingdoms of Rajputs as well as Muslims. But thereafter till 1808 A.D., the mighty Marathas rose as a national power and Maratha confederacy collided head on with the British on one side and Ahmad Shah Abdali at the battlefield of Panipat on the other. With this event died away the last hope of a Pan-Indian resurgence and the British dominion expanded, till the whole of our country was conquered. One can say that the British rule lasted from 1808 A.D. to 1947 A.D., when our country achieved its independence. With such a chequered career the biggest sufferer was the Hindu psyche. As has been brought out earlier in the Jewish history, adversity and calamity did not steel our people into a fiery nation but degraded them to a lower level of human existence. We forgot our proud heritage, our Dharma, national character and became a divided lot. In spite of all this, though the country remained divided and subjugated politically, the eternal Hindu spirit from the Sanatan Dharma remained the binding thread for the people of this landmass politically divided but emotionally united on the basis of our past culture. The nation suffered innumerable indignities. The effect of the loss of character is visible even today after 50 years of independence. Thus, it behoves on the present generation of India to use the past not as a hammock, but a springboard for future advancements. India has thus far endured but a resurgent nation, that we wish to be, must not only endure, but also prevail. In this regard, we have a lot to learn from the Israelis. Surrounded by hostile nations, tiny Israel is holding its own while India with a huge landmass and population has still to weld itself into a nation of steel, capable of protecting its sovereignty and integrity against it's hostile neighbours.

India was left in peace for a comparatively longer period and it was only from 10th century A.D. onwards that sporadic raids of Muslim adventurers began. Then from 14th century till 1707 A.D. the Muslims ruled almost the whole of India except parts of Bengal and some Southern states. After the death of Aurangzeb, the disintegration of the Mughal empire commenced with frequent change of rulers at Delhi, concurrent with the shrinking of the central Muslim rule to areas around Delhi, with a highly tenuous and tentative reach upto the Vindhyas. In the south a few independent Muslim Sultanates had come into existence but major parts of India came under the sway of the Maratha Confederacy. This period lasted a hundred years from 1707 upto 1808 in which year the Marathas were decisively defeated by the British. This century could truly be called the age of Maratha supremacy. From then onwards followed the period of British rule, which ended with the attainment of Independence in 1947. All this has been stated earlier. Israel on the other hand, at the crossroads of the Middle East, invited invasions from its very inception. The sound of marching feet and hoofs and horses never really died down except for a brief period of peace under David and Solomon. The "Chosen People" were mercilessly attacked and enslaved, exiled and deported while the land was devastated right from the early days of Nebuchadnazar, followed by slavery in Egypt and the return led by Moses, fights within the land and then Diaspora. Since the Jews were never really allowed to settle in the land that their Lord had granted to them, they developed a deep attachment to the soil of their land. On the other hand, Hindus were never deprived of their land and thus did not develop the deep devotion and attachment to the soil of this land, as they took God's plenty for granted and never suffered the longings of the deprived.

When given a chance, both people progressed rapidly, and reached high levels of excellence. The Jews achieved this in the countries where they lived whenever disabilities and the stigma of being a Jew were removed. The Hindus did so only when the conquerors allowed them peace. But throughout their periods of extreme hardships, both people took to introspection and deep inward seeking. While the Vedas, Upnishads and Samhitas are the product of the ancient peaceful times, the Torah and Talmud took shape even during deprivation and Diaspora. Both religions gave birth to new and more simplified though less profound religions, easy to follow with fewer demands. Judaism fostered Christianity and that too at a later stage had much to give to Islam. Likewise, the complicated profundities of Hindu thoughts gave rise to simpler faiths, such as Buddhism, Jainism and later Sikhism.

It is to the eternal credit of these ancient cultures that none of these ever prescribed or encouraged proselytizing and forcible conversion and none ever fought religious wars to convert those, who did not subscribe to their religion. The same was not the case with Christianity and Islam. Judaism and Hinduism alike suffered at the hands of Christianity and Islam. There were rare exceptions when the Jews and the Hindus were left in peace under a benevolent Christian or Muslim ruler. With the exception of some years in Spain and those under Suleman the Magnificent, the Jews suffered under Muslims in the Middle East, and mostly under Christian kings in Europe. Hindus too suffered in their own country under the Muslims and the British from 1300 to 1947 A.D., with a brief interlude of Maratha supremacy from 1707 to 1808 A.D. as mentioned above. Both the nations fought their wars of independence against the British. The Jews of Palestine under the British mandate fought the British as much as the people who surrounded their country. While India gained its freedom in 1947, Israel became a sovereign state a year later in 1948.

Countless conquerors strode over the land of Israel, wreaked destruction and raised great and mighty empires, but lost in the limbo of history none of these can be seen in the world today.

Yet Zion, the Jews and their Holy Land remain. Many swords and armies tried to concur India but they themselves succumbed to the culture of this land. This great and ancient civilization triumphed, while India that is Bharat survives and Hinduism endures.

Some time in 1980, when my daughter was studying Ancient Indian History, brainwashed as she was by the text books of these worthy eminences of the Leftist group, she made two startling statements. One that Aryans used to eat beef and second, that Krishna was a local God of the black skin Dasyus or what was derisively mentioned as the inferior Dravidian race. On a deeper study of the subject and after I read Arun Shouri's book mentioned earlier, he gave an account of a T.V. interview 'Apki Adalat' taken by Manoj Rajvanshi and attended by Arun Shourie and Prof. Shrimali of the leftist school. On being asked by Manoj Rajvanshi, if he could give a single reference or quote Shlokas from Vedas or any other reference to substantiate the charge that the Aryans during the Vedic period used to eat beef, Dr. Shrimali was unable to do so. Arun Shourie also pinned him on the subject, but could elicit no response except angry words. So much for the beef eating. Obviously it was a canard hatched in the conspiracy of these eminent historians still striving to disseminate the above lies in the text books or material, which they author. The other lie, regarding Lord Krishna, is nailed by studying innumerable accounts on Mahabharat and the evidence unearthed in the remains and finds of the period. The theory of Aryan invasion and the conquest of Dravidians, the indigenous people of India and their forced movement to the south are so much nonsense. First, as has been proved beyond any shadow of doubt by the research and findings of both Indian and foreign historians, there was no Aryan invasion. We shall return to this issue later in a separate chapter. Apart from the movement of races in Paleolithic times, there has only been a number of groupings and sub-groupings by the intermingling of these races. A very broad classification, which does not take into account the minor regional differences, could be on these lines. The North-West European races, which could be put into the category of

Caucasian, could be further divided into the Nordic and the Mediterranean branches. The Nordic being fair coloured with frizzy hair and blue eyes could also be found in some parts of Asia. The Mediterranean group generally white skinned, with dark eyes and black hair inhabited an area around Mediterranean Sea, and the Middle East and India. The third group was the Mongolian race with its characteristic features spread over the Central, North, East and Southeast Asia. The fourth group was somewhat similar to the Mongolian yellow colour, with high cheek bone and narrow eyes with less marked facial resemblance, of bronze colour inhabiting South American continent and parts of eastern fringe of Southeast. Then there were the other two races with dark skin, curly hair flat nose and thick lips, mainly divided into two regions. The first one the Negroid inhabiting Central and South Africa while their sister branch Australoid, inhabiting South East Pacific islands, Australia and New Zealand. In the broad historical time frame, there has been no systematic migration or invasion of the fair skinned pastoral Aryans into India or so called Aryavrata. I wish these worthies had taken some notice of the earlier histories of Ancient India, authored by Prof. Jadunath Sarkar and Dr. Ishwari Prasad. The text of Gita recorded by Vedvyasa is enough evidence of a personality much superior to any thing that can be ascribed to a so-called Dasyus or the lesser mortals. In fact, the civilization existing before the so called Aryan invasion, which included the Indus valley and many other sites with similar archaeological findings, confirm a very high level of civilization dating back to 8000 B.C.

Macaulay introduced English as the official medium of communication to produce an army of clerks to subserve British administration and create a class of Bhadralok totally alienated from their very Indian roots and antipathic to our Hindu past. Max Muller, a profound scholar of Sanskrit, mainly aimed to denigrate ancient India's civilization and culture. The third name in this trinity of India-batters was Marx and his school of historical dialectics, which aims to explain every thing in terms of economic determinism, starting from class struggle; through feudal to oppressive capitalism and finally to the victory of the Proletariat. The proletariat consisting of the working class according to his vision consisted only of industrial labour, not agricultural workers. While Macaulay and Max Muller painted ancient Indian history black, Marx took on the task of putting the medieval Indian history on its head by explaining away everything on economic grounds and class exploitation. Some of these worthies include Prof. R.S. Sharma, Bipin Chandra, Satish Chandra, Irfan Habib, Romila Thapar, K.M. Panikar and their ilk, once installed in positions of academic importance, at the Jawaharlal Nehru University (J.N.U.) and the Indian Council of History Research (ICHR). These eminent historians have produced a historical literature with a pronounced anti-Hindu bias with derisive references to Brahaminism, which they have equated with Hinduism. Textbooks in schools in West Bengal produced by the National Council of Educational Research and Training (NCERT) have totally distorted the facts of history with a view to deride the Hindu dispensation of medieval India and obliterate all the cruelty, forcible conversion and iconoclasm of the Muslim conquerors and rulers. Even their destruction of temples and loot of treasure has been attributed to nothing but whims, personal greed, administrative compulsions and economic needs of the times. Not a word about the fundamentalistic urge and the intolerance of the Islam in practice; the use of sword and the exhortations from the Prophet, the Sunna and the Hadis. They have even attributed cruelty on Buddhists and the destruction of their Viharas and places of learning like Nalanda University to the Brahminical ire and Hindu atrocities. A cursory look at what Ambedkar wrote and Swami Vivekanand preached is enough to contradict this point of view. Buddhism had already spread in Persia and Afghanistan as in the rest of Asia, before the birth of the Prophet Mohammed. There were large numbers of shrines and Viharas in these countries, which were later invaded by the armies of the Prophet and his successors. What happened to these monastries, shrines and Buddhist Viharas? Did any Hindu king venture out to these countries to destroy them? Why were these destroyed in Persia and Afghanistan only and not in the rest of Buddhist Asia? The answer is simple and in two words, Muslim conquest. Will the worthy Marxist historians, like Romila Thapar, put the blame on Brahmins and Hindus for this vandalism? The destroyers of these shrines and property were only the Muslim kings, which feats have been described in glorifying terms by their own official historians and court chroniclers, who were eyewitneses to the events. The blame for distortions in Islam and Christianity giving rise to their own caste system has also been laid at the doors of Brahaminism and Hindus. The cruelty and exploitation of Hindus, Jazia tax and destruction of temples have been described vividly by Sita Ram Goel in his learned works and in a detailed study of the destruction of Hindu temples. The reader is referred to the book *Hindu Temples-What Happened to Them*: *A Preliminary Survey*, co-authored by Arun Shourie, Harsh Narain, Jay Dubhashi, Ram Swarup and Sita Ram Goel.

Arun Shourie in his well-researched book *Eminent Historians* has cut a swathe through the thicket of lies, half-truths, innuendoes and distortions of these Leftist historians, and exposed their efforts to tarnish Hinduism and Brahaminism. For the Marxist historians the theory and cause of Marx i.e., precept and practice of socialism is paramount. The facts of history have to be doctored and contrived to substantiate these ideas. Suppresso veti, suggestion false.

One of these worthies, Dr. Bipin Chandra in an unsolicited opinion on the recent controversy regarding the historical distortion in a Bollywood film 'Ashoka' says, "One can play about with the historical facts, but one should be true to the spirit of the person. (Just) any dramatist or actor cannot be expected to rewrite history." It seems the worthy Professor is possessed of a new surgical means to X-ray the spirit and intention of a historical personality without due regard to the documented texts and evidence.These are physically documented and incontrovertible. In the lexicon of leftist historians facts do not matter, only theory does; and the facts can and should be sanitised to serve a preconceived theory or proposition. We shall see more of these clever exercises in a subsequent chapter "Ancient India and the Myth of the Aryan Invasion".

As these lines are being written a fierce controversy is raging about the so-called "safronisation" of history textbooks. Our eminent leftist historians and their fellow travellers from the Congress and Samajvadi parties have mounted a frontal attack on the Government for bringing about long and overdue corrections to history necessitated by the distortions deliberately introduced by our "friends" in the CBSE textbooks. *The Times of India* dated 25.11.2001 carried the following text in bold letters; under the screaming headline 'Talibansation of History'.

"Objectionable Text

Only 16 pages in three history textbooks for classes VI, VII and XI. But so objectionable to the BJP-led government that all CBSE schools have been directed to "delete" them "with immediate effect" and ensure that "they not be taught or even discussed in the respective classes."

Some Samples:

- For special guests beef was served as a mark of honour (Class VI,. Romila Thapar)
- Jats founded their state at Bharatpur from where they conducted plundering raids in the regions around. (Class VIII, Arjun Dev and Indira Arjun Dev).
- In 1675, Guru Tegh Bahadur was arrested and executed. The official explanation for this... is that after his return from Assam, the Guru in association with one Hafiz Adam, resorted to plundering and raping, laying waste the whole province of Punjab (Class XI, Satish Chandra).
- Archaeological evidence should be considered far more important than long family trees given in the Puranas. The Puranic tradition could be used to date Rama of Ayodhya around 2000 B.C. but extensive excavations in Ayodhya do not show any settlements around that date.
- Cattle wealth slowly decimated because cows and bullocks were killed in numerous Vedic sacrifices.

- The brahmanical reaction began as a result of the policy of Ashoka. He...derided superfluous rituals performed by women. This naturally affected the income of the Brahmans (Class XI, R.S. Sharma).

We shall briefly discuss the truth about the above statements.

Paras 1,5, & 6 have already been refuted in this book earlier and need to be dismissed with the contempt that they deserve. Para 2, regarding the Jats, also is a mischievous representation of facts. The Bharatpur kingdom of Jats was the lone stronghold defying the British expansion westwards after their conquest of Avadh. It was a well fortified fort and the fighting warriors defending the fort had to collect food and necessities by raiding areas under British occupation. These were not targeted against innocent civilians but only British garrisons.

Guru Tegh Bahadur was the militant arm who was fighting the Mughals to protect the Hindu religion. Since his forces were small, like any good military tacttitian, he had to resort to guerrilla war-fare. This involved sneak attacks on Mughal fortifications, garrisons and isolated pockets. This cannot be labelled as plundering, least of all raping, by any serious student of military history. Destruction of facilities that supported the Mughal army of occupation is not the same as laying waste the whole province of Punjab. Undoubtedly there were many Muslims in the Sikh army of earlier Gurus and most of all in Guru Gobind Singh's. Hafiz Adam may be one of such soldiers of fortune, who joined Guru Tegh Bahadur in the plunder of the property of Muslim rulers. There is no record of rape by the Guru anywhere in any history of this period. More on this later.

Coming to para 4, the study of archaeology carried out by the 'eminent historians' mentioned earlier, was not only unscientific, but totally misleading and mischievous. We shall refer to the subject in a later chapter on Ancient Indian Civilization. It is also a fact that during the Government of Prime Minister Chandrashekhar, authentic archaeological evidence in terms of old ruins and artifects was produced by the historians supporting Ram Janmabhumi Movement to prove beyond doubt that a Ram Mandir of great antiquity did exist at the same site at Ayodhya and the period was not 2000 B.C., but even earlier. The recent discovery of a sub-merged township near Dwarka dating back even earlier than 3000 B.C. puts the date of Lord Krishna and Mahabharat well before that time. Since the age of Ram is dated before that of Mahabharat, the Puranik traditions would lead to Ramayan age even earlier to 3000 B.C. and not 2000 B.C. mentioned in the charge sheet. To add insult to injury, the Congress M.P., Eduardo Falerio, Convener of the Parliamentary Forum for Education and Culture, has come strongly in support of Professor Satish Chandra, and said in his defence of this worthy the following wise words:

> "History is a sensitive and a selective subject. It is difficult to decide what should be written and what must be edited out. But this process has to be transparent. If something hurts the sentiments of a certain community then let us reexamine it but not do it in this clandestine fashion".

The Hon'ble M.P. futher states, Professor Chandra's interest are more secular. How can anyone even doubt him? Satish Chandra has well and truly found an advocate in his task of distorting Indian History!

Another secular newspaper came up with the blazing headlines "Has the Talibanising of education begun"? Sometimes one wonders if there was not an element of truth in Bal Thakrey's statement, that if Muslims in India were disenfranchised, the secularist politicians will sing a different tune and like a chameleon change their ideologies overnight. Some parties like the Congress and the Samajvadi Party, whose sole means of income or survival is Muslim appeasement, will disappear altogether. Our worthy historians will then sing paeanes to our ancient culture and the virtues of Hindutava. They will lose their enthusiasm for traducing the 'Sangh Parivar' and not run to occupy positions of eminence in history writing.

We shall now return to some more details smuggled in by Satish Chandra in regard to Guru Tegh Bahadur. The worthy Professor has insinuated that the family members of the Guru were involved in a conspiracy for his execution. They were supposed to have opposed his succession. It is intriguing, from which source Mr. Satish Chandra has obtained this fact. He has totally distorted the proceedings and sequel of the Guru's execution. Some dis-information has also been given regarding the execution of 5th Guru Arjun Dev who has written the real facts of his execution in his autobiography "Tujake-Jehangiri". Regarding Guru Tegh Bahadur's plunder, it is amazing that there is no record of any such act in the two centuries that elapsed between the first Guru and Guru Tegh Bahadur. Does it mean that Guru Tegh Bahadur set a new precedent in this regard? Satish Chandra relies exclusively on a Persian writer whose bias would certainly be for the Mughal and against the Hindu or Sikh warriors. Mr. Satish Chandra further denies a vital fact that the Hindus of Kashmir unable to bear the atrocities of the Mughal Subedaar in forcing them to convert to Islam, came to Guru Tegh Bahadur at Anandpur led by the pandits seeking his protection. This fact has also been mentioned by Prof. Jadunath Sarkar in his historical works. Mr. P.N. Kaul Bamzai in his authentic work *A History of Kashmir* has also mentioned that the Kashmiri Pandits under the leadership of Pandit Kripa Ram of Mattan did go to the Guru at Anand Pur seeking his protection. Prof. Jadunath Sarkar in his book *The History of Aurangzeb* page 313, has mentioned the following:

> "He (Guru Tegh Bahadur) encouraged the Kashmiri Hindus to oppose their forcible conversion to Islam and openly defy the emperor. In consequence, the Guru was arrested, brought to Delhi and put into jail. He was forced to accept Islam. On his refusal to comply, he was tortured mercilessly for five days and then beheaded."

Even Guru Gobind Singh in his autobiographical book *Vichitra Naiak* (Strange Drama) has given the real facts preceding the arrest and subsequent execution of his father. In his poetic words he described his father's coronation and subsequent martyrdom. There is not a single word regarding his plunder and rapine acts after his return from Assam. A contemporary poet Senapati in his work *Guru Shobha* has also mentioned the facts regarding the greatness and sacrifices of the Guru. Any number of historical works were produced in Punjab, such as – *Guru Vilas, Mahima Prakash, Suraj Prakash, Bansawali Nama* and *Sarvloh Prakash*, all describing in detail the martyrdom of the Guru. Was it not incumbent on Satish Chandra to study all this literature before pronouncing his blasphemy on the Guru? Even the foreign historians such as J.D. Cunnigham, Archer, Mecaliff, Saiad Mohammed Latif, Gokul Chand Narang, Indu Bhushan Banerjee, Genda Singh, Gopal Singh, Teja Singh and our own Khushwant Singh have all written historical works on the Sikhs and all these contradict what Mr. Satish Chandra has written.

The Guru in his wisdom told the delegation of the Kashmiri Pandits, "You go back to Kashmir, inform your Subedaar that you consider Guru Tegh Bahadur as your Guru. If he (Guru) is prepared for conversion, we too shall gladly accept the same. Till then there should be no atrocities and use of force against us". The Subedaar wrote to Aurangzeb at Lahore and conveyed this development to him. The emperor hoped that by a single stroke of converting the Guru, he shall be able to convert all the Kashmiris to Islam. The Guru refused and the rest is history. Satish Chandra has made another disingenuous statement that the death of Guru Tegh Bahadur and the subsequent demoralization of the Sikhs forced Guru Gobind Singh to flee to the Shivalik hills to escape persecution. This shows a perverted approach to historical facts. The facts are that the sixth Guru, Guru Hargobind almost forty years before Guru Tegh Bahadur had established a township named Keeratpur, eight miles away, in the Shivalik Hills. Guru Tegh Bahadur later established another one at Anandpur. Since these places of sacred importance to the Sikhs were a natural destination for the pilgrims, it was not unnatural for Guru Gobind Singh to visit these places. This was not seeking shelter but a religious visit. In the final analysis, it is good to work for communal harmony, but in the process one should not take liberties with the facts of history and resort to scurrilous writing with a distinct pro-Muslim and anti-Hindu bias.

Before the ink could dry on this paper and the controversy subside on correct history writing, another leftist ideologue masquerading as a historian has come out with an article in *The Times of India* a favoured forum for such writers. He describes the Government attempts at removing distortions from history as unbridled and unjustified nationalism. History, according to him, should consist only of facts and not be governed by extraneous considerations that have to do with national honour and glory. He moans that "this sectarian straitjacketing of our rich and complex historical legacy is a sign not of national maturity or awakening. It betrays a descent into historical nihilism". One however, wishes that the hon'ble writer had a rudimentary understanding of Sanskrit and the result achieved by scientifically working out our past which is nothing if not glorious. Decidedly, a historian has to be true to facts. But the facts in the case are in sharp contradiction to what this writer would like to see.

The achievements of ancient India are not mythology but hard proven facts. One would like to refer this writer to the long list of bibliography given at the end of this book dealing with ancient India to understand what is being said. Returning back to medieval history.

Apart from the cruelty of Delhi Sultanates so well documented by their own court chronicles, some of them having been mentioned earlier, the rule of the Sultanate was without exception dripping with the Hindu blood and destruction of their temples. References abound; just the following will serve our purpose. Sultan Alla-ud-Din Khilji (1296 –1316) and Sultan Firauz Shah Tughlaq (1351-1388) in *Tarikh-I-Firauz Shahi* of Shams-ud-Din Bin Sirajud-Din, a courtier of Firauz Shah; and *Sirat-Firuz Shahi* and *Tarikh-I-Firishta.* Mohammed Quasim Hindu Shah Firishta gives an official account of Sultan Firauz Shah Tughlaq at Nagarkot, Kangra in Himanchal Pradesh; Sultan Nasir-ud-Din Mahmud Shah Tughlaq (1389-1412) in *Tarikh-I-Muhammadi of Mohammed Bihamad Khani;* Sultan Sikandar Lodi (1489-1517) in Ahmed Yadgar's *Tarikh-I-Shahi,* Jalal-ud-Din Mohammed Akbar Padshah Ghazi (1556-1605 A.D.) in *Muntrakhabu't-Tawarikh,* are enough evidence of the fanatic Islamic zeal of the above rulers.

And here is the great deed of Akbar the most 'tolerant' and 'secular' of the Mughals narrated by a Muslim court chronicle:-

> "The temple of Nagarkot, which is outside the city, was taken at the very outset....On this occasion many mountaineers became food for flashing sword. And that golden umbrella, which was erected on the top of the cupola of the temple, they riddled with arrow... And black cows, to the number of 200, to which they pay boundless respect, and actually worship, and present in the temple, which they look upon as an asylum, and let loose there, were killed by the Muslims. And while arrows and bullets were continually falling like drops of rain, through their zeal and intense hatred of idolatry they filled their shoes full of blood and threw it on the doors and walls of the temple..."

The record of Sultans of the south is no better.

Sita Ram Goel in chapter 16 of his book gives one example after another of the biographers of the Prophet singing paeans of his deeds in the destruction of temples. The Prophet's deed defined as 'sunnas' along with the Quran is the touchstone of any act of believer or his conduct.

The reign of Aurangzeb as described by the so-called 'secularist' leftist historians is in complete contradiction to what has been said in Sir Jadunath Sarkar's well-known *History of Aurangzeb* which was written as early as 1928. One of these eminences writing in 1996 completely overlooks the facts and evidence outstanding in Jadunath Sarkar's book. The lesson is obvious. These historians are committed to their true premise i.e. to fabricate evidence to prove Hindu intolerance, and secondly to condone Muslim fundamentalism and communalism, even if it means defending Aurangzeb as a tolerant secularist. In the same way, Guru Nanak and Guru Gobind Singh have been belittled to show that since there were no atrocities and forcible conversion of Hindus to Islam, these two Gurus were mainly concerned with Reformist movement in Hinduism and had nothing to complain against the Muslim rulers. In the same way, Sir Syed Ahmed Khan has been painted as a progressive and liberal in spite of his role in the two-nation theory and assistance to the Muslim League. These theories peddled by Bipin Chandra dole out the reasons why the Muslims stayed away from the freedom movement; it was primarily a reaction to the fundamentalistic impulse of the Hindu freedom fighters. According to him the National Movement alienated Muslim masses and because of the Hindu overtones of the freedom movement the Muslims stayed away and formed the Muslim League. Again the fault lies with the Hindus. Notice the following gem from Bipin Chandra on the National Movement and its character;

> "Unfortunately, while militant nationalism was a great step forward in every other respect, it was to some extent a step back in respect of the growth of national unity. The speeches and writings of some of the militant nationalists had a strong religious and Hindu tinge. They emphasized ancient Indian culture to the exclusion of medieval Indian culture. They identified Indian culture and the Indian nation with the Hindu religion and Hindus. They tried to abandon elements of composite culture. For example, Tilak's propagation of the Shivaji and Ganapati festivals, Aurobindo Ghose's semi-mystical concept of India as mother and nationalism as a religion, the terrorists' oaths before goddess Kali, and the initiation of the anti-Partition agitation with dips in the Ganga could hardly appeal to the Muslims. In fact, such actions were against the spirit of their religion, and they could not be expected as Muslims to associate with these and other similar activities. Nor could Muslims be expected to respond with full enthusiasm when they saw Shivaji or Pratap being hailed not merely for their historical roles but also as 'national' leaders who fought against the 'foreigners'. By no definition could Akbar or Aurangzeb be declared a foreigner, unless being a Muslim was made the ground for declaring one a foreigner. In reality, the struggle between Pratap and Akbar or Shivaji and Aurangzeb had to be viewed as a political struggle in its particular historical setting. To declare Akbar or Aurangzeb a 'foreigner' and Pratap or Shivaji a 'national' hero was to project into past history the communal outlook

of 20th century India. This was not only bad history; it was also a blow to national unity."

The Prophet expects his flock to realize that Allah had given them Quran in Arabic tongue and other believer must honour the Arabic Quran. Later, the Prophet went to the extent of admonishing the faithful, "Love the Arabs for three reasons; because I am an Arab, the Quran is Arabic, and the inhabitants of Paradise will speak Arabic". If that be so did it need any instruction from the Hindus for the Muslim community to speak Arabic language in preference to the national tongue. V.S. Naipaul warms up to the same theme in his book *Beyond Belief* that these obsessions with Arab, Quran and everything Arabic makes Muslims revere Arab and the Arabic language and the lore, alienating them completely from the countries of their residency, and in the process refusing to share the collective memory of their past, excepts one that begins after the advent of Islam.

To sum up in Arun Shouri's words: " In regard to matter after critical matter the Aryan-Dravidian divide, the nature of Islamic invasion, the nature of Islamic rule, the character of the Freedom Struggle—we find this trait-*suppersso veri, suggestio falsi.* This is the real scandal of history writing in the last thirty years. And it has been possible for these "eminent historians" to perpetrate it because they acquired control of institutions like the ICHR. To undo the falsehood, the control has to be undone".

D.N. Jha in his book *Ancient India,* an Introductory outline makes startling revelation that Lord Indra was "rowdy and immoral", Lord Krishna had a "rather questionable personal record", and Lord Shiva was nothing but a development of "phallic cult", while the Bhakti movement represented "the complete dependence of the serfs or tenants on the landowners in the context of Indian feudal society". No evidence has been adduced to prove these uncalled for assertions. Based on hypothetical conjectures these statements reveal how successful the efforts of Macaulay, the Missionaries and Marx had been. If any such comments were made against members of the Prophet's own families and if even one were to reproduce what they did and said the Marxist historians would start screaming saying that this is an effort to denigrate the glorious figure of Islam. But the Hindu gods and goddeses can be calumnized with impunity i.e. *de reguer.* In brief,... nothing about Hinduism was original every evidence of greatness or sublimity was fantasy. Every achievement is contributable to the invaders, so much so that even the Maurya art is of Persian origin. Another pet theme of these historians is that the Shudras rose in revolt against the ruling classes, while none of these has ever been recorded in any history of India. That the Brahmins invented the theory of Karma to perpetuate the status quo and justify fatalism. However, they completely ignored what Krishna told Arjun, when he exhorts him on the battlefield of Kurukshetra not to accept his fate but to fight against the evil. The distortion that the Mauryan rule was oppressive, that the re-imposition of Jaziya by Aurangzeb was to enable Hindus to live a normal life without any economic pressure for conversion into Islam and this revenue was to be collected by honest God fearing Muslims and many such gems of wisdom, abounded. Thus, while Aurangzeb was exonerated of his oppressive rule, Mauryan State is singled out as coercive and overbearing. But these eminences never described the Islamic law and the armies of Sultanas and Mughal rulers as instrument of coercion, domination and control. Even Kautilya and Patanjali have not been spared. Their well meant policies on spies and laws of the State are quoted as examples of the worst construction of State policy which promotes prostitution, soothsaying, poisoning and cash rewards. But the anachronistic dictates of Quran, Hadis and Fatwas going to the ridiculous extent quoted with documentary evidence are laughed away, as fantasies, which are neither enjoined nor enforced. The two lone sentences in Quran " To you your religion, to me mine" and "There is no compulsion in religion" are touted *adnauseum* with utter disregard to actual happenings under the Islamic rule from its very inception till its decay, covering a period of almost one and a half millennia. While the Quran does not ordain the scarifice of cows, the Islamic authorities in India and the Muslim divines like Ali Mia exhort Muslim to kill cows in India for the simple reason that they are sacred to the Hindus. The exact words are "precisely because cows are revered by the Hindus". Mr. Jha in his book condemns the Hindus for animal sacrifices and their abolition by the Buddhist cult. He is silent on the uncountable number of animals such as cows, goats, chicken and sheep, which are slaughtered at every Id. According to Jha this is in order and therefore condoned. The Marxist historians have again put history on its head by their statement that the Gupta Age as 'the Golden Age', was purely a myth, and that even the so- called Golden age did not cover the whole of India, which remained beyond the pale of the Gupta Empire. This loose control and devolution of power by Gupta Kings do not redound to their credit of exercising direct control over their dominion. Thus, while Mauryas were decried for their secularist and so- called coercive administration, the Guptas are derided for decentralizing the same. In other words, there is nothing commendable about the ancient Hindu rulers and their empires. That is the central thesis of our Leftist historians. Even astronomical achievement of Aryabhatta and Varahamihira are not totally their own original contributions but were borrowed from Rome while another one from Paul of Alexandria. Aryabhatta's phenomenal insight about the earth rotation on its axis and revolution round the sun enunciated much before Copernicus and Kepler did, are undervalued because they were "contrary to the established Indian notion". The works of Kalidas are belittled as of little literary value, because their origins lay in a distant past; Puranas and Vedic literature were only compiled in their present form in the times of Gupta. No literary work is known to man, which does not have its origin and previous accounts or earlier literary forms outside India is another pearl of wisdom from Jha's "so called Hindu renaissance". Even the term Hindu is a "misnomer". "It was first used by the Arabs in the post-Gupta period and to describe the inhabitants. Ancient Indians never thought of themselves as Hindus." From descriptions compiled from the observations of Fahian, the Chinese Buddhist pilgrim scholar who visited India during the reign of Chandragupta–II .... Indian achievement in Mathematics regarding the original zero, the knowledge of Pythagoras theorem, the achievement of

Aryabhatta and astronomy, the accuracy of their calculations regarding forecast of solar and lunar eclipses and the facts of Panchang (a long-term forecast of calendar) are trivialized by these great authors.

The theory of Engels, of society passing through five stages from classless primitive societies to slaved economy, to feudalism, to capitalism, to socialism and lastly communism, is a Mantra, which our Leftist historians still chant and all facts of Indian history have been sanitized to fit into this theory. The Communists in Russian Republic had to accept that the periods and categories enunciated by Engles do not exactly represent the conditions in China and India, and the master country is prepared to accept some deviations from the original theory. But their followers in India, adopt a holier than thou attitude in fitting the Indian history in their own straight jacket. To justify this bias there is an overriding need to glorify the Islamic period and black paint the pre-Islamic era and its traditions. To sum up in the words of Arun Shourie:

> "Thus, there are two points to remember. First, our friends are not just Marxists they are also Macaulayites. Second, they are Marxists in a special sense. They are Marxists in the sense that they have thought of themselves as Marxists, in the sense that they repeatedly regurgitate a handful of Marxist phrases and assertions. But more than being Marxist historians, they have been establishment historians. Their theories and 'Theses' have accorded not just with the 'classics' of Marxism Leninism, they have accorded with the ideology, which in terms of their theory means, the needs of Congressite rules".

Macaulay's missionary technique was to enslave Indian mind, to denigrate Hinduism, their gods and goddesses, temples and idols and the texts held sacred by the Hindus and the language of these texts i.e. Sanskrit, which was the lingua franca of our country till as late as the mid 19th century, and finally to vilify the Brahmins, who were the custodians of the above features of the Indian society. The other side of the exercise was to emphasize the parts i.e. the non-Hindus, original languages, castes and the groups most vulnerable to Missionary activities in the Empire, i.e. unsuspecting tribals and the untouchables in order to reap rich harvests for Christianity. Those who stood for the whole in the Indian culture and traditions, like the towering figures such as Ramakrishna Paramhans, Swami Dayanada, Swami Vivekananda, Sri Aurobindo, Lokmanya Tilak, Gandhiji, Ramana Maharishi, the Paramacharya, Narayan Guru- were to be denigrated at the altar of the trinity of the Prophet, Missionary and Marx. It will be a Herculean task for the present generation born after Independence, fed on the history of these leftist Marxist scholars, to separate propaganda from truth and appreciate the pristine glory of our ancient past culture civilisational ethos and its past and future.

A frequently touted argument by these worthies to be little the value of our epics, is a lack of historical evidence. There are any number of ruins scattered all over India from Kurukshetra, Hastinapur, Dwarika down to Rameshwaram, which only the purblind can ignore. Be that as it may, while the historicity of the epics or Puranas can also be placed as evidence in the court of these leftist historians the lessons therefrom and the value systems they uphold are as universal and eternal as can be.

The scientific basis of the teachings of Vedas and Upnishads have been proved many times even by today's scholars. Ram stands for the ideal and ultimate in the moral code of a man; Krishna for knowledge and philosophy, and primacy of action with his teachings on Karmyog; Shiva is the embodiment of asceticism, the true worship of Satvik Tatva (the purest element) and the capacity to absorb in self-abnegation the evils of mankind. Brahma, of course, is the creator, who also writes the destiny of each living being, bringing in an element of fatalism in the Hindu thought and thereby making it resistant to unfavourable circumstances. The pantheon of Hindu gods is not obscurantism in its intent but a simple way of showing the different faces of God and all that is good and worth emulating. They are the symbols and support, the crutches on which Hindu mind ascends to celestial heights without losing sight of one Brahma, whom Vivekanand described thus:

Ekam Sadwipra Bahudha Vadanti

(The LORD almighty Braham is one; sages see it in different forms.)

Thus, the area of knowledge is finite but that of ignorance is infinite. Human mind has its limitation of perception and cannot see beyond what is possible through the tools of science and the power of reason. But there can be and is another truth that lies beyond this area of perception, which Vedanta calls *neti-neti* i.e., beyond comprehension or description.

The history of India needs a new paradigm for study, which is devoid of Marxist distortions and British colonial intent, the secularist scent, and the discursive cant of the present day Anglophilic and western clones.

Chapter 16

Truth about Hinduism

The opening truth about Hinduism is that it is not merely a religious construct, but a civilizational undertaking. Technically speaking, there is no such thing as a 'Hindu'. The original word was 'Indu', a term used for centuries by outsiders to describe the people, who lived along and east of the river Indus. Later, due to mispronouncement and inability of the Arabs to speak Indus correctly, the word came to be pronounced as 'Hindus', a construct imposed by Western colonizers, which caused disastrous consequences for Indian history and ultimately resulted in the partition of the sub-continent.

Our 'secular' and leftist historians, a pompous know-all breed, do not know the first thing about Hindu genesis. There is no fixed date for the birth of Hinduism. Unlike Christianity, which started after the crucifixion of Jesus Christ at 33 in the first century A.D., and the birth of Islam after the flight of Prophet Mohammed from Mecca to Madina in 622 A.D. called 'Hijri' dated sometime in the fifth year of his prophetic missionary years after his birth in 570 A.D., which is the starting point of Muslim calendar, Hindu origin shrouded in obscurity dated even further back to 8000 B.C. From this date downwards, the indigenous culture and civilizational ethos called Sanatan Dharma got into the psyche of the people of Indian sub-continent, continued and metamorphosed in the shape of the present day Hinduism, being a religion with no beginning or end and considered to be eternal that time cannot destroy.

It is not easy to define Hinduism, even more difficult to circumscribe it within identifiable contours of thought or benchmarks of religious praxis and rituals. It is neither parochial nor partisan, but eclectic and cosmic in it's content. Its diffusiveness and lack of cohesive inter-related literary textual forms often defy simple definitions. Better minds and facile pens have written about Hinduism, and it will be a presumptuous attempt to supersede them. Simply stated Hinduism is not about claiming proprietary rights on knowledge and truth, or to prescribe a faith that is superior to others. In any case its foundations were laid ten millennia ago when most of the countries of the world did not even exist nor were there any religions around, as we know them today. Since for a common mind it is difficult to fathom its full depth and meaning, Hinduism is often misunderstood, generally distorted and almost always ridiculed by those who seek clarity and definition. A huge corpus of Vedic thought and literature, the profoundest known to mankind, will no doubt be incomprehensible to the uninitiated. Thus to understand Hinduism better, we should start by stating what it is not. It is not rigid, not coercive, not regulatory, not limited, not conclusive, not the last word of God and does not pretend that it is the only religion that leads to God and his kingdom, not the medium of cleansing up man's original sin, not prescriptive, not pretensive, not know-all, not claiming infallibility, nor superiority. But it is the largest source of knowledge known to the world.

Hinduism derives its essence from the four Vedas, whose hymns and invocations chanted in Sanskrit, convey different symbols. Simple minds, sometimes even the more erudite, have been frustrated in their failure to comprehend the symbolism and imagery of the Vedic hymns. On the other hand, it is simplicity itself. Vedas speak of one cosmic reality, a supra-universal force, the cause and effect rolled into one, unity of the Creator and the creation, the infinite, the living force in all human beings, the unknown yet present in all living beings, the unborn, undead, eternal, unchanging yet constantly renewing itself in different forms, the invisible, the incomprehensible, and end up by saying "**Neti-Neti**" (Not this, not this). In its simple formulation, Hinduism is a universal thought with space for everyone and every thought and mode of God worship. It's waltanschaung is 'Fatherhood of God and brotherhood of men'. Its prescriptions for achieving spiritual fulfillment are many. It is not restrictive, but permits dissent and diversity. The Hindu thought of Ramakrishna, Swami Vivekananda, Sri Aurobindo, Tilak and Gandhi is the most tolerant in the world. It neither arrogates superiority over other religions, nor preaches proselytisation like other religions. Thus, there is no stress on conversion. Each thought and path to God has to be respected and there would be no competitive claim on man's mind and body or clash of one religion with other. It does not say " Come to Me so that you may enter the Kingdom of God, for I am His son". It does not clair special relationship of any human being to God entitling him to declare that "I am the last of His prophets; my word is the revealed religion given by Allah, and only those who believe in me deserve "Jannat" and the rest are doomed to purgatory".

Against this backdrop, there are serious limitations to the concept of Hinduism, in spite of its proverbial spirit of tolerance, co-existing with other religions. While we have dealt earlier with the activities of missionaries and shall revert to them later in a subsequent chapter, it is pertinent to mention what Sri Aurobindo, the Yogi, the sage and the revolutionary in the fight for freedom, who accepted Lord Krishna's message in Gita of Karma and violence, if necessary, to fight against injustice, with all his catholicity was forced to state in his magnum opus *India's Rebirth*. "You can live with a religion whose principle is toleration." But how is it possible to live peacefully with a religion whose principle is 'I will not tolerate you?' How are you going to have unity with these people?..." The Hindu is ready to tolerate; he is open to new ideas and his culture has got a wonderful capacity for assimilation". In September 1899 he stated "Every action for instance which may be objectionable to a number of

Mahomedans is now liable to be forbidden because it is likely to lead to a breach of peace. And one is dimly beginning to wonder whether worship in Hindu temples may be forbidden on that valid ground. The Hindus have discovered that the absolute can be realized or stated through the relative, and the images, crosses, and crescents are simply so many symbols—so many pegs to hang the spiritual ideas on. It is not that this help is necessary for everyone, but those that do not need it have no right to say that it is wrong. Nor is it compulsory in Hinduism".

The problem with Christianity and Islam who call themselves monotheistic religions sanctified by God or Allah, has always been their intolerance of Hindu idolatry and their God ordained mission to convert them or kill. This is what Swami Vivekananda had to say about Hindu idolatry.

"One thing I must tell you. Idolatry in India does not mean anything horrible. It is not the mother of harlots. On the other hand, it is the attempt of undeveloped minds to grasp high spiritual truths. The Hindus have their faults, they sometimes have their exceptions; but mark this, they are always for punishing their own bodies, and never for cutting the throats of their neighbours. If the Hindu fanatic burns himself on the pyre, he never lights the fire of Inquisition. And even this cannot be laid at the door of his religion anymore than the burning of witches can be laid at the door of Christianity."

The pious universality and highly intellectualized spirituality of our sages, not necessarily fully understood and imbibed by the common adherence to this faith has led to a certain vagueness in, and lack of self assertion in the Hindu psyche.

Buffetted by digital, cybernetic, consumerist and globalization oriented pressure, the modern Hindu has lost sight of the origin, history and role of Hinduism and its essence. Ill-informed and half-backed thoughts have led to a distinct dis-information about Hinduism and the Eternal Religion or the Sanatan Dharma. Since there are no precise rituals, which define the process of being a Hindu, it is little wonder that non-Hindus are as vague about its contours as the poorly informed Hindus themselves.

The absence of a single point focus and existence of a large spiritual socio-intellectual spread, which makes Hinduism more universal and capable of encompassing other religions known to mankind, has baffled simplistic definition seekers, and label choosers. A fierce debate is now raging among the Hindus themselves to circumscribe Hinduism within identifiable parameters without losing its all pervasiveness and universalism. This is essential to make a Hindu conscious of his identity by defining the paradigms of spiritual and physical existence that he has to undertake. In other words, he should be given a focus for self-assertion and his striving for perfection. The task is not easy but it is being undertaken without injecting any parochialism or narrowness of outlook in its content, which is so diffused and all pervasive that the fringes and parts are being mistaken for the whole and practised by its followers. A conscious effort is also being mounted to enunciate what Hinduttva is all about, moving away from the old benchmark of what it is, to what it is not. In an effort to unite the spiritual with the physical, harmonize the sematics with the apparent, practical and recognisable, Hinduism will hold out to the world a more focussed picture of its spiritual yearning and consummate achievement.

In a world of identifiable symbols and bench marks the Hindu has to redefine himself in visible terms. It need not be in terms of militant fundamentalism but certainly an active assertion is called for in order that the devout understand the call and readies himself for his obligations. Since the world perceives a Hindu from the geographical, historiological and philological connotation of River Sindhu; in fact in Saudi Arabia even today an Indian Muslim is called a Hindu, Hinduism will have to be based on an ethnic construct. The Hindus worldwide would then like the Jews, belong to the Hindu Diaspora. This enthnicity need not deprive Hinduism of its wider appeal of transcendental yearning and historic universality, nor this bold assertion lead to a narrow religious divide in this country, the staple on which self-serving policy of divide and rule flourishes leading to a lamentable fragmentation of society.

The message of the Vedas and Upnishads, the manifestation of "Braham" through the quantum view of a relativistic continuum of time and space, and a sense of timelessness of mind and agelessness of body is one of the most logical and scientific, modern and profund system of thought known to mankind. The Vedas provide a fertile soil for future scientific development and according to some scientists the more science advances the nearer it finds itself to the wisdom of the Vedas. Many other religions directly contradict scientific evidence and in their obscurantist zeal have punished those who have denied their basic tenets, teachings and exhortations. The Hindu too, in spite of his profound heritage, has to rise above his inherited atavistic proclivity to senseless totem worship and thought habits to an action and meditation reoriented regimen as shown by sages like Swami Ramakrishna Paramhans and Swami Vivekananda. Sitting on a treasure trove of authentic and priceless corpus of knowledge, he can no longer bask in his past glory. He has to recharge his batteries and practise his religion to benefit his fellow-being as articulated by Swami Vivekananda in his clarion call to the Hindus not to wither away in civlizational statism but to rise and act in the present. Hinduism is not atavistic but a thorough understanding of your past is essential to interpret and understand the present and plan for the future. Those who scoff at our constant reiteration of the glory of Hindu Vedic past must bear in mind what Swami Vivekananda had to say:

> "Children of India, I am here to speak to you today about some practical things, and my object in reminding you about the glories of the past is simply this. Many times have I been told that looking into the past only degenerates and leads to nothing, and that we should look to the future. That is true. But out of the past is built the future. Look back, therefore, as far as you can, drink deep of the eternal fountains that are behind, and after that, look forward, march forward and make India brighter, greater, much higher than she ever was. Our ancestors were great. We must first recall that. We must learn the elements of our being, the blood that courses in our veins; we must have faith in that blood, and what it

did in the past; and out of that faith, and consciousness of past greatness, we must build an India yet greater than what she has been. There have been periods of decay and degradation. I do not attach much importance to them; we all know that. Such periods have been necessary. A mighty tree produces a beautiful ripe fruit. That fruit falls on the ground, it decays and rots, and out of that decay springs the root and the future tree, perhaps mightier than the first one. This period of decay through which we have passed was all the more necessary. Out of this decay is coming the India of future; it is sprouting, its first leaves are already out, and a mighty, gigantic tree, the "Urdhavamumlam", is here, already beginning to appear, and it is about that I am going to speak to you."

The sweep of the Vedic thought is so vast and all encompassing, with an incredible depth of perception, that it bewilders the common man, but for this very reason makes its praxis so much easier and so unshackling. The West has only touched the fringes of physical Yoga purely for therapeutic purpose. An important element of Hinduism is 'Karma' which lays down that a man reaps the fruits of his action, good or bad, and is born to do good Karma. The other element of Hindu thought is 'Avtar'. And finally, the concept of 'Shakti', the divine energy in the shape of a goddess by different names. God, the Creator, along with the 'Shakti', the power to create, has brought into existence the universe as we know it. There are so many sub-cultures and modes of worship such as Vaishanavism, Shaivism, Shakti worship in various forms, such as Kali, Katyayini, Kalyani and the trinity of Lakshmi, Durga and Saraswati; Vaishno Devi, Jwala Devi, various occults rites of Aghories, Tantrik cults, different Akharas, including the Nirmohi at Ayodhya, Nagas; Dwait and Adwait Vad (Duality and Unity of God) and an unending array of local gods, goddesses and family deities (Kul Devta) that can easily confuse the uninitiated.

A word about polytheism. The Muslim invaders and European colonizers have often derided Hinduism on account of what they called its 'pagan character' and 'idol worship'. Nothing could be further from truth. The Hindus believe in one God, but innumerable manifestations of the same universal reality. In brief, with its vast variety of god worship from remote antiquity to present times, history has produced the webs and wafts that weave many a delicate web of golden bars and checkered shades on the tapestry that is Hinduism. The Hindus believe in 'Jiva,' the life moving force of all existence, unfathomable, eternal, indestructible, detached, free and beyond grasp.

Comparing Christianity and Islam with Hinduism, one cannot miss certain fundamental differences. Prophet Mohammed who borrowed heavily from the Old Testament and portions of the New, recognized the earlier Prophets like Abraham, Moses, and Jesus but the Last words of God's teachings according to him are the 'Ayats' of Quran. These are said to be revealed to him through Gabriel, the messenger of his Allah. His own utterances together with those of his companions and twelve Caliphs that came after him form the bed-rock of Sunnah and Hadis. They lay down prescriptions in Islam for all times to come. A totalitarian religion like Islam leaves nothing to human reason or innovation but finds atavistic solution to every small detail of day to day living, anchored entirely on the sayings and actions of the Prophet and others as stated above and propounded in the Hadith. Not one word can be added or subtracted from these sacred texts. This makes Islam a completely exclusivistic religion driven entirely by past pronouncements and actions with no room for evolution or development in the context of modern science, philosophical thought, art forms, and new discoveries. Concentrating entirely on externals with little room for spiritual insight, the Islamic injunctions issued through the Fatwas form the corpus of Islamic teachings and their jurisprudence called Shariat derives it's legitimacy from the same sources, dating thirteen centuries back. The Fatwas are the final words on such petty matters as postures for coitus, urinating, Wuzus (washing and cleaning), women's rights, marriage, divorce, inheritance, adultery, treatment of non-believers, war against qafirs, physical actions during Namaz and so on.

Christianity in comparison leaves more room for individual actions and interpretations of the religion, though it too suffers from the same insistence on the sayings and deeds of Jesus Christ, the genesis of human race, nature of universe and other temporal matters. Like Islam it insists to a large degree, on externals, with disregard for inner search and spirituality.

In the praxis of their faith, both Christianity and Islam give almost equal importance to God and His son or the Prophet. In Christianity, unlike Hinduism no salvation is possible without Jesus, the son of God. In fact, in Christian theology Jesus holds the key to the communion of ordinary mortals with God. Similarly, there are more references to Prophet Mohammed in Muslim literature than to God Himself. In every Qawwali, almost the entire emphasis is on Mohammed and Kaba rather than Allah. Even the prescriptive words on the entry permit for conversion to Islam read, "Ya ilah-Lilillah Mohammed Rasul Allah". (There is but one God and Mohammed is his prophet). As opposed to this, Hinduism concentrates directly on God and the minor gods of Hindu pantheon, merely represent different traits of this God, which are easy to grasp and worship and act as symbols, comprehensible to ordinary people who lack the erudition and yogic power of concentration and the ability thereafter to become one with the cosmic consciousness called "Nirakar Braham", eternal without beginning or end, all pervasive, the creator and creation itself. But these gods have not been given the same importance as God nor the key to man's communion with Him. Even salvation is possible by entirely concentrating on the "Param Braham" without the aid of intermediaries. In the case of Judaism there is no interlocutor between God and His people. The role of various prophets had been merely to educate the Jews in the path of righteousness and obeying the dictates of God alone.

To the early Christians Jesus came first, and it was he who explained the nature of God and His Kingdom to the Jews and the pagans. In the same manner, Mohammed came first and it was he who explained existence and the nature of a monolithic and shapeless God to the desert tribes who used to worship various local gods and stone idols in and around Mecca and

Medina. This is in sharp contradiction to Hinduism where God came first and the prophets, sages and seers came later. In a latest effort to pronounce the supra-state of Jesus Christ, the Vatican in it's annual Diwali greetings sent to India, has asserted that Christ is God himself and the ultimate fulfillment of the "human heart's restless searching". This has embarrassed even the officials of the Indian Church themselves.

Hindutva is the cultural essence of Hinduism and is the end-product of three elements—cultural nationalism, intense patriotism and a pride in the collective memory of India's past glory. I have mentioned this subject in brief in my book on Nehru, but the subject bears repetition. The canard about 'Hindutva as a fundamentalist, misguided Hindu communalism is the worst kind of pamphleteering from the English speaking so-called elite and half-baked westernized intelligentsia, consistently listing to the left. They are still willing slaves to their imported socialistic, Leninist, Marxist thought, which has lost its rationale and relevance in the world in general and the country of its origin in particular. This breed nurses a pathological hatred towards anything Indian or indigenous. For the last 50 years since Independence, under the garb of progressivism a well-orchestrated campaign has been unleashed to revile the tolerant, mild, liberal and accommodative Hindu religion and the culture and civilization that it has spawned. Through chartered media, dedicated to destroy the self-respect and pride of this ancient civilization, they have spared no pains to traduce every thing Indian or Hindu.

In spite of the risk of incurring the opprobrium of the secularist brigade, a Cartesian dialectic statement about Hinduism can be made without any hesitation. That India's ancient ethnic native genius forms the colour and content of its Hindu heritage and there is no reason whatsoever to be apologetic about it. Like Christianity in western countries, Hindus form the majority community and thereby have the right to be called the natural civilizational core of India. They have, are, and will in future determine the structure and ethos of our civilization and nationality. There is no need to shy away from this reality. The dragon seeds sown by Nehru, who can be well and truly called the greatest Hindu baiter, have taken deep roots and his caucus of leftist intellectuals, communists and JNU academia are simply incapable of facing the fact that Hindu spirit and resurgence is the natural order of the day.

The composite nature of our culture has often been touted by our secularist brigade, discussed earlier and the impossibility of the proposition have been established. Those, who wax eloquent on the multi-cultural, multi-ethnic, pluralistic and composite culture must realise that 95 percent of the minorities, who claim a separate culture are born out of the Hindu stock. They must realize that it is possible to change your religion but not ethnicity. You can change yourself by giving yourself any name but you cannot disown your ancestors or forebears. The genetics and DNA code runs through centuries from generation to generation.

British rulers believed, with some element of truth, that if mental slavery in India is to be perpetuated as a natural corollary to political domination, the first thing to do is to destroy Hindutva. Unfortunately, they have found many Indian collaborators in their grand design. To prove their secular credentials this group finds it necessary to vilify Hindu religion and society. The Supreme Court in its landmark judgment has upheld the proposition that Hindutva is synonymous with India's culture and is a way of life and has no communal overtones whatsoever.' Hindutva' is a product of the geography and history of this land mass called Bharat, moulded and nurtured through millennia of traditions, thoughts and beliefs, enunciated by our seers and sages. It is through their constant search for truth regarding God, universe, man and earth, and a selfless striving for perfection that they passed down to generation after generation, that the essence of Hindu thought received its natural form. Inimical to none and friendly to all it allows dissent and encourages reasoned argument. Not being a closed system, it is open to constant development and evaluation for ever revitalizing itself through assimilating new ideas, while it raises ever new edifices on the foundations of universal cosmic truths. It is unlike other so called well-defined religions with their teachings and practices frozen forever in a time-warp of original thought and wisdom, thus denying alternatives as a sequel to new discoveries, and in spite of expanding horizons of human knowledge and perceptions with each passing day. Evolving civilizations, as opposed to the decadent, are not content with "what is, but strive for what can be". Thus striving for achieving the highest in achievable, is a common running thread in Hinduism. As opposed to this, both Christianity and Islam prohibit any need for readjusting the enjoined sayings and practices mentioned in their holy books. No line written more than a thousand years ago can either be questioned or erased, even though their validity and raison-de-'etre is open to scrutiny. Mere material well-being has never been the end all and be all of the Hindu thought. While they accept the need for freedom from want and never frown upon material progress, the ultimate goal however had always been much beyond satiation of physical needs and a constant striving for perfection, spiritual achievement and even a final search of and immersion into the universal God-head. A feature, however, unique to Hindu thoughts is the importance of four 'Ashrams' – Brahmacharya, covering the first 25 years, aims at asceticism, scholastic pursuits, building of character, health, acquisition of knowledge and sharpening of skills as a preparation for the life ahead. Thereafter, Grahasth, which lasts for the next 25 years, means entry into married life in the material world, providing for earthly needs, excellence in profession, utilization of knowledge, efforts at worldly success and raising a family as per the needs of the society and the country's, demands, fulfilling the material and worldly obligations. Vanprastha, which commences after 25 years of Grahasth life seeks something beyond the material and routine, or acquisition of wealth and worldly satisfaction. Social and national service and dedication to the real issues of enrichment of society and the country exploring the frontiers of knowledge and quest for truth super cede, purely material pursuits. In the world and yet outside it action without desire for rewards one strives, to achieve the state of Sthitipragya, which means raising oneself above worldly concerns and total detachent from the fruits of endeavour. Serving the world to the best of one's ability, without a desire for personal gain and supreme mental equipoise is the essence of *Vanprasth*. Finally, man is ordained to achieve *Sanyas*, meaning total renunciation of the world at 75 years. It involves meditation, devotion, 'Yoga' and the attempt to reach the sublime, by cutting loose from the worldly concerns and aiming to achieve salvation through *Sadhna* (intense spiritual striving). With minor adjustment, the system should and can continue in the present world order. Though present longevity is less than 100 years, the time span for each 'Ashram' can be suitably curtailed by devoting the first half of life for self-improvement and family and the second half for impersonal ends. This system is unique and different from all other religions and systems of thoughts.

The Brahmin, the twice born, and who according to Indian mythology came out of the head of the Creator Brahma, was ordained to live the life of an ascetic. His was not the luxury of palaces but to learn, meditate, acquire knowledge and wisdom and disseminate it to all mankind. He was not to think of himself but others and live for others. To lead and guide man in the ways of God, to prepare them for the ultimate spiritual perfection and salvation. Brahmins were not to earn or store money but depend entirely on alms from the laity and material and protection from the Kshtriya princes. From womb to tomb a Brahmin had to perform "anusthans" (rituals) and "Sanskaras" for all Varnas or castes, educate the un-initiated, teach the ignorant and remonstrate with them, to the extent of chastisement, to bring them back to the narrow path of virtue and "Raj Dharam" (the duties of the king). In brief, their duties lay in ushering into the world the rule of Dharma, which does not mean a sect. Dharma was a very sacred and emotive world during the times of our proto history. One hears of the splendour of the kings or Kshtriyas; the material wealth of the Vaishya or the treasury of Kuber, but the Brahmin is always referred to as ascetic and poor. With the passage of time and the coming of priesthood many evils and covetousness entered the lifestyle and the conduct of Brahmins.

The early Rishis, who shunned the comforts of cities lived in jungles and far off places to carry out their Sadhna and run the Gurukuls (the family of teacher or a place of learning) and train their disciples in godly pursuits and knowledge of the world. As brought out earlier, these teaching places, or the sanctuary for the Rishis, almost all of whom came from Brahmin class, are the greatest assets of our civilizational foundations. Since they did not work for themselves, these Ashrams were maintained by grants released by the kings and princes of Kashtriyas' class. As pointed out earlier, the prisesthood as distinct from Brahminism entered into our society much later.

To unlock the doors of this storehouse and repository of profound learning, the key is a good knowledge of Sanskrit, which is totally lacking in our present day intelligentsia. Even Hindi, our national language is derided as a language of country cousins and 'desi behanjis'. It is a crying shame that the post graduate course in Hindi in Shri Ravi Shankar Shukla University in Madhya Pradesh had to be cancelled because there were no students opting for the subject. When asked the reason for this, a girl student interviewed by a Television staff replied that if they apply for Hindi, they are made to feel inferior by their own English class colleagues. Returning to Sanskrit, this is what Swami Vivekananda had to say:

> "The attempts of the great Ramanuja and of Chaitanya and of Kabir to raise the lower classes of India, show that marvelous results were attained during the lifetime of those great prophets; yet the later failures have to be explained, and cause shown why the effect of their teachings stopped almost within a century of the passing away of these great Masters. The secret is here. They raised the lower classes; they had all the wish that these should come up, but they did not apply their energies to the spreading of the Sanskrit language among the masses. Even the great Buddha made one false step when he stopped the Sanskrit language from being studied by the masses. He wanted rapid and immediate results, and translated and preached in the language of the day, Pali. That was great, he spoke in the language of the

people, and the people understood him. That was great; it spread the ideas quickly and made them reach far and wide, but, along with that, Sanskrit ought to have spread. Knowledge came but the prestige was not there, culture was not there. It is culture that withstands shocks, not a simple mass of knowledge. You can put a mass of knowledge into the world, but that will not do it much good. There must come culture into the blood. We all know in modern times nations which have masses of knowledge, but what of them? They are like tigers, they are like savages, because culture is not there".

It is hardly surprising that almost all contributions in all branches of knowledge and facets of civilization such as arts and music, architecture, literature, grammar, medicine, astrology, astronomy, mathematics, science and physics, botany and chemistry, human biology and science of health (Ayurveda), all came down from these scribes of Vedic knowledge.

Two greatest sons of India during the late nineteenth and early twentieth century were Swami Vivekananda and Mahatma Gandhi. Both were deeply imbued with the spirit of Hinduism and both served Mother India in their own way. While Vivekananda dedicated himself to religion and awakened our people to their greatness and inspired them to greater endeavours, Mahatma Gandhi sacrificed his all to enter politics in order to lead us out of slavery to freedom. Both were deeply conscious of their religiosity and proud of being Hindus. Vivekananda made religion the foundation of a successful temporal world, Gandhiji made spirituality and truth the essence of his political philosophy. Both succeeded beyond measure in their God ordained mission.

In Young India his weekly journal, Mahatma Gandhi wrote, that nothing could be further from his thought than that "we (Indians) should become exclusive or erect barrier. But I respectfully contend that an appreciation of other cultures can follow, never precede an appreciation and assimilation of our own". His views on borrowing foreign values were very explicit, and he said, " I do not want my windows to be stuffed. I want the cultures of all lands to be blown about my house, as freely as possible. But I refuse to be blown off my feet."

And then Swami Vivekananda declared, " The old religion said that he was an atheist who did not believe in God. The new religion says that he is an atheist who does not believe in himself. It is the coward and the fool who says this is his fate. But it is the strong man who stands up and says I will make my own fate."

The process of learning never stops. I was amazed to learn how scanty was my knowledge about our urban English speaking elite. On a chat show " We the People" compered by Barkha Dutt on NDTV programme on 21st July, 2002, at 8.00 p.m., everytime the speaker who attempted to speak of Hindu nationalism or tried to put Gujarat riot tragedy in its proper perspective was booed down by the crowd. These youngsters were either totally alienated from our cultural roots or completely under the influence of New Delhi's English chatterati, or what seemed more likely, was a crowd of camp followers gerrymandered by the NDTV staff. The very mention of the word 'RSS' "Rastriya Swayam Sevek Sangh" or Hindu nationalism was met by sniggers and jeers by some of these social upstarts. Hinduism and the Sangh Pariwar were targeted as the social pariahs. To my horror, I realised that what medieval Muslim rulers, Macauley, Max Muller and Marxists could not achieve in a millennium was accomplished by our own nationalist governments since 1947, their Marxists friends and the English educated elite. Although the medium of discourse in the above show was both Hindi and English, I did not find even by mistake a single speaker except one from the B.J.P. and that too, a Muslim, who could speak a single word of Hindi or express himself in our cultural medium.

Now a look at the strength and weakness of Hinduism, the biggest strength is its power of assimilation, open endedness, continuous evolution and eclectic response to all that is progressive and new. Hinduism can absorb and co-exists with people of any faith as long as they owe allegiance to this mother country. Even a Hindu converted to Islam who shares the same collective memories with the Hindus is welcome in its fold. Hinduism being progressive, the genius of its people can be seen in entrepreneurial skills, business acumen, technological expertise and excellence in all forms of human activities. Unfettered and uncontrolled by a tyraneous state Hinduism encourages self-actualization, and abjures acquisitive or imperialistic tendencies.

The weaknesseses, though endemic, are curable. There is an excessive stress on the individual which led to his neglect of organized effort. Lack of development of social institutions community alliance and collectivism has led to the weakening of our polity and social fabric. Proverbial Hindu tolerance has often verged on cowardice and projected an image of weakness leading to foreign invasions and defeats in battles. Indian history from 700 A.D. onwards with a few exceptions is a monotonous story of defeats. In spite of Kautilya's Arthshastra Hindus took little interest in military methods and political sciences. The caste system though well intended in its inception degenerated into a cruel caste divide and led to internal conflict an enfeeblement of the Hindu nation. And last but not the least is the "crab in the can" mentality of Hindu individuals who cannot see their brothers rise to excellence and often attempt to drag them back to their level of incompetence.

To conclude we can do no better but quote what Sri Aurobindo had to say about Hinduism:

> "Something has been shown to you in this year of seclusion something about which you had your doubts and it is the truth of the Hindu religion. It is this religion that I am raising up before the world, it is this that I have perfected and developed through the rishis, saints and avatars, and now it is going forth to do my work among the nations. I am raising this nation to send forth my word... When therefore it is said that India shall rise, it is the Sanatana Dharma that shall rise. When it is said that India shall be great, it is the Sanatana Dharma that shall be great. But what is the Hindu religion? It is the Hindu religion only, because the Hindu nation has kept it, because in this peninsula it grew up in the seclusion of the sea and the Himalayas, because in this sacred and

the ancient land it was given as a charge to the Aryan race to preserve through the ages. That which we call the Hindu religion is really the eternal religion, because it is the universal religion which embraces all others. If a religion is not universal, it cannot be eternal. A narrow religion, a sectaraian religion, an exclusive religion can live only for a limited time and limited purpose.... I say no longer that Sanatana Dharma is for us nationalism.... Sanatana Dharma is nationalism."

Chapter 17

Ancient Indian Civilization & The Myth of Aryan Invasion

In the long march of Indian civilization a historiographic disaster overtook our people in the second half of the nineteenth century. Flying in the face of all textual and scientific evidence and for reasons that have more to do with politics than science and scholarship, a colonial missionary construct was foisted on our ancient history to subserve the interests of colonial rule Christianity and Europe. An Anglo-German, philologist and 'scholar' Frederick Max Muller worked out a chronology and thesis, unquestioned by the academia till today, and actively supported by the leftist historians, that hangs more on fatuous fancies than facts. This is the myth of the Aryan invasion and the story of the Vedic civilization as retold by these worthies.

A deep study based on a combination of astronomic, literary, ecological, mathematical, scientific and meteorological data will establish that the Rigvedic civilization formed an earlier layer of world civilizations that flourished before the rise of the civilizations of Indus Valley, Sumeria and Egypt, and can be dated back well before 7500 B.C., approximately about the date when silver was separated from natural brass casting. Rigvedic period would be even earlier. The theory of Aryan invasion invented by Max Muller has its roots in the nineteenth century political concerns of Germany and British colonial India. The Aryan theory has its genesis not in India but Europe. Let us examine the facts. People of North and South India speak languages from different families. The two are derivatives from the Aryan and Dravidian families of languages. We shall soon realize that separating the two people on linguistic basis is a gross distortion of facts. First a look at the motivation of Max Muller's theory in the nineteenth century Europe, and the political, racial, religious and nationalistic forces at work at that time. There was no Indus archaeology and there was no known co-relation between Indian and European languages. The two important pillars of the Aryan theory were European racism, mainly anti-Semitism and German nationalism. Comparative linguistics and archaeology did not exist at this time and the fact is that Sanskrit was the source of most European languages. Instead of the 'theory' being the result of archaeology and comparative philology the position is the other way round. Indus archaeology itself contradicts the invasion theory. The invasion of the dark skinned people by the light skinned ones was really a replay of the European strategy of colonizing Asia and Africa. Substituting European for Aryan, and Asian and African for Dravidian, you have the leit motif of the European colonial campaigns in the two continents. This makes the Aryans a replica of the European colonizers. The archaeological finds of the Indus Valley civilization were made to fit the Aryan invasion theory which was supposed to have come later and destroyed the former. In fact, the ruins of Harappa and Mohenjo-daro were interpreted as the result of the destruction caused by the Aryan invasion. The myth of the invasion was thus invented to corroborate the tautology or a circular argument, as a proof that the Aryans came after the Indus civilization, which they destroyed. This effort totally ignored the fact, as we shall see later, that most of the artifects found in the Indus valley excavations were in use much earlier in the Vedic period. The destruction of the Indus valley civilization was not due to any invasion but the drying up of the river Saraswati, which flowed across the Thar desert and watered this civilization to prosperity. Later, as the river dried up, the civilization too came to an end, but this happened much later after Rigveda period. Certain Shaivic remains found in Harappa with similar finds in Gujarat, and the phallus worship of Dravidian Shaivites led to the belief that the people of Harappa were Dravidian, completely ignoring the fact that the stronghold of Shaivites is not the Dravidian south, but the Himalayan regions of Nepal, Kashmir and the northern parts of Uttar Pradesh and Himachal Pradesh. This was the cradle of the earlier Vedic people, whose legacy was passed later to the Harappan civilization. To quote the famous historian, Talageri, "The negative evidence in the form of absence of the horse and rice in the Indus civilization, which was taken as evidence of its Dravidian origin is no more tenable in view of the occurrence of horse bones and rice at Lothal, Kalibangan, Surkotada and Ropar in India and Mohenjo-daro in Pakistan. On the other hand, there is enough positive evidence in support of the religious rites of the Harappan being similar to those of the Vedic Aryans. Their religious motifs, deities and sacrificial altars bespeak of Aryan faith..." The word Druids of England sounds strangely like 'Druhyus', who were driven out of India in sustained campaigns and had their Asian origins in the early fourth millennium B.C. Thus there have been so many Indo-European migrations and this points to India as the original home of the speakers of Indo-European dialect, who migrated to the West and North-West in pre-historic times, the exact reverse of the facts of the Aryan invasion theory. I have discussed the subject of the Aryan invasion in some detail in my book on *Nehru*. The Aryan invasion theory requires a negation of a substantial body of literary and archaeological evidence. How could the Aryans, who were basically supposed to be nomads, evolve such a refined language as Sanskrit, its sophisticated texts and generate a vocabulary that spread to the rest of the world, influencing Greek, Latin, Sumerian and Egyptian languages. The sophistication of Panini's grammar three thousand years ago, the *Astadhyayi* and Patanjali's *Mahabhasya* will make one wonder how such a linguistic perfection can be achieved by a nomadic people so late to arrive on the historic scene. This leads to a paradox of a 'history' without a literature and literature without a history. The fact of the matter is that the word 'Arya' did not denote a race but was used to address a person of noble origin. There are examples galore in our epics of queens addressing their husband kings as 'Aryaputra'.

The Harappans of the Indus Valley have left vast archeological evidence over a million square kilometer area from Iran and beyond Afghanistan to Eastern UP and the Tapti Valley and yet left absolutely no literary records. The Vedic Aryans and their successors on the other hand have no archaeological record of their existence. Thus, we have a concrete history and archaeology of thousand of years but no literature and the ancient Vedic Aryans, who left no history or archaeological records.

The Harappan society of 3000 B.C. precedes the Dravidian-Tamil literature by 2000 years, since the latter dates back to fist century B.C. only. Thus, there can be no comparison between Harappans and the Dravidians. The Harappans, we know, were literate, but left no literature, while their so-called illiterate Aryans have left a mass of literature behind. There is another hole in the Aryan invasion theory; that geometry and astronomy were borrowed by the Indians from the Greeks after Alexander's invasion. A cursory look at the Harappan ruins shows a very well developed art of town planning with straight lines, squares and rectangles, used in making streets, houses, courtyards, baths, aqueducts and a drainage system. These could not have developed without a thorough knowledge of geometry and mathematics. The late American mathematician and historian of science, Seidenberg, has pointed to certain Vedic sacrificial altars called 'Yajnasalas' from the past Vedic period, which contained technical details for the construction of these. All these are detailed in 'Sulbasutras', the mathematical texts of the post-Vedic period. The mathematics of 'Sulbasutras' dates back to long before 2000 B.C. The Egyptian pyramids of the Third Dynasty and before dating back to 2500 B.C. were most likely based on the Vedic funeral altars known as the 'Smasana-cit'. Seidenberg has conclusively proved that all ancient mathematics is derived from Vedic mathematics or the 'Sulbasutras'. All this preceded

Pythagoras, the father of the Greek geometry'. Thus, there is a paradox that the construction in the supposedly antique Dravidian-Indus sites, came earlier, while the instructions for building them are found in the Vedic literature of the supposedly invading Aryans, who came much later.

Einstein often said, ' A Theory must not contradict empirical facts;' the Aryan invasion theory does precisely that. Reverting to 'Sulbasutras', my grandfather was born well before 1870 A.D., the time of the invention of the Aryan invasion theory. He had no formal education, but was a scholar of all Shastras and Vedic writings, including 'Sulbasutras'. He often posed me this question:

"Nam chaturgun panchmil tako dwigun praman, va me asthi se bhag de, shesh me Ram hi Ram."

Stated simply

'Imagine any number and multiply it by 4, add 5 to the product. Double this amount and divides the result by 8. The reminder shall always be 2.'

This is an algebraic problem of the 'Sulbasutras' when there was no Aryan invasion theory, nor were the Vedic Indian, considered ignorant, of any knowledge of Algebra as a corollary to the so-called theory. Does it not prove that algebra as explained in 'Sulbasutras' existed well before the Greeks and Egyptians came to know of it. We will revert to the other mass of compelling evidence against the Aryan invasion theory later but a mention here should be made that this move had far-reaching consequences on the Indian polity resulting into a skewed and degraded perspective of our past and a permanent Aryan-Dravidian divide. In the *Amarakosa* the Sanskrit lexicon dating about 500 A.D., an "Aryan is: *mahakula-kulinarya-sabhya-sabhya-sanjjana-sadhvah.*" This is unambiguous and means: "an Arya is one who hails from a noble family, of gentle behaviour and demeanor, good natured and of righteous conduct." It has nothing to do with race. Manu, the first man and a seer, much hated by the leftist and today's Dalits, had said that people of all nationalities were Aryan or non-Aryan depending on their culture and conduct. The word Aryan denoted a very high moral code of behaviour and adherence to sacred laws. Manu's list of such people included those from all parts of India, neighbouring countries like China and Persia, Kambojas from the North East Afghanistan, Yavanas from North West Afghanistan and beyond. The Dravida probably refer to people of the south west of India and the south. The following texts occur in an ancient literature:

"Praya arya jyotiragrah

Children of Arya seeks and are led by jyoti"

RV VII 33.7

"One who destroys life is never an Arya, and one who desists from taking life is an Arya."

Dhammapada 270

This clearly puts the Nazi's out of the community of Aryans. Ramayana of Valmiki, is not without a message:

"Aryah sarva-samascaiva sadaiva priyadarshanah

Arya-who cared for the equality of all and was dear to everyone."

The Ramayana I 1.16

The Holy Bible has two parts- The Old Testament and the New Testament. The Old Testament is a Jewish litany and deals with ancient times till the emergence of Christianity. To sever its umbilical cord from its Jewish heritage the Christian Europe looked East, mainly towards India to seek its origin from a new race or civilization. This is the time when the word 'Aryan' as a race was invented, sometime in the middle of nineteenth century. There were two civilizations in the East—Indian and Chinese. The Europeans preferred the Indian Aryans as their forebears and adopted the word Aryan to dissect themselves from the rest of the people. With this master stroke they adorned themselves with the nobility of birth and a higher civilizational pedigree. Thus, anti-Semitism and a colonial drive were the main impulses for the nineteenth century Europe to give themselves on Aryan heritage and invent the theory of the Aryan invasion of India. The logic of a superior race invading the lesser mortals. The author of this effort was Frederick Max Muller (1823-1901).

The similarity between Sanskrit and European languages prompted the linguists to add their might to the anti-Semitic impulse of Western Europe and give themselves an Aryan heritage, based entirely on a pseudo-scientific presumption. Colonel Boden, God bless his soul, established a Professorship of Sanskrit at Oxford University, whose aim, according to Monier-Williams, was "...to promote Sanskrit learning among the English, so as to enable his countrymen to proceed in the conversion of the natives of India to the Christian Religion". Later, prizes were also offered to literary works that undermined Indian tradition. The first holder of the Boden Professorship was Horace Hyman Wilson (1784-1860). Writing about a series of lectures he gave, Wilson himself noted, that "These lectures were written to help candidates, for a prize of £ 200 given by John Muir,... for the best refutation of the Hindu religious system." Frederick Max Muller, generally regarded as the greatest Indologist and a Vedic and Sanskrit scholar of his times, which credit he did not possess, was favoured by circumstances to write extensively on Rigveda with a view to denigrate Hindu religion. Later, challenged by his critics on the inexactitude of his theory, he had to admit, "whether the Vedic hymns were composed in 1000, 1500 or 2000 or 3000 B.C., no power on earth will ever determine!" Max Muller combined in himself a romantic temper with a Protestant missionary zeal. He wrote in 1868 to the Duke of Argyle, then acting Secretary of State for India: "The ancient religion of India is doomed, and if Christianity does not step in, whose fault will it be?" Another aberration in the so-called "race science" was the invention of the superiority of the European whites over the blacks, which forced the British writer Nancy Stephan to charge that, "On examination it is found that the European whites are at the top and the African blacks at the bottom, with others coming in between." While Max Muller gave credence to the Aryan theory in England and Germany, his friend, E. Renan popularized the same in France, and Sanskrit thereafter became a popular reading in the nineteenth century Europe, especially Germany, the home of Indology. However, the credit for the first premise that European languages were a branch of Sanskrit goes to Filippo Sassetti, a Florentine merchant, who stayed in Goa between 1583 to 1588.

Now the fortunes turned. Germany had lost its self-esteem after continuous defeats from the Thirty Years War to Napoleon's victories and found itself a pawn in the power game of the contemporary great powers of Europe. As a reaction, the unification of Germany began and was completed around 1870, making Germany the greatest European power. The pride in its Aryan ancestry played no mean role in resurgent Germany's new found strength. Their over-weaning confidence forced contemporary Britishers to observe that – "...a nation has been born out of Sanskrit." The British were already traumatized by the 1857 revolt in India and were deeply conscious of the reality that if India united under a single leadership, nothing can stop the end of the British Empire. To them the obvious leaders were the Brahmins, who had been respected for generations and traditionally provided all guidance in matters temporal and spiritual. This forced the British Government to remove all Brahmanical influence in India and put Indian history on its head, by using the missionaries, not only to spread Christianity but to undermine Brahmanical influence and denigrate our past. In this effort the greatest contribution came from Thomas Babbington Macaulay (1800-1859), the Education Member of the Governor General' Council, who wrote in 1836: "Our English schools are flourishing wonderfully. The effect of this education on the Hindus is prodigious... It is our belief that if our plans of education are followed up, there will not be a single idolater among the respectable classes in Bengal thirty years hence. And this will be effected without any efforts to proselytize, without the smallest interference with religious liberty, by natural operation of knowledge and reflection, I heartily rejoice in the project." This diabolical plan was aimed to turn the strength of the Brahmins against themselves by using their commitments to scholarship in uprooting their own tradition. The assistance of the Indian educated elite in this regard was most valuable. Macaulay's hired agent in this effort was Max Muller. He, on a stipend of Rupees one lac a huge sum at that time, was asked to undertake the study of Rigveda and use this knowledge against India's past. With time as the German nationalism and its antagonism to British interests grew, Max Muller had to do a volte face and attempt to wean away Western Europe from their Aryan origins. This was not an easy task, since Max Muller had already made too many bargains with the devil. With the resurgent Germany as the spearhead of the Aryan race, his own handiwork, and Max Muller being a loyal citizen of England, his own theory became an embarrassment, casting aspersions on his loyalty. He had no recourse but to recant his own theory of Aryan race and the Aryan invasion of India. Unfortunately, Indian academia and leftist historians are still obsessed with the same old pseudo-scientific version of the race theory. What are the textual sources that we can search for evidence?

The ancient Indian texts in addition to the four Vedas, and 100 Upnishads and other literary corpus consist of two epics i.e. *Ramayana* and *Mahabharata* and 18 *Puranas*. The word Puranas means "that which had lived from ancient times" or "a work containing records of past events". In addition to 18 Puranas, there are another 100 Uppuranas. The sequence of the 18 Puranas is as follows:

1. *Braham Purana*
2. *Padma Purana*
3. *Vishnu Purana*
4. *Sri Vayu or Shiv Purana*
5. *Bhagvat Purana*
6. *Naradiya Purana*
7. *Markandeya Purana*
8. *Agni Purana*
9. *Bhavishya Purana*
10. *Brahmvaivarta Purana*
11. *Linga Purana*

12. *Varah Purana*
13. *Skanda Purana*
14. *Vamana Purana*
15. *Kurma Purana*
16. *Matsya Purana*
17. *Garuda Purana*
18. *Brahmad Purana*

It is amazing to note that no author has attached his name to any part of the Vedas or Upanishads and Puranas. The Vedas are an important source of political history for two reasons. First, which is unique, is the incorruptibility of the Vedic Text, handed down obligatorily through recital by learned Brahmins, who had memorized these with perfect pronunciation. Second, the Vedic Sanskrit differed from the later or classical Sanskrit in that the accent indicated the intended compound.

A study of the above literature raises a number of intractable problems if the Aryan invasion theory is to be accepted. The entire mass of Vedic texts has no reference whatsoever to any invasion. Any attempt to justify the Aryan invasion based on Vedic literature is flawed, due to selective references picked up from isolated passages. The nomadic Aryans, by no means possessed an organized instrument of war, unlike the Mongols, who conquered half the known world, and yet according to Western scholars the nomad Aryans, who had no knowledge of the art of war or any worthwhile instruments to wage it, are credited with the conquest of the main land mass from West Anatolia to Babylon, to Persia, to Afghanistan right upto the Indian heartland. The aggressive trait of the Aryans alone cannot explain this great military achievement. Any invasion or war attributed to the Aryans is only between the Aryan subgroups or amongst members of the community itself.

In the entire Vedic literature there is not a single reference to any information regarding the place of origin of the invaders themselves. The Vedic exegesis too, such as the Brahmans, Puranas and other texts, are also silent on the subject. An ancient primitive people arriving in scattered waves through a sub-continental movement, could not have successfully covered up the fact of their arrival from outside, nor suffer from a selective amnesia, and a collective loss of memory of any such odyssey. There also does not exist any such mythology of the central Asian desert or mountain region, except one of a riverine and ocean culture in the literary corpus of these people. The oldest texts in Rigveda only refer to the rivers of the Indian sub-continent, its climate and the topography. The Rigveda, consisting of 1,017 hymns and around 10,000 verses, the four Vedas and the related Brahmans, Aranyaka and early Upanishads, all pre-Buddhist, running into 5000 pages, also do not mention any such event. No contemporary civilization or one before the Vedic can boast of such a vast literature. Even if a portion of this was produced outside, how could this be grafted on to a different continent without leaving any trace of its place of origin. The inevitable conclusion, therefore, is that this literature was indigenous to these people in their habitat. The Vedic Sanskrit is a complex poetry with precise metrical forms and an ideal language for computers, because of its lack of ambiguity. To attribute the knowledge of this profound language to primitive invaders is a most unlikely proposition. The primitive invader matrix just does not gel with the complex traditions of literature and civilization recorded in the language of a highly civilized community. The Vedic people identified with a high level of civilization and possesser of a profound literature have been made an instrument of the destruction of the so-called earlier Harappan civilization. This is a bizarre fact of literary history, as pointed out earlier. The highly advanced Harappan culture that had been destroyed has no history or literature, while a much more advanced language is left with no culture to hang on, both occurring in the same part of the world at the same time, Thus the word Aryan has no racial connotations. Buddha declared his religion as Aryan and when Arjuna refused to pick up arms at the battlefield of Kurukshetra, Lord Krishna accused him of behaving in an un-Aryan or ignoble manner. It was not a racial slur on Arjuna. Cyrus, the First, Emperor of Persia, also called himself an Aryan or a noble person. The term Aryan denoted an elevated or evolved state of man. The battle between light and darkness is well described in various religions as in Vedic texts and denotes a fight between good and evil. It does not have a racial metaphor. There are innumerable myths in Persian, Celtic, Germanic, Egyptian and even the Christian religious texts, describing such fights between good and evil or power of the light and darkness.

Another commonly abused term is 'Varna'. Varna does not mean the tint of the epidermic or colour in the racial sense, or caste. A Brahmin is white because of his purity and power of intelligence (Sattva). A Kshtriya, due to his quality of energy, will and action symbolizes red; the Vaishya, who deals with trade and commerce, is referred to as yellow, while with his quality of ignorance and servitude, the 'Dasyu' or 'Shudra' is termed black. Thus, 'Varna' in the Vedic Aryan lexicon denotes quality of the spiritual level of light, truth and friendliness, while the Dasyu varna stands for the opposite i.e. the quality of darkness, enmity and falsehood.

Manu is the first Vedic seer king as mentioned in Satha-Patha Brahman (1.8.1), who took shelter in the Himalaya during the great flood. As per Rigveda (x.63.1), he is the original man whose descendants were Pururvas, Ayu, Nahusha and Yayati. Yayati gave birth to five Vedic families called Purus, Anus, Druhyas, Turvasas and Yadus. Human beings are referred to as 'Manusa' or 'Manav'. These five groups of man or 'Panch Manav', which are generally recorded as the five Aryan tribes, similar to the twelve early Jewish tribes, which crossed the Jordan river under Joshua can be identified in the Puranas as belonging to the Lunar dynasty of kings. The Turvasa relate to southeast, Bihar, Bengal and Orissa and are the likely forebears of Dravidas and Yavanas. The Yadu relate to south or southwest Gujarat and Rajasthan traced in the historical times to Mathura, south of Delhi in Dwarika and Somnath. The Ayus related to the north or the Punjab and some parts of Bengal and Bihar too. The Druhyas inhabited the west or central-west including Gandhar, Afghanistan and were later driven to central Asia, while the Purus dwelt in the central region later called Ganga-Yamuna region. All, except the Purus, were denounced for having sinned against 'Dharma' at various times and the main wars involved conflicts between different varnas and Vedic groups as recorded in Puranas, the Yadus, being the most turbulent. Any resemblance to the Yadavas in today's Indian politics is purely accidental. These intra-Aryan wars were conflicts between the virtuous and those that had fallen from grace and by no imagination related to the Aryan Dravidian divide. There is also references in the Vedas to the Great War of Ten Kings.

> Ten united unholy kings could not defeat Sudas.
>
> Oppressed on all sides in the Battle of the Ten Kings.

RV.VII.38.6-8

All the four 'Varnas' had their share of the demons and the divine; Brahmins and Kshtriyas included the good, bad and the ugly. There had been many wars between Kshtriyas and also between Brahmins and Kshtriyas. The idea of the Dasyus as fallen descendants of Vedic people occurs, early in Vedic literatures.

The *Manu Samhita,* a post Vedic text similarly states:,

> But in consequence of the omission of sacred rites, and of their not consulting the sages, the following peoples of the noble class have gradually sunk in this world to the condition of servants – the Paundrakas, Codas, Dravidas, Kambojas, Yavanas, Sakas, Paradas, Pahlavas, Cinas, Kiratas, and Daradas. All those peoples in this world, who are excluded from the community of those born from the mouth, arms, thighs and feet of Brahmin (the four Vedic classes), are called Dasyus, whether they speak the language of the barbarians or that of the Aryans.

Manu Samhita X.43-45

These texts from the Vedas indicate a highly civilized origin of the Aryans and the Dasyus, both being part of the same culture except for their different proclivities. Dasyus even had the same accouterments such as horses and implements of war just as the Aryans. The Aryans described in the Vedas had a large number of cities inconsistent with the nomadic origin attributed to them. The Vedic sages invoked the Gods to protect them with cities.

O Fire, protect us with a hundred metal cities.

RV. VII.3.7.

Agni, thus be like a wide unconquerable metal city multiplied a hundred times.

RV. VII 15.14

Protect us with a hundred cities, O Agni

RV.VI 48.8

With a hundred fold cities protect us from evil and deceit, O Maruts.

The Vedic people lived along the great rivers in the land called Sapta Sindhu. Vedic hymns sing glory to the rivers of which the most sacred was Saraswati frequently mentioned in Vedic literature. Due to climatic and environmental changes, the river dried up leading to the fall of Harappan culture and the movement of Aryans eastward, marking the end of the Vedic age. Dholavira a port city of the Harappa Mohanjo-Daro complex was once a seaport at the mouth of the river Saraswati, which sustained the existing civilization. As per the present archaeology, it is known that the river Yamuna stopped flowing into Saraswati well before 2300 B.C. With the drying up of Saraswati this part of the river basin turned arid and could no more sustain life nor an urban civilization of the Harappan kind. The site of the great 'satras' or sessions by the Brahmin priests were situated along the confluence of the above streams.

Five rivers converged on Saraswati along with their streams. In consequence, Saraswati became five-fold in this region. These five were identified as Drashavati, Sutudri (Satluj), Chandrabhaga (Chenab), Vipas (Vyas) and Eravati (Ravi). (*Sukla Yajurveda* – 34.1).

When we add river Yamuna to these, the above rivers became Sapt Sindhu, the highly lauded Saraswati, which became the largest river system of the Vedic times. Gandhar and Afghanistan as brought out earlier were part of the Vedic civilization and included Shortugai, Harappan site located in Balkh or Bactria mentioned in *Atharvaveda* (V.22,14,17). *Attareya Brahman* (VII.34) also mentions the use of camels during the Vedic age. There is also evidence of the existence of Lapiz-Lazuli mines near Balkh, the main source of precious stones to the ancient world. The growth of barley (Yava) and copper (Ayas) during the Vedic times point to a date earlier then 3000 B.C. The other Vedic lands of Anga and Bang i.e. Bihar and Bengal formed the eastern extremity of the Saraswati region of the Vedic people and was called the land of the unorthodox religious practices.

The Saraswati region lay midway between Balkh and Bengal. The origin of the Rigveda age dates back to the end of the Ice Age, when Saraswati, the heart of the Vedic India, was a mighty stream, which flowed through the desert and had a length of 40 days journey time on horse back from its origin. This is one basis on which the Aryan invasion theory falls flat on its face and their origin in the Central Asia or Europe suffers the same fate due to the irrefutable evidence of the existence of the perennial stream called Saraswati in Vedic texts. That the westward flow of Yamuna supplied Saraswati with most of its water is mentioned not only in *Rigveda* but in *Atharvaveda* as well. This single evidence of the change of flow of Yamuna places the chronology of the Vedic period much above the Harappan civilization, which according to accepted dates goes back to approximately 3000 B.C.

The river Ganga where the Vedic people moved after the drying up of Saraswati became the symbol around which legend and lore were woven without end and formed the life-blood of our ancient civilization. Believed to have descended from the heavens to the head of Lord Shiva, it became the river divine. However, in more earthy terms Ganga has a never-ending source of water not only at its origin at Gangotri from the Gaumukh glacier, but also all the way down up to the sea. For instance, even after the diversion of a large part of its waters into irrigation canals, least of which is at Roorki, Ganga replenishes itself through many hidden sources of subterranean water along its course.

Unlike the Saraswati, the Ganga has never dried up nor shall it do so in future. It is a hydrological miracle for the present day marine engineers. If besides the gods, one were to identify one single symbol of Hinduism in our Vedic culture in the past and present civilizational anthology, there shall be only one name, Mother Ganga or *Ganga Mata.*

The Aryan invasion theory as pointed out earlier received its impetus from the early philologists, who depended entirely on commonality of words between Sanskrit and Indo-European languages with the movement not from East to West but from West to East. This theory dated the arrival of the Aryans at 1500 B.C. and the writing of Rigveda around 1200 B.C. For a long time, the linguistics vetoed all scientific and mathematical evidence to the contrary, i.e. the movement of languages from India westwards. As we shall discuss later the epicenter of the Indus valley civilization along with Mohanjodaro and Harappa was somewhere in the east of river Indus and along the course of the river Saraswati., The Aryan invasion theory creates an improbable hypothesis that the invading Aryans crossed all the six rivers i.e. the Indus and its five tributaries to establish themselves along a river which had gone dry almost 500 years earlier. As per this theory the chronology of the various Vedic texts would be as follows:

Chandas (Rigveda)	1200 to 1000B.C.
Mantras (Later Vedas)	1000 to 800 B.C.
Brahmans	800 to 600 B.C.
Sutras	600 to 200 B.C.

The relationship between old Avestan i.e. Zoroastrian (Persian) and Vedic Sanskrit has led to further complications, regarding the relative chronology of the Vedic Aryans vis-à-vis the Persian civilization. Let us now evaluate the new evidence. David Frawly had noted the mention of a deity named 'Himalaya' in the Kassite records of 1750 B.C. The Kassites appear in history around the time of the final desiccation of river Saraswati when the focus of the Indian civilization shifted from its basin to Ganga eastward and the political supremacy shifted from the Bharatas on the Saraswati to Magadh on the Ganga. The above facts are well-documented in Puranas and other texts. The origin of Kassites is not very clear and they may have possibly originated from the marsh lands of southern Babylonia. Some records suggest that the mouth of river Saraswati was near ancient Dwarka known earlier as Kushasthali (place of Kusha). The phonetic resemblance between Kusha and Kassites is too strong to be ignored. The Kassites having defeated the Babylonian rulers settled near the Indus site and the Himalayas under their king named Kashtiliashu and are known to have used horses and chariots. Baudhayana, a Vedic scholar who designed the spoked wheel in his mathematical works, is also documented in the *Rigveda,* thus pointing towards Indian antecedents of the Kassites. The ancient *Vendiadad* Persian text also mentions the 'hapta hendu' (Vedic 'Sapta Sindhu') .... of times when Saraswati was still flowing. A passage from *Bhavisya Purana* referring to Jarathushtra Mag later known by the name "Mag (Shaka), denotes a semblance to 'Mag Brahmins'. The word 'Mag' and 'Shaka' also stand for people of Iran as well as India. These two will suggest a linkage westward from India to Iran, which places Indian civilization much earlier to Iranian Zoroastrianism. The theory of the Aryans moving from an interior land in Eurasia, far from the sea is further rebutted by countless references to the rivers and the seas so frequent in *Rigveda* and subsequent texts.

We now return to the mathematical basis for the interpretation of our ancient civilization. The pioneer research in this regard has been carried out by Feuerstein Kak and Frawley in their book *In Search of the Cradle of Civilization* (1995), which conclusively proves the origin of all mathematics, algebra and geometry to be in ancient India. To this list of authors the most important addition would be A.B. Datta and A. Seidenberg. They repeatedly refer to Veda's texts called the 'Sulba Sutras' and its mathematics based on religious rituals. The word 'Sutra' means 'string' and the 'Sutra' works are composed in the form of a string of short statements, undoubtedly for easy memorization. Panini's masterpiece *Astadhyayi* with its cryptic statement described as 'aphorisms' by modern scholars enunciates the principles (formulae) of algebra and geometry. While 'Grhayasutra could be termed 'principles' for the householder 'Sulbasutras' meant principles of geometry, and the whole corpus contains material, both sacred and secular. The 'Grhayasutra' is a mine of useful information on architecture and mathematics. The sulba of Baudhayana, Apastambe and Katyayana with the mathematics of old Babylonia and Egypt enables us to establish 2000 B.C. as the absolute lower limit for the early 'Sutra' literature. Taking this fact along with the astronomical data from *Asvalayana Grahysutra* and other works, pushes this date back by another thousand years, the traditional date of Mahabharat War (3102 B.C.). Gradually, as the miasma of misdirected linguistics lifted under the glare of scientific evidence, the real source of all mathematics was traced to Sulba Sutras in the Vedic texts. The Pythagorean Greek, Old Babylonian and Egyptian mathematics came to be derived from a single source of *Sulbasutras.* The credit for this achievement goes entirely to A. Seidenbeg, who conclusively proved that instead of being the recipient, Vedic India was the donor of all mathematical science to the ancient world.

Seidenberg's mathematical methods clashed head on with the contemporary entrenched theory of the Aryan invasion, but he refused to compromise and stated in no uncertain terms that "the elements of ancient geometry found in Egypt and Babylonia stem from a ritual system of the kind observed in the Sulbasutras." From his profound study of Sutra literature containing the works of Baudhayana, Asvalayana, Apastamba and Katyayana, he concluded that the Sutra mathematics dated much earlier than the old Babylonian and Egyptian middle kingdom (2050-1800 B.C.), both deriving from the Sulbas. Ashvalayans's astronomical works too place the Sulba literature to around 3100 to 2600 B.C. This was the time when the star Dracoinis (also called Thuban in the constellation of Dragon) was the pole star, also mentioned in *Satpatha Brahman.*

The Sutra literature premises the pre-existence of the four Vedas, which would have been in existence much before. This date agrees with the tradition of Vyasa, who edited the four Vedas and Mahabharata (3102 B.C.). A date, which is in accordance with ancient mathematical and astronomical data. There are clear connections between the so-called Step Pyramid or the 'mastaba' (2650 B.C.) built by Djoser (2686-2613 B.C.) and Samasana-cit (cemetery shaped altar) of Baudhayana dealing with Vedic funerary rituals. The mathematical as well as religious connection between the Vedic altar and the mausoleums called the Pyramids are not accidental. We now come to the Pythagorean theorem. It was Thibaut, who first explicitly made out the case that the Pythagorean geometry derived from Vedic mathematics. This is rooted in a statement of Baudhayana that the diagonal of a rectangle produces both squares which its length and breadth produced separately.

He first tried to derive the theorem from the square noting that the diagonal produces an area twice as much as one produced by either side. A common figure in the Vedic altar is given below.

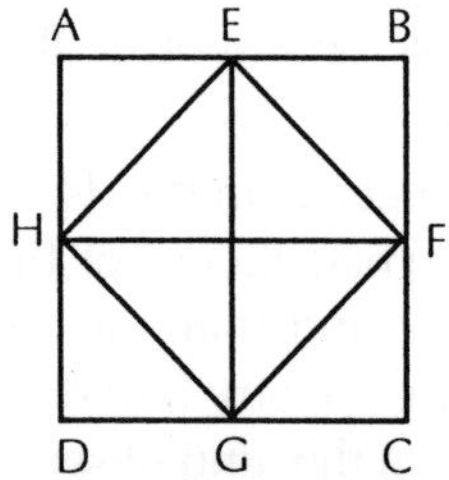

It shall be seen that the square on GF, ie GHEF has an area equal to half of the square ABCD or the total of the square on side FC and CG. Thus, Baudhayana, who derives his theorem from this figure as early as 3000 B.C. could legitimately be the father of the theorem of Pythagoras. The Greek followed this much later, in the works of Democritos (c.440 B.C.).

For the Indians and the Greeks geometry was primary, while for the Egyptians and Babylonians it resulted from arithmetic. In Vedic India geometry sub-served religion and ritual. In Babylonia and Egypt it has no such religious affiliations.

The unit fraction approximation that frequently appears in the Egyptian and Old Babylonian texts can also be traced back to the Sulbas. Consider the following:

$$\sqrt{2} = 1+1/3 + 1(3.4) - 1/3.4.34)$$

Such unit fractions appear at several places in the Sulbas too. Also the value of π used by Ahmes of Egypt (1550 B.C.) is the same as mentioned in the *Manava Sulbasutra* in precisely the same manner i.e. $\pi = 3.160.49 = 4x(8/9)^2$. This conclusively proves that Ahmes and *Manava Sulbasutra* used the same approximation or the value of π. The two examples given above leave no room for doubt that the Babylonian and Egyptian mathematics have a common source in Sulbas. We now come to the structure of the Pyramids. The Vedic altars shaped like trapezoidal figures are also found on Egyptian monuments. Two samples from *Histoire de l'art Egyptian d'apres le monuments* as given below are also found in the Sulbas.

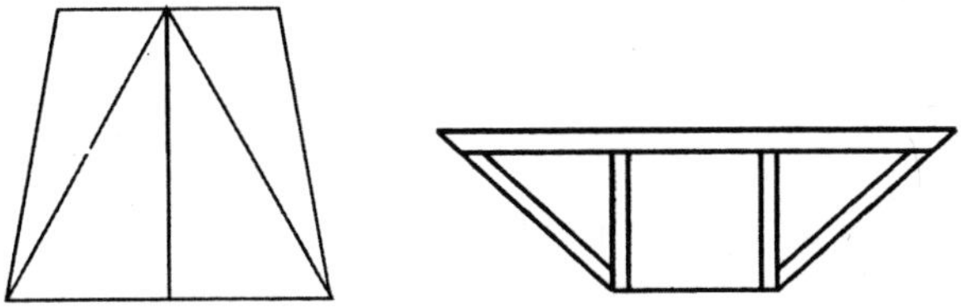

The trapezoidal shapes and their sub-division are noteworthy. The first figure is shown in *Sulbasutras* and the second dealing with computation of the area (and its proofs appears in *Apastamb Sulbasutra*). The trapezoid has connotations to health and wealth, an Indian concern, while in Egypt, they are useful in pyramid constructions.

There is also a mention in Rigveda of large numbers such as the series: 2,4,8,20,30,40,50,60,70,80,90,100 (RV,II.18.4-6). There is also mention of a limited decimal system and terms like dasa (10), sata (100), Sahasra(1000), ayuta (10,000) and 'parardha', which stand for trillion (10^{12}) are also mentioned in Yajurveda (17.2). Trisaptah which stands for various types of combinations of threes and sevens like 3+7=10; 3x7=21;

3+5=8 and others appear in the very first verse of Atharvaveda. The astronomy and Vedic mathematics are closely intermingled in Vedic texts. For example, Jupiter being the heaviest of the planets is called Guru (heavy) while Saturn, which has the slowest orbital velocity amongst all visible planets is called Shani (slow). The Rigveda also mentions the orbital period of the five major planets as well as the sun and the moon. An interesting feature of geometric algebra of Baudhayana is the construction of spoked wheels. The chariots with spoked wheels appear in West Asia around 2000 B.C., but in Rigveda they do much earlier. An interesting feature in *Baudhayana's Sulbasutra* is the ingenious method for designing the chariot wheel using the Pythogorean triples and circulature of the square as illustrated below:

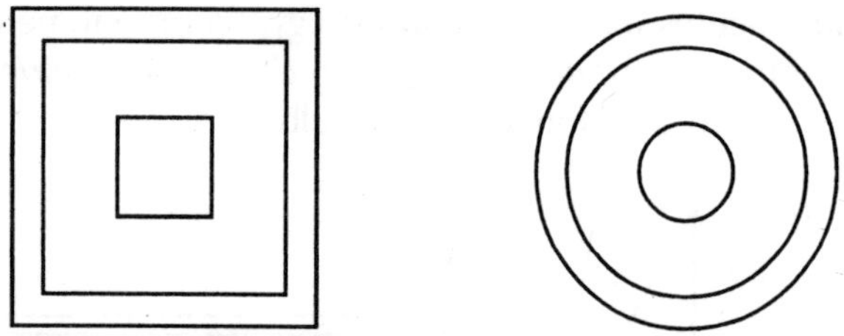

Drawing a 12x12 and 4x4 square and placing them concentrically in 17x17 square shows that the difference between 289 (17) and 144 (12) covers the felloe of the wheel. By converting the outer (17x17) square into a circle using the Sulba method and then repeating the procedure with the interior 12x12 square and removing it the result makes up the outer and inner boundaries of the felloe. Converting the 4x4 square into a circle makes it the hub. The area left for the spokes became 144-16=128. Since half of 128 is 64 one should place eight spokes in each one of them. Though easy it is an amazing conclusion.

The spoked wheel which played an important role in ancient history will now appear to be born out of the mathematics of the Sulba, dealing with the construction of altars and circling of the square. The inverse problem of squaring the circle was a further refinement. Thus, there should be no doubt in the mind of any serious student of ancient history that all mathematics, geometric and algebraic knowledge disseminated from Vedic India westwards.

We should now return to astronomy and its related chronology highlighting some vital chronological landmarks and relate them to archaeological finds, which taking mathematics into account shall help us, to arrive at a chronological synthesis. Very few identifiable archaeological remains are available that relate to the Vedic periods but the oral evidence is vast and unimpeachable. Frenchman Jean Le Mee a modern student of Vedic time states:

> "Precious stones or durable materials- gold, silver, bronze, marble, onyx or granite have been used by most ancient people in an attempt to immortalize their achievements. Not so however the Aryans. They turned what may seem the most volatile and insubstantial material for all the spoken word- and out of this bubble of air fashioned a monument, which for more than thirty perhaps forty centuries later stands untouched by time or the element... The pyramids have been eroded by the desert wind, the marble broken by earthquakes, and the gold stolen by robbers, while the Veda is recited daily by an unbroken chain of generations, travelling like a great wave through the living substance of mind".

The Arabs are generally credited with the first knowledge of astronomy. The western thinking on the "Semitic source" of astronomy is contradicted by a statement of the Spanish Arab astronomeı Sa'id Al-Andalusi himself, known also as Qadi-Sa'id (1029-1070BCE), who said:

> "Of the Indian astronomical systems, the three that are well known are the Sindhind ... the Arjbadha....and the Arkand... we have received correct information only about the Sindhind system, which was adopted and further developed by a group of Muslim scientists"

"Sindhind is Sinddanta or Surya Siddhanta and Arjbagh appears to be the Arabic distortion of the name of the great Astronomer Aryabhatta". The theory propounded by Keith that Indians borrowed their astronomy from the Arabs can again be contradicted on sound technical reasons. The equinoctial position of Western Zodiac is identical to that of Varahmihira (500 B.C.) but is no longer the same today due to the shift of the equinoxes. However, the Middle Eastern "Tropical" Zodiac of the West remained frozen and did not account for the precession of the equinoxes, while the solstices and equinoxes have regressed by about 23 degrees, a fact known to Hindu astronomers and Panchang (Calendar). Corrections required in the Indian calendar based on the motion of the sun and moon through the fixed stars are a vital achievement of the Indian astronomy dating back to 4000 B.C. Thus it would have been impossible to fix the Indian sidereal Zodiac of 27 Nakshatras by a reverse calculation, since the orientation of the Zodiac requires continued correction for the precession. This effort would require a thorough knowledge of the Law of Gravitation and differential equations. Later day astronomers could not have worked out such a data stretching thousands of years merely by borrowing and superimposing upon a later Zodiacal system.

The Indian Zodiac consists of 27 approximately equal parts, each measuring 13° 20′ of arc, and while the solar Zodiac is related to the seasons with respect to a fixed star, the 27 Nakshatras (constellations or 'lunar mansions') indicate the progress of the lunar month and the movement of the sun along its ecliptic annual solar orbit. The start of a particular season is worked out by the entry of the sun, i.e. noting the sunrise, in a particular constellation. The seventh Mandala of the Rigveda mentions vernal equinox in Mrigashira, indicating a date near 4000 B.C. A landmark date when the sun entered the constellation Krittika (Pleiades in Taurus) indicates an era that lasted about a thousand years after 3000 B.C. The Satapatha Brahmana also specify Krittika heralding the vernal equinox, which proves this date to lie between 2900 and 1900 B.C. Both Satapatha and early Sutrakara Asvalayana record sighting of a pole star, possibly a Draconis (c.3000 B.C. to c.2500 B.C.). The three constellations relevant for our purpose with their Indian and modern names are given below:

Mrigashira or the Orion	**c. 4500-3500 B.C. Rigveda**
Rohini or the Aldebaran	**3100 B.C. (Transition) Mahabharata**
Krittika or the Pleiades	**c.2900-1900 B.C. Sutra and Brahmana**

As per tradition Asvalayana was born around 3000-2900 B.C. following the five generations after the Mahabharat war during the Krittika equinox. The Egyptian mathematics and Sulba point 2000 B.C. as a date much later than the Sutra period and thus, there is the convergence between the two evidences. *Satapatha Brahmana* also indicates Yajnavalkya's birth about three generations following the Mahabharat war very near to the time of Asvalayana, thereby proving that the Brahmana and the Sutra periods did overlap. This fact receives a confirmation from the observation of the pole star mentioned in *Satapatha Brahmana* and *Asvalayana Grihyasutra*. "Dhruva star" the "unmoving" (literally meaning 'certain') is so important that it is shown to a newly married couple to enjoin constancy. The present α-Ursa Minoris (Polaris), a star of second magnitude that indicates the north pole today did not do so in ancient times. Since the orientation of the North Pole moves with the precession of the equinoxes, during much of human history there has not been a pole star. The fact that *Asvalayana* and *Satapatha Brahmana* do mention the pole star, an observable pole star, is a matter of great chronological significance. Our evidence thus far indicates 3000-2500 B.C. as the period of the earliest portion of the Sutra literature. This also brings the date of the Mahabharat war to the traditional 3102 B.C. The Greek chroniclers after Alexander's invasion of India were aware of the date of Krishna, the principal figure in Mahabharat. The evidence, however, is confusing when it comes to Sandrocottos-Chandragupta's identity. Pliny refers to Krishna as Hercacles, a word derived from Hari Krishna. He also mentioned that Krishna was held in high esteem by the Sourseni (Present 'Suraseni') tribe living around Mathora now known as Mathura. Sourseni, (read Sura), was the father of Vasudeva. Krishna or Heracles according to Greek records is said to have lived 138 generations before the time of Alexander (325 B.C.). At a rough estimate of 20 years for each generation, a good average by any standards, this leads to 2760 +325 i.e. 3058 B.C. as the date of Krishna, which tallies with the beginning of Kaliyug from 3102 B.C. onwards. While the chronology of the West and leftist Indian historians is based on "a conjecture supported by other conjectures" as Sri Aurbindo put it our method has been entirely based on mathematics and science. Thus the Mahabharata war preceded the Harappan civilization. With so many present day relics, such as Hastinapur, Kurukshetra, Indraprastha and Dwarika it is difficult to believe that the knowledge of cities and town planning was not passed down from the Mahabharata era to the later day Harappan civilization.

Let us now sidestep a little to have a deeper look in to the Puranic chronology. The Adiparva of Mahabharata mentions a period of 630 years between Sudas and Arjuna. With a date of 3100 B.C. for Mahabharata, according to the method used by Hicks and Anderson in their work, the date for Sudas and the battle of 10 kings would come to 3730 B.C.

(Continued)

Proposed Chronology
of
Ancient Indian and Contemporaneous Civilizations

Date	Geography: Clim. le	Astronomical Era	Technology	Indian Hist ry	Indian History (Periods)	Indian Literature	Indian Authors; Kings	Mesopotamia	Egypt: (Elsewhere)
9000	Ice Age								
8000	Ice Melts								
7000				Mehgarh					
6500				Horse					
4500		Mrgasiras (Orion)		Mandhatr fights Druhyus					
4000					Early Vedic	*Rg Veda*	Atri		
3800				Decline of Rg Vedic world					
3700			Silver Purification of Copper	Battle of Ten Kings			Sudas Visvamitra Vasistha		
3600					Late Vedic	*Yajur Veda* *Sdma Veda* *Atharva Veda*			
3500	Sarasvati perennial	Rohini (Aldebaran)							
3100	Sarasvati loses Yamuna Desert divides east-west			Kali Yuga Mahabharata War Vedas canonized	Post-Vedic	*Mahabharata*	Vyasa, Krishna		

3000	Desert expands Flooding	Krttika (Pleiades) era reckoning	Cotton	Harappa Mohenjodaro vajasaneyi orthodoxy (east) Taittiriya heterodoxy (west)	Late Brahmanic Early Sutric	*Satapatha* *Brahmana* *Sulbasutras* *Asthadhyai* *Nirukta*	Yajnavalkya Baudhayana Apastamaba Katyayana Panini Asvalayana Yaska		
2900				Vedic altars				Rise of sumer Rise of Akkad	Old Kingdom Mastabas Pyramids Zoser Snerfu Imhotep
2200	Major drought begins		Decline of Harappa					End of Akkad	
2100									
2050								Horse	
2000	Sarasvati loses Sutlej				End of sutric period				Middle Kingdom
1950									
1900	Sarasvati dry			Harappa ends				Old Babylonia	
1750									(Zoroaster)
1550								Kassites Spoked wheel Chariot	New Kingdom Ahmose

The Puranas mention the passage of about 31 generations between Rama of Ikshvaku dynasty and son of Dasharatha, upto Brihadabala in Mahabharata records. Brihadabala was slain by Abhimanyu, Arjun's son, at Kurukshetra. Again computing on the basis of 20 years per generation we come to a date of between 3800 and 3700 B.C. for Rama. This date is further confirmed by the fact that Vashistha a senior contemporary of Rama was also present at the Battle of 10 Kings. To sum up in David Frawley's terms, the chronology of the Vedic age would be as given below:

Proto-Rigvedic Period	**Around 8000 BC and before 6000 B.C.**
Early Rigvedic Period	**6000 to 4000 B.C.**
Later Rigvedic Period	**4000 to 2000 B.C.**
Transitional	**2000 to 1000 B.C.**

A chart showing a proposed chronology of ancient Indian and contemporary civilizations is given in the chart opposite. *(Vedic Aryans and Origins of Civilization- A literary and scientific perspective* – By N.S. Raja Ram and David Frawley).

Let us now deal with the scientific evidence. Domestication of the horse was perfected in India well before it was done in Central Asia and South Russian steppes around 4000 B.C. Along with the recent findings of S.R. Rao, a marine archaeologist, at the site of Dwarika the above date is further confirmed. There is a mention of gold in Rigveda but not of silver, which should have come after the Rigvedic period. The above facts are in accordance with astronomical and geographical data particularly the record of vernal equinox in Orion and the perennial Saraswati- both facts being mentioned in the Seventh mandala of the Rigveda. The above together with the evidence of astronomy and the Sulbas and Egyptian mathematics, all independent determinations, indicate the same period of i.e. 4000 B.C. for the ending of the Rigvedic age, The archaeological remains found at Mehrgarh and other places in Gujarat and elsewhere alongwith the submerged city of Dwarika discovered recently date the earlier Indian civilization as far back as 7000 B.C. With more research in charting the river Saraswati and it's dessication leading to the shift of ancient civilization from the centre of Saraswati-Drishadvati doab to the south west, more convincing evidence will emerge on the Rigvedic society and our ancient settlements. The ecological disruptions in the Saraswati basin led to the move of that civilization eastword to the Ganga valley and south westward into Gujarat and Maharashtra. What further proof of this movement is required than the fact that both Baudhayana and Apsthamba belong to the south? While this dichotomy further explains the Yajurvedic tradition into Vajasaneya and the Taittreya schools, it also proves that the so-called Aryans and Dravidian divide is so much historical humbug. Sethna from his laborious works brings out the fact that cotton was a commodity of daily use in the Harappan times. The Vedas and Brahmanas also mention the making of cloth, and terms like weaving, war, and weft. The discovery of Indian cotton in Peru during 2500 B.C. and even earlier in Mexico accords with the common usage of the cotton and its extensive trading abroad and across the seas during the Vedic period. Further findings, tested with calibrated C-14 methods, show that 'the Harappan culture should be dated to the period 2700-2000 B.C. This along with the fact of climatic change of 2200 B.C. recently discovered explain the sudden ending of the Accadian empire and the shift of Saraswati based civilization to the east and confirms the data brought out thus far. We now come to the question of silver when did it come to India? It was well known to the Harappans but not the Rigveda. The use of silver in other parts of world goes back to 5000 B.C. This is not a certified fact. Silver as we know is not mined in pure state but is separated from copper after a purification process of the latter. The discovery of the silver ornaments at the Pre-Harappan site of Kunal near Ambala points to a date not later than 2000 B.C. With the application of dendrochronology as practised by European archaeologists such as Colin Renfrew that date could go back to 4000 B.C., several centuries before the Vedic people had learnt to separate silver from copper ore. In 1958, a famous casting known as "Vashistha's head" was discovered by Hary Hicks, an American collector.

Subsequent metallurgical tests have shown a high silver content which points to the art of casting of an ancient era. Laboratory tests in California and Zurich on this artifect showed carbon deposits, which according to Radio Carbon dating leads to a date between 3800 and 3700 B.C. This conclusively proves that the Vedic age should have ended well before this time. This is also corroborated by Mrigashira vernal equinox, which dates closer to 4000 B.C. With the evidence adduced thus far the brief chronology of events can be inferred. Close to the end of the last Ice Age before 8000 B.C., the river Saraswati, the greatest in India started flowing from the mountains to the sea around 7000 B.C. during the Rigvedic age.

It remained a mighty river joined by two other great rivers, the Satluj and the Yamuna, which followed the course of the dry river Drishadavati. This was the situation around 4000 B.C., when North India was watered by the three major river systems of the Indus, Saraswati and the Ganga. There was no Thar Desert separating the regions as it is today. Astronomically this was the Mrigashira era. Sometime around 3100 B.C., when the great Mahabharata took place the Yamuna changed its course to empty itself into the Ganga resulting in the diversion of the waters from Saraswati, which gradually dried up. The expanding desert began to separate the western people and their Sindhu-Sauvira culture from the Kuru heartland around the Ganga. The desiccation of Saraswati along with recurring floods resulted in the shift of the heart of the Vedic religious praxis eastward to the Kuru-Panchala territory adding to the alienation between the east and the west. These were the times of the rise of the Sumerian civilization and the Sutra period, when the western people were derisively called 'Melcchas' by the orthodox of the Vedic heartland. Subsequently, a center of Vedic tradition grew up in the Gujarat – Maharashtra region anchored on Taittiriya thought led by Baudhayana. While the Vajasaneya school of Yajyavalkya settled in the east, the Yajurvedic tradition as brought out earlier was split into its northern and southern components following the Mahabharata war. The desert continued to encroach on the river Indus and the Harappan civilization, a branch of the main Vedic heartland around Ganga, and along with the drying up of river Saraswati caused the extinction of the Indus valley civilization.

As these lines are being written, a land-mark discovery in the Gulf of Cambay by a team of oceanographers followed by the combined efforts of National Institute of Ocean Technology, the Birbal Sahani Institute of Palaeobotany and the National Geophysical Research Institute, has conclusively proved the existence of a civilization in that area much before the Harappan and contemporary civilizations in Egypt, Sumeria and Babylon. Artifects such as construction material, wood with holes and studs, pot shreds, beads and fossil bones, after the process of carbon dating, point to a date around 7500 B.C., almost the same as the proto-Vedic civilization that came into existence after the melting of the Ice Cap around 8000 B.C., as discussed earlier. Professor S.N. Rajguru, former Joint Director and Head of Department of Archaeology at Deccan College, said, "These collections represent an exciting breakthrough in offshore archaeology. The findings indicate that the entire landscape between Bhavnagar and Hazira were probably connected around 7000 B.C.

The acoustic images of the area present channel like features, indicating the presence of a river in the region. "Geometrical structures and the antiquities have been discovered in an area only within 200 miles adjoining the channel indicating human activity on the banks of the river that was present at that time".

These findings also conclusively prove the existence of river Saraswati in the early Vedic period and its subsequent desiccation. The above effort by the National Institute of Ocean Technology (NIOT), which led to an accidental discovery of this sub-merged township was further supplemented by the following factoid published in many Indian news magazines.

The town lay at a depth of 40 meters below the sea, 30 kms off the Gujarat coast and the dredging efforts spread to an area of nine kms, situated on the mouth of a river with signs of a masonry dam. Geometric forms like those at Harappa in various forms and sizes were found. An Olympic size sunken area with steps going down as for a swimming pool and resembling the great bath of Mohenjodaro was discovered, through photographs and sonar soundings. Rectangular platform of 200x45 meters, almost the same size as the Acropolis in Greece, was also found as earlier in Harappa. A large granary structure made out of mud 185 meters long could also be seen. As part of this township rectangular basement resembling remains of homesteads and tiles of a drainage system and mud roads too were found. About 2000 artifects including polished stones, tools, ornaments, figurines, broken pottery, some precious stones, ivory and remains of human vertebra, jawbone and human tooth were also found. But the clinching evidence of antiquity was provided by a fossilized log of chopped wood that dated back to 7500 B.C. The only other settlement of this antiquity was found earlier at Mehargarh in Baluchistan, which was basically an agricultural settlement in the Bolan river valley.

We shall sum up by stating that the entire linguistic, literary, mathematical, scientific, archaeological, metallurgical, carbon, radio, and ecological evidence, which we have listed in some detail, points to the indisputable facts that that there was no Aryan invasion, which led to an Aryan-Dravidian divide; that Sanskrit was the mother of all Indo-European languages; that all knowledge, mathematical, scientific, astronomical, medical (Ayurvedic) and literary flowed from India westwards and not the other way round; and that ancient Vedic civilization the oldest in the world, had reached a very high level of perfection known to mankind.

Chapter 18

The Fall from Grace

Mention has been made earlier of the legacy of the three M's avidly followed by Nehru and his dynasty, his camp followers led by Leftists, Congressmen and the Jawaharlal Nehru University (JNU) school of thought, all aimed at vilifying Hindus and their culture.

Hindus can rightly be proud of their oldest culture and Sanskrit, which is the mother of all languages. Hindu philosophy has formed the basic foundation for the development of Greek mythology and Celtic thought as pointed out by a French Indologist, Guy Deleury, who mentions that the above two cultures in turn led to the flowering of all the European cultures. In fact, we all know that the discovery of atomic nature and zero concept originated from India, but what is not so well known is that the Egyptians used Hindu arithmetical concept to build their pyramids and that Hindu mathematicians inspired Pythagorean theorem. An 18th century French astronomer Jean Claude Bailly had remarked that Hindu calculation of the position of the stars and of solar eclipses were so precise that we are still using them today. In 'The Ferengi's column' titled "Hindus: majority yet minority" contributed by Francois Gautier in the *Indian Express,* he makes certain startling observations, which should make all right thinking Indians to sit up and think. Some of excerpts:

"Thus the Hindus, inheritors of an immense, noble and age-old culture, constitute 85 percent of India and represent the social, religious and cultural majority of this emerging Asian superpower of the 21st century. And yet, their voice is rarely heard in India. They are respected neither in home, nor abroad, and they generally lack self confidence."

"Could it be that Hindus are a psychological minority in India whereas minorities, such as the Christians, which constitute only 3 percent of the population, wield an enormous moral power in this country...."

To quote further:

"All European children, Italian or German, are brought up on Christian values and Greek philosophy. It would be impossible, in France for instance, for the Muslim minority-immigrants from French ex-colonies such as Algeria or Morocco to impose their views and culture on the government. In fact, Muslim girls are not allowed to wear a veil when they go to French schools; ' you are in France, you have been given the French nationality, so behave like a French first, and like a Muslim second', they are told bluntly."

And he makes a point further:

"Would that be possible in India? Would any Indian, except the much-maligned RSS (Rashtriya Swayam Sevak Sangh), have the courage to ask Muslims to be Indians first, and Muslim second? Or tell Catholics and Protestants that they have to revert to a more Indianised Christianity, such as the one that existed in Kerala before the arrival of the Portuguese Jesuits? And see how stridently Muslims and Christians backed by most of the media react when the Human Resource Minister, Dr. Murli Manohar Joshi, wants to teach Indian children a little bit of the greatness of their culture.

"There are two sets of standards used in India amongst intellectuals; one for the Christians or the Muslims; and one for the Hindus. When the Australian missionary Graham Staines and his two sons were killed the Indian and foreign press spent weeks – if not months – in eulogizing Graham and making Nazis of all Hindus held responsible for his murder. But if a few days later 20 labourers, as innocent as Stains' two sons, are savagely assassinated by separatists in Kashmir, it will only warrant a few lines in Indian newspapers, without any of the outraged comments, which followed Stains' murder."

Thus, he leaves no doubt on his proposition and adds:

"When the Ayodhya mosque was brought down, it was as if eternal shame had descended upon India. 'Death of Secularism', 'Hindu fundamentalists have taken over the country', ' a Black Day in the history of our democracy', the newspapers screamed. However unfortunate the Ayodhya episode was, nobody was killed there, but the terrible Bombay blasts, which followed, orchestrated by Indian Muslims, with the active help of Pakistan and the silent approval of Saudi Arabia, which took the life of hundreds of innocent Hindus, never warranted the kind of moral indignation, which followed Ayodhya".

And he goes on:

"Hindus are, ironically, chased from their own ancestral lands. There were one million of them in Kashmir in 1900 but only a few hundred today, the rest having been made to flee through terror. In the North East, Hindus are being outnumbered by Bangladeshi illegal immigrants and terrorized by pro-Christian separatist groups, such as the Bodos or the Mizos."

And then on the Hindu psyche he says:

"In Karnataka, a bill will bring more than 43,000 Hindu shrines and matthas under the Commissioner's control. This act does not apply to Christians and Muslims. The Indian Government still sponsors the Haj pilgrimage".

And finally his advice:

"Hindus should become a little prouder of themselves; there is ample talents and brains in India today. Hindu children regularly top their schools and universities in the US, they are the best programmers of this planet and are amongst the richest people in the UK, the US or Canada. Why cannot the majority of this marvelous diverse, ancient and extraordinary country stop behaving as if it was a moral minority?"

Tell this to the leftists, their fellow travellers, the worthies of the JNU, the "secularists," Congress Brigade, our Friday Club chatterati of the India International Centre and the Samajvadi Party zealots and they will squirm in their seats.

Besides being a majority with a total loss of self-esteem another trait in our national character is the tendency to genuflect to everything, western, our English print media be praised. Unlike Indian leaders, who lay a red carpet for the Western visitors and even the non-descript Under Secretaries from the U.S. State Department, the other Asian countries behave differently and we should learn how they treat them. The facts would be revealing. The Chinese accept unlimited foreign aid and technology from Europe and the United State of America. But they do it on their own terms, and having extracted the maximum benefit of foreign investment and trade, show them the way out. Even senior bureaucrats and businessmen have to cool their heels before they can meet someone in the Chinese bureaucracy. The Chinese in a more subtle way show them their place, treating them with cultural disdain. Much to the embarrassment of the white men they are not even given fixed tenures in the Japanese Universities. Malaysia, while accepting foreign direct investment (FDI) shows no eagerness to borrow western cultural values of a dying species against their own Asian values. In spite of a deceptive facade and mannerism their core remains basically Asian with impenetrable cultural walls. Tokyo and Seoul have absorbed modern industrial development but kept their ethnic identity intact. The western historians and ideologues are baffled at this phenomenon and find them-selves at sea when they observe this clash of civilizations and cultures. There is a fundamental chasm between the American civilization with its high emphasis on material progress, consumerism and social disarray against Asia's social institutions and value systems. As opposed to this the Indians take Europeans and Americans a bit too seriously and ape in undignified imitation all that is western. The gullible amongst us have tried to graft western images on their eastern roots and native thought. Sooner or later the asymmetry is bound to prove a disaster, resulting in a clash of civilizations as foretold by Professor Huntington. Our colonial experience has coloured our perception and left a permanent Anglophylic psyche amongst our intelligentsia.

No nation can ape its way to greatness. Our motto should be, "Do not preach to your enemies; first copy their nasty habits, if they look effective. They will then treat you with circumspection." This is more than true of the militant activities and terrorism in Kashmir and the rest of the country spawned by the Inter Services Intelligence (ISI) of Pakistan, the terrorism let loose by Lashkare-Toiba and its ilk. Unfortunately, Indians in general and our leaders in particular wish to be loved and are susceptible to international flattery. These are serious handicaps both in human and international relations. With all our pleadings and wish to placate the US administration, they will scarce take notice of us at the cost of their strategic perceptions and national interests. The US in particular respects a bully as is evident from their different approaches to India and China. Toughness pays as it has done in the case of Israel. In the same vein, though in a different context, our great national poet, Ramdhari Singh 'Dinkar' wrote :

Kshama Shobhati Us Bhujang ko jiske Pas Garal ho.
Usko Kya jo Dantheen Vishheen Vineet Saral ho.

Literally meaning that 'forgiveness befits the snake with poison in its fangs; it is meaningless for one, which is toothless, poison-less, humble and simple.' The Hindu race suffers from this congenital weakness.

The Jews though small in numbers were never a walk- over for the invaders. They behaved like a porcupine deterring any beast of prey. Unfortunately, India though much larger and better endowed, through its pacifist outlook developed into a soft state, which over the ages became easy prey for prowling invaders and armed adventurers. The country is still suffering from the same syndrome. Even today with hostile neighbours all around, with persistent offers of peace against a congenitally hostile and inimical country like Pakistan, which spares no effort to dismember and disintegrate our country, our leadership keeps on hoping against hope that Pakistan will reciprocate in a similar manner. Such a posture encourages further intrusion and cross-border terrorism into our territories eating at the very vitals of our national integrity with loss of precious lives and a feeling of insecurity. Thus, India has forgotten the basic lesson that its national interest can never be served by an impression of a weak and soft state. While Pakistan has a free run in our country, we have no such plan for today or tomorrow. No wonder our armed forces today operating in such regions are totally demoralized with constant extensions of cease-fire and overtures of peace. This is not what Lord Krishna had taught us and the basic tenets of our Vedas are, which propound:

> *"AGRATE CHATURO VEDA PRISHTHATE SASHURAM DHANU"*

Which means, 'keep the four Vedas in front but keep your bow and arrow behind'. In simpler terms, while we can reason and negotiate, we should also have our weapons ready, should the other party refuse to play ball. The world does not respect a weak nation, least of all a bully like Pakistan. Unfortunately, we have, in spirit and substance, developed into a weak state. This is the one area where we should learn from the Jews and their history.

Why did the Jews fight, when the odds were heavily stacked against them, and there was an easier way out, to submit and survive rather than fight huge armies of Greece and Rome with tiny forces at their command? Six million Jews died fighting Romans only resulting in destruction and devastation all around. They chose to adhere to their faith rather than succumb to expediency and adopt discretion as the better part of valour. They could have submitted politely and forsaken their faith. That was the wisdom of the worldly. However, the Jews were made of sterner stuff and they protected their faith and law with stubbornness unheard of in human history. Not atavistic by nature like the followers of Islam, the Jews like Hindus, could adept to changes while keeping their core of spirituality untouched. This flexibility of Jewish mind is reflected in the fact that the largest number of political figures, visionaries', poets and scientists in the world came from the Jewish stock.

Recent secularists and leftist historians in India have criticized Maharana Pratap for carrying his fight against Mughals to a disastrous extreme, causing destruction and devastation all round and the loss of his kingdom of Mewar. But Pratap thought differently. To him his faith was more important than his kingdom. He believed that compromise is the weapon of the weak, and great nations are not made that way. Likewise, Jews did not submit, they fought. Dying by the millions they kept their faith with their Lord.

This tenacity to stick to one's faith is not confined to the Jews. It is inspiring to find that the oldest religion in the world Sanatan Dharma still dominates the largest section of humanity in our country. At the site of Maha Kumbh, which showcases the tradition, culture and civilization of this land the sight of Dharam Sansad, naked Sadhus, devotees and a sea of ordinary poor and illiterate humanity taking a holy dip in the Sangam at Prayag in the freezing temperature of 2.5 degree Celsius at the break of dawn should be enough to convince even the worst cynic and our so-called rationalists about the deep roots of our culture and the staying power of our faith. On 25th January, 2001, on the occasion of Mauni Amavasya, in the chilly cold in the morning darkness, a total of thirty million people took their dip in the sacred Sangam. This number is higher than the total population of the ¾th of the countries of the world. There is something in our culture that defies explanation. Ancient civilizations like India and Israel live on their faith defying all logic of history. Great nations like India and Israel not only endure but prevail.

But let us add a footnote, how the sublime can be reduced to the ridiculous. Instead of understanding the abiding faith of the multitudes in our religion and its praxis with such fervour, the Western media, which covered the Mahakumbh at Prayagraj could only find the naked Sadhus and half-naked women, taking the holy dip, of any photographic interest. Such is the perversion of our educated elite and the so-called civilized Western media. Rather than emphasizing the spirit of the event the so-called literatti could only focus on such trivia, which to them, was better news than the underlying eternal spirit of the great Sanatan Dharma, the life-thread of the Hindus, who constitute 85 percent of the population of this country.

A lack of attachment to the symbols of our national honour is a failing that afflicts a large part of our intelligentsia. No institution is immune to this virus of cynicism.

We as a people are proving ourselves to be a nation of somnolent conscience that occasionally splutters, sleep walks and then subsides into an unseemly slumber again. Such a society has never produced a great leader or a nation. We are not even aware of our duties, while we keep on demanding our rights by all possible means. It is the Western mindset, which emphasizes the rights at the expense of duty. Our scriptures and culture teach just the opposite. For us action and duty is more important than the right. That is the message of the Gita. Article 51 A of our Constitution lays down the singing of the National Anthem as a fundamental duty. But strangely, in a reference to the Supreme Court on this issue, the highest judicial authority of the country decided that discretion is the better part of valour and refused to give a substantive decision. Contrast this with the spirit of Israelis who during the freedom struggle gladly climbed the gallows and put the noose round the neck singing "Hatikvah". Our freedom fighters too sang "Vande Mataram", while gladly embracing death.

While the Jews throughout their existence had to struggle hard to retain or regain their Promised Land, the Hindus inherited a sub-continental mass without any effort. It was a gift of nature's bounty and history. As history unfolded itself countless invaders, ruthless marauders and soldiers of fortune and those in search of a kingdom invaded our country and met unexpected success despite larger armies opposing them. This was due to the fact that Hindus took the gift of nature and their land for granted. This is the fundamental difference of approach between Jews and Hindus towards their land. The Hindus could never develop the same attachment and zeal for their native soil as the Jews did. The early Huns, Sakas and Mongols, and later the Turks, the Mughals and finally the British all had a free run of our country and the population stood a mute onlooker as the aggressor established himself on our soil. Even today, we lack that indestructible bond with our land. There are innumerable cases, where our politicians have gifted our land away to our neighbours for ephemeral gains. Starting from Beru Bari and Tis Bigha in Bengal, they allowed vast territories to be occupied by the Chinese by force in 1962. Subsequently, they gave back the strategic battle gains like the Haji Pir Pass after the 1965 war to Pakistan and finally the whole territory conquered in the west during the 1971 war against them. Even at the birth of our country, Nehru gave on a clean plate one-third of the state of Jammu and Kashmir to the tribal invaders led by Pak Army soldiers by calling for a premature cease-fire and referring the case to the United Nations.

Even today, there is an illegal infiltration of population and enemy agents into the eastern states from Bangladesh and Nepal abetted and aided by the ISI in Pakistan. This ingress continues unabated leading to a total demographic change in the map of Assam and the neighbouring states. In the United States, there is a constant search of and surveillance on the illegal immigrants and aliens and they are regularly detected, de-franchised, and deported without much ado. But in our country, there is an unending stream of illegal immigrants in North Eastern States and West Bengal, which has not been stopped till today, thanks to the politics of vote banks of our worthy-politicians. This lack of attachment to the land endemic to our culture and an effete leadership has persisted down the ages. Even the independence that we got from the British in 1947 did not change this basic impulse. This love of the land is the one single most important lesson that we must learn from the Israelis. We as citizens of this sacred land owe it to ourselves, in spite of our politicians. India is a free country, free to be intruded in and free to settle in. There are few disabling provisions in our immigration laws, and fewer still for the sanctity of our borders, and none whatsoever in the enforcement of these.

If this process of Open Door Policy continues the demographic pattern of the border states of West Bengal and Assam will change drastically. In fact, Assam will become the second Muslim majority state in India after Jammu and Kashmir.

One Night, 15th/16th April, 2001, a force of 30 armoured personnel carriers supported by a brigade strength of Bangladesh Army assisted Bangladesh Rifles to intrude in the territory controlled by a post of 106 BSF Battalion at Pyrdiwah, Meghalaya, on Indo-Bangladesh border. This operation was accompanied by similar attacks at the villages of Boraibari and Mankachar. It was a meticulously planned operation, launched by the Director General of Bangladesh Rifles (BDR). Maj Gen Fazalur Rahman, nick-named as the 'local Napoleon', a hard- core Islamic fundamentalist. While our mandarins at the Ministry of External Affairs described him as acting without the permission of Prime Minister Sheikh Hasina, the fact strains credulity. To ease this pressure, the B.S.F. troops at Golaibari village sent out a strong patrol inside Bangladesh territory where a BDR force was waiting for ambush. In the encircling operation 19 B.S.F. jawans were captured and taken away to captivity. Local Bangladeshi villagers also activily helped their troops while other villagers residing in the Indian territory looked silently on. It was obvious to the most naive that any Bangladesh Rifles operation could not be assisted by the regular Army without the knowledge of the Army High Command and the consent of the Prime Minister.

Sixteen bodies of the captured B.S.F. jawans mutilated beyond recognition, badly burnt with eyes gouged and carrying brutal custodial injury marks were returned to our border forces on 22nd April, 2001. They were spread-eagled and tied on poles in public view as common criminals and their dead bodies paraded as war trophies. It is incredible that our national leadership was so puissant that instead of taking retaliatory military action the Prime Minister on April 22, only expressed his deep sense of "hurt and anguish" over the barbaric torture of our jawans in captivity and gave a clean chit to the Bangladesh Government even before extracting a 'regret' not to say 'apology' from Prime Minister Sheikh Hasina.

There was no resolve to demand war reparations, the compensation for the damage of village properties and the 16 valuable lives lost. The matter seems to have ended with the Bangladesh Prime Minister promising to investigate the matter. While all the national newspapers screamed for revenge and the nation was seething with rage, imploring our leadership to act and not to genuflect, against this act of barbarism, their response was nothing but pusillanimous. A country, which cannot protect its citizens and avenge the death of its soldiers has no right to call itself a nation. The world has no respect for a sissy. A weak nation can neither win diplomatic points and the respect of nations, nor can have any true friends. The weak-kneed response of our Government, to say the least, to this barbaric act is shocking. If our aim was to ensure the political survival of Sheikh Hasina, who is weak enough to fail in controlling the anti-Indian elements in her territory, her continuation in power would be of no political advantage to our country. It is better to have a known enemy than a weak friend, who can neither be trusted nor expected to address our legitimate concerns. We were fooled by Pakistan at Shimla, and now we were fooled again by Bangladesh. The civilizational identity of Bangladesh as an Islamic country is not different from Pakistan. Despite our gift of freedom for erstwhile East Pakistan with the blood of our jawans, Bangladesh remains ungrateful. Soon after the surrender of Pak forces in Dhaka on 16th December, 1971, I flew to Dhaka as part of the vanguard of a Civil Affairs Team to the State capital to revitalize the economy of the devastated country, restore its rail, road, telecommunications, kick start its industry, rehabilitate the refugees returning home and establish a semblance of effective governance. But for all this hard work we put in, some times frustrating, we got no thanks. Even before I flew out of Dhaka back to Delhi on 26th February, 1972, there was a large section of Bangladesh population, which was openly hostile to India and our presence there. It has become worse over the years. The rationale for the existence of Bangladesh or erstwhile East Pakistan remains the same, as it is for Pakistan "Two Nation" theory and nationality based on religion. We should not fool ourselves into the belief that Bangladesh is and will remain friendly to us. There are already reports of incursion of Bangladesh into our eastern borders, as is happening in the west in Jammu and Kashmir, and from the north through Nepal, the ISI being the principal instigator of this armed subversion.

With the victory of Bangladesh National Party headed by Begum Khalida Zia, things are going to get verse. Already there were reports of minority bashing in Bangladesh and the leaders of minority community had appealed to the Government to ensure that they were allowed to celebrate Durga Puja in peace and tranquillity without interference from criminals and fundamentalists.

Under the Muslim fundamentalists and the cheer leaders of the new government, atrocities on Hindu minorities have increased manifold. About 702335 hectares of land and 22835 Hindu homes have been forcibly confiscated and the occupants rendered homeless. The common refrain of the BNP is "Ekta ekta Hindu Dhar, Hindu Dhare tiffin kar" i.e. catch the Hindus and chew them. The future forebodes even worse.

We have tried to stick to our premise to restrict our study of the vast Indian history to only the special points of emphasis where distortions have been deliberately slipped in by our so-called eminent historians mentioned earlier. India woke up from its slumber of slavery in the beginning of twentieth century and through various stages of awakening of national conscience, and struggle for freedom. India was lucky in its gift of outstanding leaders like Bal Gangadhar Tilak, Gopal Krishna Gokhale, Lala Lajpat Rai, Bipin Chandra Pal, the father of the nation, Mahatma Gandhi, Sardar Patel and to an extent Jawaharlal Nehru. Gandhiji brought the freedom struggle out from drawing room discussions to the average man tilling his field and the labourer at the machine wheel. He did not preach, he acted. By this simple gesture of being one of the masses, the masses became one with him. Without going into platitudes and following the tortuous movement of freedom struggle a few statements can be made. Gandhiji introduced non-violence to raise politics to a high moral level. The Empire could not suppress or enslave those who refused to be suppressed or accept slavery. Gandhi's non co-operation and non-violent movement was the praxis of this thought. Needless to say the mighty British empire bucked before this saint-turned-politician and found no answer to his civil disobedience movement. However, as true Indians, while we acknowledge the greatness and the teachings of Mahatma Gandhi, we should not forget what Lord Krishna had said in Gita, i.e. to pick up arms against injustice and fight for Dharma against evil. Gandhiji did not wish our country to be a nation of cowards, he wanted us to be brave. Gandhiji's methods may not succeed in today's world where our country is surrounded by hostile neighbours and the law favours the mighty. We as a nation will have to shed the inhibition of the past and don the mantle of a strong nation. Our freedom obtained without much fight need not put us into a state of complacency. We should pro-act rather than react. In today's battle against worldwide terrorism, we need not be shy of using force and fight the terrorists with the weapons and methods they use.

Nurtured on the literature of Ramayan, a household sacred book in all Hindu homes, our psyche has been moulded on the character of Maryada Purushottam Ram. While we have internlized his qualities of piety and forgiveness, we have ignored his fight against evil and a determination to take up arms against injustice. As a result, through centuries of slavery, rapine and destruction of Hindu population we stood mute spectators and offered a pacific response to injustice. The Jews, however, except for the early part of their history, reacted differently and aggressively. Like Hindus they too blamed their misfortune on the wrath of the gods and their defeats as the wages of sin. But this was for a short period when they learnt their lesson, and thereafter there was no looking back and much later, the cult of Gun Zionism emerged. But for the Hindus in their long history of ten millennia the period of Muslim and British rule, lasting nearly six and a half centuries was a period of unmitigated disaster. We lost most of our battles and much worse our very vitality and the capacity to stand up and fight. We forgot the teachings of our God, Lord Krishna, who on the battlefield of Kurukshetra exhorted Arjun to take up arms against evil and injustice and fight Adharm with a Dharm Yudh. To tolerate injustice, He emphasized, was a worse sin than to perpetrate it. Even the apostle of non-violence, Mahatma Gandhi, gave his blessings to the Chief of the Armed forces fighting in Kashmir against the Pak invaders in 1947 to go ahead and fight the aggressors. But somewhere down the long road of history we have forgotten this lesson and even now have earned the dubious distinction of being a soft state. The sobriquet of the 'mild, tolerant and submissive Hindu' is not far from truth. G.K. Chesterton put it even more succinctly. "Tolerance is the virtue of those, who do not believe in anything." While the oppression of Jews and the indignities suffered by them throughout history have been dealt with in some detail earlier in this book, there was a continuous struggle after the Balfour Declaration in 1917 announcing the creation of a national home for Jews in Palestine. They struggled for every inch and every moment of their existence to retain their Promised Land. Before we return shortly to the struggle after Independence, a few points can be made here. The aggressive spirit of Jews, under the British mandate, could not be suppressed by any amount of repression or threats. For every Jew hanged by the British, the Jews in return hanged a Britisher in public, thus squaring the score. The same was true for the Arabs. For every Jewish settlement, attacked or destroyed, there was an instant and fierce reprisal through similar destruction of the Arab villages. For every Jew killed, there were more Arabs killed. The lesson was clear. The cost of destruction of Jewish life and property would be prohibitively high. This was not the way Hindus reacted to oppression. Their fatalism was unbounded, though difficult to explain. It is to our eternal shame that when Mahmud of Ghazni attacked and destroyed the temple of Somnath, the Hindus who were numerous enough to destroy his army, even with knives and bare hands, hid themselves in the temple premises praying to God. This aggressive spirit and faith in oneself and destiny is something, which we could emulate from the Jews. It is understandable that in a large country like India, with difficult communications, it was not easy to organize a united response and counter-measures. Thus, there was never a coordinated resistance to an invader. But this does not explain our defeat when the opposing armies were equal in size and numbers. Sometimes the Indian side was larger. During the process of habitation in Palestine Jewish migration increased manifold. From a trickle it changed into a flood, and the British were not long in imposing punitive measures. But they reckoned without the Jewish spirit and their leader David Ben-Gurion. During the first World War when the Jews were fighting on the British side, and the restrictions on the number of migrants was imposed through a White Paper, David Ben-Gurion gave his clarion call, "We shall fight the war as if there is no White Paper, and we shall fight the White Paper as if there is no war". Such a leadership and a nation of doers need no one's help to endure and to prevail. The latest example of Jewish tenacity and self-reliance came to light in the earthquake devastated Bhuj, where all the international rescue teams and medical personnel were waiting for instructions and guidance from the local civil authorities before commencing operations. The Jewish team of doctors set about their task without delay. The fact that the Jews have won almost half the number of Nobel Prizes in Medicine is proof enough of their excellence in the Science of Medicine. But here they achieved the miracle of reclaiming a marshy land and established a hospital in tents offering immediate relief and succor to the suffering and the wounded of Bhuj.

The German philosopher Friedrich Nietzsche (1844-1900) came up with a novel but dangerous idea of a superman and a master race, which shall dominate the world. The idea was avidly picked up by Adolf Hitler, who decided to produce a master race of German Aryans by systematically cleansing the German society of the weak, the disabled, the infirm and the slow witted. His target, however, was mainly the Jewish population. Unfortunately in India, we are unknowingly involved in a process of social engineering of the reverse order. Instead of taking the hard road of education, empowerment, development and conferring dignity on the under privileged and the *dalit* masses, our leaders took a short cut, based entirely on electoral considerations, by creating reservations in Government and other professional jobs without regard to merit. This has caused severe erosion in the level of merit and excellence in our society leading to two far-reaching consequences that threaten the very fabric of our society. First, reservation has led to an inadequate ability in the echelons of governance and other professional jobs with disastrous consequences. Second, talent and merit in society are marginalized, on account of the caste of birth, leading to frustration in the upper castes. It is sad to note that after 55 years of reservations not a single person from *dalit* or scheduled castes or scheduled tribes has reached anywhere near the level of intellectual eminence or material prosperity. Even Dr. B.R. Ambedkar had to struggle his way to his position by sheer hard work and education. Recently, the Supreme Court struck down a controversial proposal to extend reservations in specialty and super-specialty jobs in the All India Institute of Medical Sciences with this remark, "Shall the Government ensure that the treatment of VVIPs is carried out only by the physicians of reserved category?" If they accept, there is no harm in reservation. The answer to the problem is not reservation but education and empowerment of the *dalits*. These reservations have not only spawned a conflict of interest and avoidable strains in the social milieu but also resulted in a fractured polity. The inevitable result of this insidious process has been a devastating brain drain to foreign countries, mainly the United State and Europe. Thus, while foreign countries are enriching themselves with our talent, our own country is slowly being deprived of its best material. Unless this evil is removed immediately (in any case reservations were to be removed after ten years of the adoption of our Constitution) we shall end up with a society with the lowest possible index of merit, highest poverty rate, lowest educational standards and an inferior race, which our forefathers neither anticipated nor desired.

The dis-service done to our polity by the leftists and pseudo-secularists is evident by their effort at denationalization of our polity. Their specious projection of Hindu culture as Hindu fundamentalism is a contradiction in terms. I have dealt with some length on this theme in my book on 'Nehru' and also in some pages of 'Indian History', while defining Hinduism earlier in this book.

Adding further wounds to our badly damaged polity is the constant cacophony of the leftist forces from West Bengal. This anti deluvian relic of the Marxist dinosaur tries to meddle in the politics at the Center with an authority out of all proportions to its size and substance.

The fractious nature of our polity and personal ambitions of our so-called leaders has resulted in the emergence of a large number of political parties in our country, which could easily obtain an entry into the *Guinness Book World of Records*. With so many parties babbling their shibboleths and competing for public votes, it is a complete bedlam in a Tower of Babel, which not only confuses the average citizen, but makes him cynical in the exercise of his franchise. India's present does not inspire.

The all-pervasive corruption has reached such a level that a convict can be elected a Chief Minister of a state as in Tamil Nadu and another one charge-sheeted in fodder scam is aspiring to be another one in the state of Bihar. It is about time that our people rose against this loot and plunder of public money. How fragile is the democratic edifice of our country? To say that our electorate though illiterate is wise in their judgment at the ballot box would amount to being economic with the truth. Most elections are won through the use of money, criminal and muscle power. The voters are mainly affected by local issues, personal interests, caste considerations and fear. National issues seldom enter their calculations. To quote Margaret Thatcher:

"There is little hope for democracy if the hearts of men and women in democratic societies cannot be touched by a call to something greater than themselves." Democracy in our country is a farce and mobocracy rules the roost. I have mentioned this aspect in my book on 'Nehru', how mobs and crowds can be sentimental, irrational and often wrong. The case in Tamilnadu is one such example.

The nation today needs a leader of resolve, who could put the nation above ambition. Someone in the mould of George Washington of whom Major General Francois Jeande Chastllur, a member of French Academy and one of Europe's leading men of letters, wrote thus:

> "Bravery without temerity, laborious without ambition, generous without prodigality, noble without pride, virtuous without severity.... He had nothing to reproach him with".

Can we hope to get such a leader?

PART - IV

The Future

Chapter 19

Civilizational Fault lines

Before early nineteenth century state boundaries were decided by the princes of small kingdoms based on their ambitious, military might and expediencies, as given in the teachings of Machiavelli in the European context and Kautilya in the Indian. Their two books, *The Prince* and *Arthshastra* were the Bible of state policy in those days. Later from early nineteenth century onwards a new phenomenon called "nationalism" determined statecraft and political boundaries. Nationalism was defined as the pursuit of a common objective, feeling of oneness, sharing, past history, ethnicity, and a common striving for future that moved a community. Thus emerged various nations in the world, both western and eastern—Canada, the United States and countries of South America, Western Europe, Middle East, Asia and far east. They all had their own national forms. This continued till the beginning of the Russian Revolution. After Marx and Engels re-wrote history in terms of economic determinism, ideologies transcended national and political boundaries. In consequence, three world groups emerged—capitalist west, including Western Europe and countries of America, Japan and South East Asia, while another block subscribing to Marxist ideologies of communism came into being and coalesced around the Soviet Russia including East European countries, Cuba and China. The remaining countries untouched by polarization around these two nodes, declared themselves as the third block. Non-aligned and not attached to any of these two capitalist and communist poles nor encumbered by any military alliances spawned by them, they created a political space for themselves. This era lasted till the break up of the Soviet Union into independent states and the fall from grace of communist ideology, except for some anachronistic entities like Cuba, Indian communists and the left. This is the present scene. But a New World order is in the making, which will be based on the civilizational identities and their fault lines. The originator of this theory is Prof. Samuel P. Huntington of Harvard University, who in his book "The Clash of Civilizations and the remaking of World Order" has expounded the theory that the future politics and the world order will be decided on the basis of civilizational identity. I can take some consolation from this thought, which in my own way I had expressed in my book " *India Betrayed – The Role of Nehru*". There I had emphasized that the civilizational entities such as Hinduism, Islam, Christianity and Judaism will be over-arching national identity to form patterns of civilizational formations. To quote Micheal Dibdin:

> "There can be no true friends without true enemies. Unless we hate what we are not, we cannot love what we are. These are the old truths we are painfully rediscovering after a century and more of sentimental cant. Those who deny them deny their family, their heritage, their culture, their birthright, and their very selves! They will not lightly be forgotten."

The running thread in all that follows is the hypothesis that cultural identities, which at the broadest level conform to civilizational identity, are and will be shaping the future world dispensation in the post-cold war era. Prof. Huntington has divided the world broadly into nine civilizational entities viz, the Western, which comprises Western Europe and North America; the Latin American; the African, which includes the southern half of Africa, areas south of Sahara and some sub-Saharan states; the Islamic Asian nations; the orthodox Christian, which includes areas east of Germany upto the whole of Russia and the Bahrain straits; the Sinic or the Chinese which includes the whole of China, the two Koreas and further north; the Hindu comprising India and Nepal; the Buddhist comprising some Southeast Asian countries and finally Japanese.

The learned Professor, however, forgot to include Judaism, which will be even more important than the Buddhist civilization of Southeast Asian countries. According to Dr. Henry Kissinger:

> "The international system of the twentyfirst century will contain at least six major powers- The United States, Europe, China, Japan, Russia and probably India –as well as a multiplicity of medium sized and smaller countries."

To this list we shall like to include two important civilizational entities i.e. Islam and Judaism. The rivalry of earlier supreme powers will be replaced by that of the civilizations. Prof. Huntington defines the nature of civilization in the following manner:

> "Human history is the history of civilizations. It is impossible to think of the development of humanity in any other terms. The story stretches through generations of civilizations from ancient Sumerian and Egyptian to Classical and Meso American to Christian and Islamic civilizations and through successive manifestations of Cynic and Hindu civilizations. Throughout history civilizations have provided the broadest identifications for people. As a result, the causes, emergence, rise, interactions, achievements, decline and fall of civilizations have been explored at length by distinguished historians, sociologists and anthropologists including among others, Max Weber, Emile Durkheim, Oswald Spengler, Pitirim Sorokin, Arnold Toynbee, Alfred Weber, A.L. Kroeber, Philip Bagby, Carroll Quigley, Rushton, Coulborn, Christopher Dawson, S.N. Eisenstadt, Fernand Braudel, William H. McNeil, Adda Bozeman, Immanuel Wallerstein, and Felipe Ferman-dez-Armesto. These and other writers have produced a voluminous, learned and sophisticated literature devoted to the comparative analysis of civilizations. Differences in

perspective, methodology, focus and concepts pervade this literature. Yet broad agreement also exists on central propositions concerning the nature, identity, and dynamics of civilizations."

Civilization, which is our concern in this chapter, is "a cultural entity'. Nineteenth century German thinkers drew a sharp distinction between civilization, which involved mechanics, technology and material factors, and culture, which involved values, ideals, and the higher intellectual, artistic, moral qualities of a society. This distinction has persisted in German thought but has not been accepted elsewhere. Some anthropologists have even reversed the relation and conceived of cultures as characteristic of primitive, unchanging, non-urban societies, while more complex, developed, urban, and dynamic societies are civilizations. These efforts to distinguish culture and civilization, however, have not caught on, and, outside Germany, there is an overwhelming agreement with Braudel that it is "delusory to wish in the German way to separate culture from its foundation, civilization."

Civilization and culture are indivisible, referring as they do to the overall way of life of the people. The present cry of cultural pluralism in India touted by our so-called secularists and leftists is a contradiction in terms. To quote Huntington again: "a civilization is a culture writ large. They both involve the values, norms, instructions, and modes of thinking to which successive generations in a given society have attached primary importance. A civilization is, for Braudel, a space, a 'cultural area' 'a collection of cultural characteristics and phenomena". Wallerstein defines it as "a particular concatenation of worldview, customs, structures, and culture (both material culture and high culture) which forms some kind of historical whole and, which coexists (if not always simultaneously) with other varieties of this phenomenon." A civilization is, according to Dawson, the product of "a particular original process of cultural creativity, which is the work of a particular people." While for Durkheim and Mauss, it is "a kind of moral milieu encompassing a certain number of nations, each national culture being only a particular form of the whole".

Another emphasis on the synergy between culture and civilization is provided by Athenians when they talk about the Persians:

> "For there are many and powerful considerations that forbid us to do so, even if we were inclined. First and chief, the images and dwellings of the gods, burnt and laid ruins, this we must need avenge to the utmost of our power, rather than make terms with the man who has perpetrated such deeds. Secondly, the Grecian race being of the same blood and same language, and the temples of the gods and sacrifices in common; and our similar customs; for the Athenians to become betrayers of these would not be well."

The most important component of a civilization is religion. History is a witness that in spite of common ethnicity and language, people slaughtered each other, as happened in Lebanon, the former Yugoslavia, and the Indian subcontinent.

Physical characteristic and races do not form an essential ingredient of a civilization. A race can be divided into civilizations and the same civilization can have more than one race, just as Christianity and Islam have more than one race. The crucial distinction among human groups are related to their beliefs, institutions, values and social structure and not the shapes of their heads, size and colour. Civilizations are comprehensive inasmuch as they are constituent unit and have no locus standi without reference to the encompassing civilisations. A civilization is a totality. According to Melko;

> "Civilizations have a certain degree of integration. Their parts are defined by their relationship to each other and to the whole. If the civilization is composed of states, these states will have more relation to one another than they will do to states outside the civilization. They might fight more, and engage more frequently in diplomatic relations. They will be more interdependent economically. There will be pervading aesthetic and philosophical currents."

As per the earlier listing the following civilizations outside the Euro American can be identified today:

Sinic: The Chinese civilization dating back to 1500 B.C. or even earlier, is mainly dominated by Confucianism and the term "Sinic" aptly describes the Chinese community outside China in Southern Asia, Vietnam and Korea.

Japanese: This culture emerged out of the conglomeration of Chinese-Japanese culture into a distinctive identity between 100 and 400 A.D. And like Chinese Confucianism is anchored on Shintoism.

Hindu: This is described in great detail under Indian History and related issues.

Islamic: Originating in Arabian peninsula in seventh century, Islam spread west and eastward, covering the areas described earlier. Because of its fast spread many distinct cultures or sub-civilizations exist within Islam such as Arab, Turkey, Persian and Malay.

African: The northern half of Africa is basically Islamic, while the southern half comprising the natives and the European and later English settlers created a distinct society in South Africa as its core.

Apart from four world religions i.e. Christianity, Islam, Hinduism and Confucianism, Buddhism does not really form a separate civilization as far as population and area are concerned, and therefore, its role in making or unmaking the new world order is minimal.

The above analysis and the treatise on the clash of civilizations by Professor Huntington though sound in outline, suffers from some glaring infirmities in details. He has failed to emphasize adequately the importance of Israel. Possibly due to reasons of its small size and population as also its supposed status as a satellite state of the U.S., which it is not, Israel is bound to rise like a phoenix out of the ashes of its past as it has done so often in the long march of history. There is absolutely no doubt that Judaic civilization will emerge as a potential power center, fueled by the inherent strength of its civilization and its mighty power of survival through millennia. The learned Professor misses the point that the durability of a civilization does not depend merely on its economic wealth and technology, natural resources, large size and military might, but the power of its institutions and the dedication of its people to the identity and substance of their culture. India and Israel stand alone in this regard as they share these attributes in ample measure. Greece, Rome, Egypt, Babylon, Assyria and Persia were great empires of their time, but where are they today? But the Judaic kingdom or the Hindu land has stayed not merely as a geographical expression of a state but as a civilizational entity with a glorious past that overshadows its present and the impulse of its history ever drives it to greater endeavours. The U.S. centric West is a fairly young civilization in comparison. Its state has military might; but so had Greece and Rome. The fault lines in their structures were evident even at the height of their power. But the appetite for material gains and a lack of spiritual content and a shared belief of the people in their value systems were the cause of their downfall. Unless cured immediately, the U.S. centric Western societies will reach a state of terminal decay, mainly due to a philistinic over insistence on the material factors, consumerism and abhorrence of spiritual values.

One can safely eliminate the Slavic Orthodox, Latin American and even African civilizations for their lack of roots, continuity and uniqueness of their spiritual values. Japan though identified as a separate civilization, is very close to the West in all its thought and practice except a token adherence to its history and Shintoism. This ambivalence will give Japanese civilization a doubtful longevity.

The simple teachings in the profound thought of divinity and human virtues propagated by Prophet Mohammed have gradually been forgotten and replaced by a blind adherence to the letter of Koran and Hadis. The form remains but the spirit is lost. The stranglehold of the clergy, ulema and the vested interest of the ummah have led to the fossilization of Islam into a rigid time warp. Any move towards modernity or rational development is stonewalled by these interests through their edicts and fatwas, which shackle the minds of the unquestioning masses and the innocent believers. As brought out earlier, the recrudescence of the regressive impulses in some otherwise progressive Islamic countries and recourse to fundamentalism in many others lies to a large extent in the atavistic urge of Muslim societies to seek a solution to the present day problems by cat-scanning the Koranic texts to discover hidden meanings where none exist. This lack of rationality has led to many incongruous situations in the daily life of a Muslim; the issues of personal law, penal and civil code, economic and scientific discoveries and so on. The few voices of reform have been drowned in a general cacophony of the extremist fundamentalists. This is particularly true of Pakistan and India, which have the largest population of Muslims.

America centric West is plagued with internal problems of economic slow-down, stagnant population, unemployment, fiscal deficit, poor work ethics, low saving rates, social disintegration, drugs and crimes. Inevitably, the economic power and consequential military strength is gradually shifting eastward, mostly China and Japan centric, while India is on the verge of an economic takeoff. In consequence, the dominance of the West would be eroded sooner than later, compounded by an increasing hostility of Islam. In short, the balance of power is shifting to modern civilizations, which are increasingly turning atavistic and searching their moorings towards God away from modernism. Secularism is on the retreat as fundamentalism rapidly fills its space. With the second evangelization of Europe, the present idiom is no longer to modernize Islam but to Islamise "modernity'. This 'unsecularisation of the world' will be a prominent social fact in the new twentyfirst century. The number of orthodox churches increased considerably in the Slavic republics while an Islamic revival swept through Central Asia. The number of churches, mosques and madarasas increased manifold between 1989 till the end of 20th century. As Islamic countries abandon western ideologies and culture, there is an emphasis on recommitment to Islam. To quote a Saudi Arabian official,

> "Foreign imports are nice as shiny or high-tech 'things'. But intangible social and political institutions imported from elsewhere can be deadly—ask the Shah of Iran.... Islam for us is not just a religion but a way of life. We Saudis want to modernize, but not necessarily westernize."

This resurgence of Islamic awakening in personal life has many facets. To quote John L. Esposito:

> "The indices of an Islamic awakening in personal life are many; increased attention to religious observances, (mosque attendance, prayer, fasting), proliferation of religious programming and publications, more emphasis on Islamic dress and values, the revitalization of Sufism (mysticism). This broader-based renewal has also been accompanied by Islam's reassertion in public life, an increase in Islamically oriented governments, organizations, laws, banks, social welfare services, and educational institutions. Both government and opposition movements have turned to Islam to enhance their authority and muster popular support... Most rulers and governments, including more secular states such as Turkey and Tunisia, becoming aware of the potential strength of Islam, have shown increased sensitivity to and anxiety about Islamic issues."

In brief, the countries of Islamic civilization are re-inventing themselves by falling back on Islamic education through multiplicity of Islamic schools, Islamisation of the curricula, adherence to the words of Koran and Hadis and development of solidarity amongst Islamic states and societies. Returning to the basis of our thesis, the important constituents of civilizational identities are blood and belief, faith and family, common language, religion, ancestry, values and institutions. The inevitable result would be a reconfiguration of global politics on civilizational basis and their conflict will lie along the fault lines separating these groups. Though identity is generally the most meaningful at the immediate contact level along with a single dimension, narrower identities within these do not necessarily conflict with the whole. The increased importance of lower level identities may well reinforce their salience at the higher level of cultural identities of ethnic groups, nationality and religion of a particular civilization. To quote Edmund Burke : "The love to the whole is not extinguished by this subordinate partiality ... To be attached to the subdivision, to love the little platoon we belong to in society, is the first principle (the germ, as it were) of public affections."

In global politics with the disappearance of secular ideologies, the differences between various liberal democracies and liberalization of civilization per se can be debated but not resolved. To quote Huntington again:

> "Differences in material interest can be negotiated and often settled by compromise in a way cultural issues cannot. Hindus and Muslims are unlikely to resolve the issue of whether a temple or a mosque should be built at Ayodhya by building both, or neither, or a syncretic building that is both a mosque and temple. Nor can what might seem to be a straight forward territorial question between Albanian Muslims and Orthodox Serbs concerning Kosovo or between Jews and Arabs concerning Jerusalem be easily settled, since each place has deep historical, cultural and emotional meanings to both people. Similarly, neither French authorities nor Muslim parents are likely to accept a compromise, which would allow schoolgirls to wear Muslim dress every other day during the school year. Cultural questions like these involve a yes or no zero sum choice".

Political leaders chasing the illusion of fundamentally reshaping the culture of their societies are doomed to failure. They can merely introduce a cosmetic layer of Western culture, but they are sadly mistaken if they think that they can suppress or eliminate the core element of their indigenous culture. They can make history but they cannot escape history. With the best will in the world to inject Western culture into these societies, they will only end up by creating cultural schizophrenia, which would continue to be their defining characteristic.

Just as demography creates destiny, population movements form the motor of history. Centuries past, economic conditions, government policies and differential growth rates have caused numerous immigrations within Europe and Asia. Though some of these were peaceful the others were violent. However, once the settling process was completed, civilizational identities emerged. It will not be incorrect to say that civilizations are the ultimate human tribes and the clash of civilizations is a tribe conflict on the world scene. In the emerging scenario even states and groups from different civilizations may form opportunistic coalition to further their interests against an inimical civilization to share common interests. The foundations of such coalition however, will never be strong and will remain cool and even hostile.

Arnold Toynbee describes Judaism as an 'arrested civilization' and a product of an earlier Syriac civilization. The learned professor is widely off the mark in not fully understanding the developmental vitality of Judaism. It is unfortunate that by affiliating Judaism to Christianity and Islam he has put history on its head. He has conveniently forgotten that Christianity was born out of Judaism, while Islam mentions Judaism as its parental faith, and Mohammed the last of the prophets of this common genealogy dating back to Abraham.

To quote Huntington again on the expansion of Western culture, "It was also facilitated by the superiority in organization, discipline, and training of its troops and subsequently by the superior weapons, transport, logistics and medical services resulting from its leadership in the Industrial Revolution. The West won the world not by the superiority of its ideas or values or religion (to which few members of other civilizations were converted) but rather by its superiority in applying organized violence. Westerners often forget this fact, non-westerners never do."

The political ideologies of the twentieth century i.e. Liberalism, Socialism, Anarchism, or Corporationism, Marxism, Communism, Social democracy, Conservatism, Nationalism, Fascism and Christian Democracy were all products of western civilization. But west has never produced a major religion. All the great religions of the world predate and do not belong to the western civilisation. The demographic pattern of the world forecasts a phenomenal increase in the two major proselytizing religions of

Islam and Christianity, but in the long run, Mohammed will outpace Jesus. Christianity spreads mainly through conversion, while Islam by conversion and rapid reproduction. The percentage of Christians in the world on its all time high of 30% of the world population in 1980s has since been declining and will probably reach 25% by 2025. But the extremely high growth rate of Muslim population will continue to increase and will reach 30% by the same date. This enormous population impelled by religious fervour poses a great danger to the rest of the world including Judaism, Christianity and Hinduism in particular and the remaining parts in general. Westernism, which till yester year was synonymous with modernization, is no more so. Again to quote Huntington:

> "Modernization, in short, does not necessarily mean westernisation. Non western societies can modernize and have modernized without abandoning their own cultures and adopting wholesale western values, institutions and practices. The latter, indeed, may be almost impossible; whatever, obstacles non-western cultures pose to modernization pale before those they pose to Westernisation. It would, as Braudel observes, almost "be childish" to think that modernization or the "triumph of civilization in the singular" would lead to the end of the plurality of historic cultures embodied for centuries in the world's great civilizations. Modernization, instead, strengthens those cultures and reduces the relative power of the west. In fundamental ways, the world is becoming more modern and less western."

The first fault line between Christian west and Israel against Islam would lie along the territorial boundaries of Middle East and the whole of North Africa with the possible exception of Egypt and Saudi Arabia. More likely than not these two countries may also defect from their neutral position to join the Islamic Middle East. North of the Middle East and below Russia, the second threat to Western civilization may come from China. As far as the Hindu civilization is concerned, the fault line would lie along the Pakistan border continuing north of Kashmir, against Islam while the other line of conflict will lie against the Sinic civilization to the north along the Himalayas and in the North Asia and further east against the rapidly Islamizing Bangladesh. Just as the Hindu civilization is hemmed between Islamic and Sinic civilizations, so is Israel surrounded by militant Islam on all sides except the sea westward, beyond which may lie a friendly Christianity with an American dominance.

The lynchpin in the Confucian-Islamic entente controls a conveyor belt, which moves a large amount of nuclear technology and arms to Pakistan and that is a direct threat to the Hindu civilization. Though Chinese exports do trickle, to an extent, to North Korea, the main recipients between 1980 and 1991, were Iran and Pakistan, Iraq being a close second.

In recent years violent conflicts between the Muslims and local non-Muslims have taken place in a number of places. In Bosnia, bloody conflict raged between Muslims and orthodox Serbs and also in Kosovo between Muslims and Catholic Croatians. Albanian Muslims carried out an underground war against the Serbian rule, while the Albanian and Greek Governments fought it out over the rights of their minorities in each other's country. The historic antagonism between Christian Greek and Muslim Turks goes back to the times even before the rise of Alexander and lasted till only a few decade back in the partition of Cyprus along religious lines, the way it happened in India. Turkey and Armenia are old enemies and Azeris and Armenians have been constantly fighting for over 200 years for the control of Nagorno-Karabakh. Muslim ethnic groups like Chechens and Ingush have been fighting on and off for their independence from the Russian Republic and the war still goes on. The fight between Ingush and the Orthodox Ossetians continues, as in the Volga basin the Tatar Muslims continued their fight against the Russians till 1990s and finally settled for a limited sovereignty under Russia, balanced precariously on an uneasy compromise.

Consider the following scenario. Since 1958 there have been fifteen major Muslim inspired political confrontations in the world, resulting from the Muslim point of view, in a significant revision of the rhetoric of revolution. There is a double speak, which makes Geoge Orwell's prophecy seem mild by comparison. They fight their revolution to decolonise the world, shouting death to the imperialists and racist governments. But these wars always result in a new form of imperialism under Islam. While they brand others as racists, their own dispensations are visibly more rabidly racist. The votaries of Islam are still dreaming of a new version of Islamic expansion, which followed the death of Mohammed. Its forces are poised to sweep three continents from the Atlantic to the Indian Ocean, converting virtually every nation in its path. The significant confrontation was the Arab-Israeli conflict closely followed by the one between India and Pakistan, and the latest accounted for till 1993, was the fight between Islamic "freedom fighters" and Government forces of Philippines on the Island of Mindanao. In 1947 in India during the exchange of populations, when India surrendered 400,000 sq. miles of sovereign territory to create Pakistan, which broke up into two Muslim countries that never existed, there was a blood- bath unparalleled in history. When in Nigeria, the prominent Christian segment, Beaver, amongst a majority Muslim population, attempted to form an independent state to escape death and persecution, the Nigerians were not as human as the Indians during the partition. A bloody war followed against the Christian population and the Christians beaten and battered became a second class citizenry. The same phenomenon is happening in Bangladesh today where women are being raped and the minority is being forced out of the country. In Algeria, one million French Catholics had to leave after the country gained independence. Earlier Algeria was as much a part of France as Alaska is at present a part of the United State. Moving eastwards, Libya, a conglomeration of local ethnic groups, pushed out nearly 25,000 Italians resulting in the loss of some $300,000,000 worth of property confiscated by the government. The Sacred Heart Cathedral was converted to a mosque and dedicated to Gammal Abdul Nasser. This gesture was to be a reminder to the world that the Holy War of the Prophet 1000 years earlier was not for conquest but to wipe out the infidels symbolically and materially. Libya has been at war with Chad overrunning its northern region and continues its conquest and campaign of conversion, seeking help from their Islamic countries for a 'just and noble' task. The greatest orgy of slaughter took place in Sudan where approximately 500,000, non-Muslim blacks in its southern region were put to death in a glaring genocide, unequalled in the African continent. Moving further to the east, in Egypt, considered to be a moderate Islamic Arab State, it's Coptic Christian population, barely 12 percent of the whole, almost the same as the black population in the United States, has been brutalized and kept under constant fear. The atrocities ranged from burning of churches, arrest without warrant, house confinement and wanton slaughter of those suspected as unbelievers. According to a source, the Islamist expansionism, slaughter and persecution, is not confined to these areas. There was an attempt on the life of Pope some time back by an Islamic fanatic, under the misguided conception "kill the head and the body dies", a recipe for destroying non-Islamic civilizations. Christians and Hindus are not the only enemies of the Islamic movement, but also Syrian Kurds and the Druse, who are being robbed of their farm lands, denied access to schools, access to press and the right to serve in the military or the government. Between 1920s and 1948, both Iraq and Iran tried to wipe out the Kurds sacrificing 25 million in this long conflict. In the near past, Lebanon provided the fighting ground between Muslims and the rest. The present Christian crisis in Lebanon originated in 1958, when Nasser declared this country as a part of the Islamic world, under a veiled threat of a total take over. This effort was aborted by President Eisenhower's intervention. The timely landing of the United States' forces prevented the radical take over of the Labanese government, but a half-hearted follow up action opened the door for the "Cairo Agreement" which document technically resulted in an Islamic terrorist state within a state. Taking advantage of the situation around 1970, a majority of PLO members, fleeing for safety landed along with those escaping from Jordan, where they faced execution at the hands of their own people, and found a safe haven in South Lebanon. These refugees explaining their status as a nation within a nation attempted to take over Beirut between 1975 and 1982 resulting in a loss of 25,000 lives. In 1976, the Syrians joined the fray, settled in Beirut and never left. The much maligned offensive by General Arial Sharon under Menachin Begin, the then Prime Minister of Israel, destroyed the PLO power base in Southern Lebanon, provided a temporary reprieve to the Maronite Christians and Shiites by forcing the PLO to flee Southern Lebanon. Philippines is burning as the Islamic group called the Moro National Liberation Front, plays havoc in the country and the fire has scorched even Indonesia. The leader of the Moro National Liberation Front, Sharif Zain-Jali, announced that a separatist group representing a mere 5% of the population in Philippines will "become a nation in the eyes of the Islamic world". In Pakistan, Bangladesh, Sudan and in parts of Southern Lebanon, Islamic law has been proclaimed as the law of the land. In any country with Muslim majority, the Muslim law prevails, but wherever the Muslims are a minority they insist on a secular state and equal rights for the minorities forgetting completely how they treat their own minorities. The series of terrorist acts against non-Muslims are legion. From the blowing up of Pan Am 103, the air heist from Kathmandu to Kandhar involving more than 200 Indian passengers, bombing of the United States Embassies, destruction of the statues of Buddha in Afghanistan and the latest bombing of the World Trade Center in New York on 11th September,2001, the raid on the Legislative Assembly of Jammu and Kashmir Government at Srinagar on 1st October, 2001, an attack on Indian Parliament on 13th December, and now the recent attack on Swami Narain temple in Gandhi Nagar, Gujarat, on 24 September, 2002, should leave no one in doubt about the intention of the Pan-Islamic fundamentalism trying to overtake other civilizations.

Since, 1500 A.D. there was hardly any period lasting more than five years when the Muslims did not pick up arms against Europe, somewhere in the Muslim world and in more than one country simultaneously. The Muslims see a fundamental chasm between Islam and the West. The two cannot co-exist, if the west is to flourish, Islam has to be suppressed and vice versa.For the Muslim world there is a widespread belief that 200 years of

Western colonialism, which oppressed and kept the Muslims poor and backward with loss of initiative, are going to end and the future belongs to Islam. The past 150 years, during which the Muslims were culturally smothered and their institutions and way of life destroyed, will be a thing of the past. They envy the prosperity of the West and hate its success and their own deprivation. In the words of Malise Ruthven, a British Arabist, "The West like its women has been a simultaneous source of attraction and repulsion; admiration for its institutions and for the technical prowess that has enabled so many of its citizens to enjoy the undreamed of freedoms and opportunities, disgust at its vulgarity, its seeming callousness and spiritual emptiness combined with a deep sense of unease that Allah, whose way has been shown for all mankind in the holy Koran and the Sunna has been one-upped."

Recently, recruited by one of the religious organisations preaching holy war against the US as an Islamic obligation, the foot soldiers of Mullah Mohammed Omar, meant to be used as canon fodder in the recent war in Afghanistan, had confessed the futility of their cause. On pain of death these innocents were separated from their families and were ordered by the Taliban to fight in Kandhar to the end or till America is destroyed. They could meet their families only after this sacred task was completed. One of these fundamentalists, 23- year old Abu Kalam confessed, "god was kind to make me realize that it was sheer distortion of the concept of Jehad".

The demographic challenge posed by the Muslim émigrés to European countries is real. They account for 10 percent of the births in Western Europe, while the Arabs alone in Brussels constitute 50 percent of this figure. Whether they be Turkish in Germany or Algerian in France, they refuse to be assimilated into the host culture. Jean Marie Domenach in 1991 remarked that "there is a fear growing all across Europe, of a Muslim community that cuts across European lines, a sort of thirteenth nation of the European Community." The French are basically less racists than culturists. While they can accept black Africans speaking perfect French as their legislators, they are averse to

Muslim girls wearing headscarves in their schools. The public perception about this suffocating by increased presence, when analyzed reveal the revulsion by 76 percent of the French against Arabs, 46 percent against blacks, 40 percent against Asians and 24 percent against Jews. In Germany in 1994, the picture was somewhat different, being mainly directed against the Turks. In 1990, Bernard Lewis, a leading scholar of Islam, analyzing "The Roots of Muslim Rage" observed that the Muslim ire though irrational, was definitely a historic reaction of an ancient rivalry against a Judeo-Christian heritage, its secular content and worldwide expansion. An Egyptian journalist, Mohammed Sid-Ahmed, pronounced in 1944 that there was a growing clash between the Judeo-Christian Western ethics and the Islamic revivalist movement, starting from Atlantic and ending up at China in the East. Similar sentiments were expressed in 1992 by a prominent Indian Muslim, that the next confrontation from the Muslim world would be along the fault line, coterminous with the sweep of Islamic nations from the west to Pakistan. In a similar vein a Tunisian lawyer observed that "Colonialism tried to deform all the cultural traditions of Islam. I am not an Islamist. I don't think there is a conflict between religions. There is a conflict between civilizations." As far as the USA is concerned, a sample survey of 3500 respondents revealed that 61 percent considered 'Islamic Revival' as the main threat. A similar survey to identify 'critical threats' had revealed that 72 percent of the public and 61 percent foreign experts believe nuclear proliferation as No. one, while 69 percent and 33 percent of these categories pointed their fingers at 'international terrorism', both closely associated with Islam. Similarly, 33 and 39 percent of the above categories of the respondents saw a threat in the expansion of Islamic fundamentalism. The Secretary General of NATO in 1995 went to the extent of saying that Islamic fundamentalism was as dangerous as communism had been to the West. However, in the America centric west there is an unanimously growing apprehension against a 'Tehran-Islamabad-Beijing axis'., to counter, which the west will have to ally with India. Should these three states form the underpinning of a larger grouping of other

Muslim Asian countries, an informal 'Confucian-Islamist alliance', will emerge, on the world scene. A consolidation would occur not because Mohammed and Confucius are anti-west but because these cultures perceive the west as the main colonial persecutor. This sentiment was echoed in 1994 when Mu'ammar al-Qadhafi declared:

> "The New World order means that Jews and Christians control Muslims and if they can, they will go after Confucianism and other religions in India, China and Japan... What the Christians and Jews are now saying "we were determined to crush Communism and the West. We must now crush Islam and Confucianism."
>
> "Now we hope to see a confrontation between China that heads the Confucianism camp. We have no justifications but to be biased against the crusaders. We are standing with Confucianism, and by allying ourselves with it and fighting alongside it in one international front, we will eliminate our mutual opponent".
>
> "So, we as Muslims, will support China in its struggle against our mutual enemy..."
>
> "We wish China victory..."

Communal conflicts and fault line wars are the staple of history, and Islam's borders have always been drenched with blood. In the thirtytwo ethnic conflicts during the Cold War, which included fault line wars, between Arabs and Israelis, Indians and Pakistanis, Sudanese Muslims and Christians, Sri Lankan Buddhists and Tamils and Lebanese Shi'ites and Maronites, identity wars constituted half of all such wars. The largest number involved were Muslims. To quote Huntington again:

> "The overwhelming majority of fault line conflicts, however, have taken place along the boundary looping across Eurasia and Africa that separates Muslims from non-Muslims. While at the macro or global level of the world politics the primary clash of civilizations is between the West and the rest, at the micro or local level it is between Islam and the others..."

Though Muslims constituted only one-fifth of the world population they, more than any other groups, were involved in the violence of civilizational clashes. In a study carried out by Ted Robert Gurr, the Muslims were participants in twenty six out of fifty ethnopolitical conflicts in 1993-94 alone. Out of twenty of these conflicts, between different civilizations, those between Muslims and non-Muslims alone amounted to fifteen. In other words three times as many inter-civilizational conflicts involved Muslims, as opposed to non-Muslim civilizations. In terms of casualties, the conflicts involving Muslims had been most bloody. In the six wars, analyzed by Ted Robert Gurr, 200,000 or more people were killed. Three conflicts were between Sudan, Bosnia and East Timor – Muslims and non-Muslims, two (Somalia, Iraq-Kurds) were intra-Muslims and only one(Angola) was non-Muslim.

The primal causes of the involvement of Muslims in most conflicts are history. Intermittent fault lines bred violence between different civilizational groups causing fears and insecurities on both sides—Hindus and Muslims in South Asia, Russians and Caucasians in the North Caucasus, Armenians and Turks in the Transcaucasus, Jews and Arabs in Palestine, Catholics, Muslims and Orthodox in the Balkans and many others.

The moot question before the twentyfirst century is,: why are the Muslims more involved in inter-group conflicts than other people. Six possible causes can be traced—the main three explain violence between Muslims and non-Muslims, and the other three are slowly emerging into focus. Firstly, Islam has been a religion of the sword, glorifying military valour, born among "warring Bedouin nomadic tribes" and this ''violent origin is stamped in the foundations of Islam. Mohammed himself is remembered as a hard fighter and a skillful military commander." Islamic doctrines ordained a fight against Kafir " non-believers" and when this was accomplished, the same impulse led to fighting among themselves. There are few prohibitions in Islam on violence and any thought on non-violence is absent from Islamic doctrine and practice.

Secondly, the rapid spread of Islam from Arabia to West in Africa and even in south Spain and north and eastward to

Central Asia, the Balkans and the Subcontinent juxtaposed Muslims against the local populations to be conquered and converted. The doctrine of Koran is based on the assumption that there are two worlds – *Dar-ul-Islam*, which belongs to the believers and *Dar-ul-Harb*, which belongs to the non-believers or the Kafirs. It is the duty of the faithful to expand the boundaries of *Dar-ul-Islam* to absorb *Dar-ul-harb* within its confines by all means including violence. This is the fundamental basis of conflict between Islamic and other civilizations.

The third potent factor is the "indigestibility'" of Muslims in any other society. This process work both ways i.e. Muslim minority against any non-Muslim society turns aggressive to maintain its identity, while the Muslim majority tends to eliminate, suppress or convert any minority in their midst. The latest example was a decree by the Taliban government of Afghanistan that all Hindus and Sikhs in that country must wear yellow clothes and put yellow signs on their houses. Who says that we have not left behind the era of anti-Semitism in Europe and the days of the ghetto when the Jews were forced to wear a distinctive badge of dishonour. The consequence of this 'indigestibility' is that Orthodox Christians, western Christians, Hindus, Buddhists and Confucians find it easier to adapt to each other than to Islam. Coming to the other three subaltern causes, the first one is a historical feeling of subjection and oppression of Muslim societies by the Western colonial powers in the nineteenth and twentieth centuries. Akbar Ahmed, a Muslim writer, feels that the West looks upon the Muslims as "Red Indians, depressed groups, shorn of dignity, trapped on reservations converted from their ancestral lands".

A persuasive factor, which can explain both intra and extra Islamic conflicts is the result of the absence of one or more core states in Islam. The Muslims feel that there is a lack of such a central coordinating force, conspiratorial in nature, directed against the West. This may not be true. Islam is a source of instability because there is no dominant centre and so many states aspiring to become leaders of Islam. Countries such as Saudi Arabia, Iran, Pakistan, Turkey and possibly Indonesia have been competing for this position. Thus, there is no central authority in Islam, which can deal with conflicts within and outside Muslim groupings.

Lastly, the population explosion in Muslim societies and the presence of a large number of unemployed males between the age of fifteen and thirty is a major source of instability and violence within and outside Islam. This single factor alone can explain the Muslim violence in 1980s and 1990s.

As a final footnote on the above, it could be submitted that Prof. Huntington's analysis is an empirical one. Einstein once remarked that "no theory should contradict empirical facts." That is all very well as far as deductive logic goes. But if one postulates through valid reason and an inductive process of logic, the following assumptions and conclusions are inescapable.

The simple and earthy teachings of the Prophet based on a profound thought of divinity and human virtues, through a process of cultural arthritis, have resulted in their fossilization into a rigid time warp. The stranglehold of the clergy over the believers, championing to be the sole interpreters of the teachings of the Prophet, left little room for debate or a move towards modernization of these thoughts through a rational development. Even the understanding of Islam through Hadis has often been flawed by a subjective approach and vested interest of the self-appointed mullahs and the Ummah, who laid the law for the mass of the unquestioning faithful.

This insistence on uniformity, rigidity of procedure and cruelty of its expansion by violent means, its intolerance of dissent, lack of rationalism and stifling free thought provided the seeds of inherent instability, schism and the ultimate burn- out. Thus the only three civilizations that will defy time and hostile surroundings will be Hinduism, Judaism and Confucianism. They shall write the next script of history and decide the fault lines of civilizations. The lasting value system of Hinduism and Judaism has much in common. That is the theme of modern thinkers on the longevity of these civilizations. Confucianism too shall endure not merely on the merits of its antiquity, soundness of thought and depth of its culture but also due to its military might that pervades China. Israel and India have a sounder and more lasting edifice of thought, a basic pre-requisite of their endurance. Down the course of history an increase in their economic and military might will give rise to a potent mix of thought and might that will be irresistible and difficult to counter. That shall be the shape of the coming millennia.

The life-blood of any civilization is a common sharing of value systems, it's ancient heritage and pride in the past. Civilizational contours overarch narrow political divides drawn by conquering nations afterwards and during enforced treaties to suit their political interest. These being merely state boundaries, artificially delineated against ethnic, rational and cultural continuities and civilizational inspirations, create so-called nations that are surreal and brittle. The erstwhile Republics of Soviet Union or the states created in the Middle East after the First World War under the Sykes Picot agreement, dividing the landmass under British and French areas of influence are some recent examples.

Israel, the home to the Judaic civilization, is the arrowhead of the western civilizational phalanx pointing at the heart of Islamic Middle East. The U.S. and Russia can co-exist, but America centric west is incompatible with the Confucian- Islamic axis. Thus, west needs India to play a key role in containing the Chinese hegemonistic impulse assisted by Islamic fundamentalism as articulated by Gaddafi. Thus the civilizational factor reinforced by considerations of balance of power induce India and Israel to form a natural alliance to act as a non-Islamic outpost. They need to be actively assisted by America centric west. India and Israel need America as much as America needs them both.

While America is threatened only indirectly by a hostile Islam, Israel is threatened directly and lives from day to day, fighting for its survival against a hostile Islamic terrorism. There are regular clashes between Israel and Palestine provoked mainly by the latter. But Israel is no walk-over. For every act of violence by the Palestinians there is a swift and strong retribution from Israel. The very low population of Israel makes it imperative that no Jewish life is lost without a heavy price. How different is the case in India where human lives have no premium and we continue suffering casualties without initiating offensive or proactive war measures against cross-border terrorism sponsored by Pakistan. Extension after extension of ceasefire would undoubtedly lead to a total demoralization of Indian troops fighting desperately to contain and eliminate militancy in the troubled state of Jammu & Kashmir. India's threshold of patience is unlimited.

Coming back to Islamic Middle East, the U.S. has no choice but to reinforce India and Israel to contain the Confucian- Islamic heartland on its periphery. The enormous nuclear and military might of this power block can lead to a Muslim revival, and jingoism, which will translate itself into International Islamic terrorism. This has to be contained and defeated. Gun-Zionism of the Jews was the answer to centuries of humiliation, indignities and oppressions. And now in their new state, this forms the core of Israeli identity and value system, without prejudice to their spiritual and moral impulses. India should do the same instead of continuing in its excessive tolerance of injustice and violence. All the four Vedas, eighteen Puranas and two hundred fifty Upanishads, all Samhitas and Smrities that form the bedrock of the Hindu culture do not teach weakness as a virtue. Lord Krishna said in Gita that to submit to injustice is worse than perpetrating it. Even Lord Ram, when the cussed Varun, the god of seas, refused to give a pathway to his army to enter into Lanka, had this to say:

"Vinaya na manat Jaladhi Jad, Gaye Teen Din Beet,

Bole Ram sakop tab Bhay Bin Hot na Preet."

(After three days of futile prayer to the adamant Lord of the seas, Ram angrily spoke thus" There is no love without fear.")

India should now strive to convince its enemies not through pusillanimity but by a show of its muscle power that violence against it will be a high cost game. Those who are gratuitous enough to counsel restraint must remember that force is the only language understood by those who refuse to see reason or heed repeated warnings. The lion gives but one final roar before it leaps to kill.

The United States of America props up Pakistan, a failed state and an exporter of terrorism to India, as its frontline state, in its war against terrorism. In the process it has no compunction in roughriding Indian feelings and interests and treading heavily on India's feet. But this short-term policy may prove counter-productive and detrimental to its long term interests in regard to the clash of civilizations. India and Israel can and will never fight America and its way of life. The same is not true of Pakistan. Pakistan is nothing if not fundamentalist Islam. To India this marriage of convenience between a democracy and a dictatorship may be an amusing transience and even a short spell of rough weather. But ultimately America has no choice but to befriend India, not only for its own long term strategic gains but also as a civilization that can be trusted to keep their cherished values alive—values of freedom and human development, spiritualism and piety.

To a perceptive observer of the current national scene in India, there is very little to be proud of. Except for the competence and dedication of our scientists and the strength of our technological advances in Information Technology, India is otherwise a somnolent nation. We seem to have forgotten our proud heritage and sunk into the morass of immorality, betrayal of the country and all forms of social, political and economic vices. There seems to be nothing correct going with our nation. Abysmal poverty and hunger, unemployment, low literacy rate, poor growth of national wealth, economic stagnation, political instability, lack of national character, an all-pervasive corruption, lack of civic sense, abject surrender to criminality and viles of politicians, stand out as a sore thumb in our body politic. We have no national leadership worth the name which has the courage, character, integrity and conviction of its own. Chasing illusive popularity, they sadly lack a vision of the future India. The paradigm of our political discourse and conduct and the state of affairs needs a total overhaul. With our ostrich like vision we have made no marks on the geodetic panorama of history in the making. Stumbling from crisis to crisis, events have overtaken us. We do not make history but are prisoners of history. A soft state like India, that is Bharat, is an open land to all hostile forces, terrorists, ISI agents, saboteurs and illegal immigrants from our Islamic neighbours from east and west. Any ISI agent or saboteur who comes to blow, blast, destroy and kill finds easy shelters in the spawning Muslim localities, which form more than 15 percent of our population, not to talk of twenty million illegal Bangladeshi immigrants. According to international convention during war, even a proxy war, which is even worse than an open war, the only punishment for a spy is death. But in our country every ISI agent caught is placed in a jail with all possible comforts. Any number of lawyers who can sell their souls for a petty monetary gain at the cost of their country fight with alacrity the cases of such criminals. The endemic delay in the courts prolongs the process and in almost all cases the culprits go scot-free. We have yet to hear any ISI agent being executed in our country. In a recent case hardcore militants were set free in return for Indian hostages. It happened during the hijacking of the Indian Airlines flight IC 814 in December 1999, and the subsequent drama at Kandhar airport, when our Hon'ble Foreign Minister carried with him the most dreaded militants including their leader Azahr Masood in return for Indian hostages. It was a day of national shame. The release of these dreaded militants has caused a formidable list of casualities of the Hindus and others in the troubled valley in Kashmir amounting to more than three times the number of Indian hostages released. One wishes that our Hon'ble Foreign Minster and Defence Minster had remembered how Israel set free its hostages during the Entebbe operation from a far off location in Uganda flying by night across continents, taking the hijackers by surprise and killing them all.

Our leadership has a chronic weakness for squandering away military gains at the negotiating table; Nehru in 1948 in Kashmir, Lal Bahadur Shastri in 1965 at Tashkand. Our jawans had shed their precious blood to win these crucial territories. The prisoners in Kargil war were allowed to return with honour to their homeland after inflicting severe casualties on our troops and sending back mutilated bodies of our five prisoners of war. The same namby pamby approach was visible against Bangladesh, when the mutilated bodies of sixteen BSF jawans were returned to our country.

What is the way out? After centuries of degradation in the life of a civilization the worm has to turn. Israel had suffered for centuries and rose back again from its ashes.

Indian civilization is even older. With the new archaeological finds of a submerged town off the coast of Gujarat dating back to eighth century B.C. which dates even earlier then the Harappan culture, the life of our civilization now spans a longer period. In such a long civilizational history, a mere four centuries of Muslim rule, followed by one and half century of British, the total span of foreign cultural influence amounts to a mere five and half centuries of our history. But the last 54 years of national degradation after independence is a very short span in the lifetime of a nation and a mere comma in the textbook of human history. We too shall rise again if we keep our heads straight. First we should have a national leader of great consequence with courage, character integrity who has a vision instead of hankering after cheap popularity and appeasement. He should have a bold and a well-defined road map of India in the days to come. When such a leader who enjoys the trust of his people, gives the clarion call, the multitudes shall follow his footsteps as they did follow Gandhiji during the freedom movement. But we, as Indians, too have a heavy responsibility. It is we who shall throw up such a leader. Therefore, we should know our past, take pride in our culture and civilization and strive for a better future. We need to pull up our bootstraps, square our shoulders, take a deep breath, straighten our spine and look to the future with confidence. Struggle, struggle, struggle and to strive is the motto for the future. To quote poetess Sarojini Naidu:

"Sons of Hind, why sit ye idle;
Wait ye for some Deva's aid?
Buckle to, be up and doing;
Nations are by themselves made"

If we fail now history will never forgive us.

Chapter 20

The Reckoning

The time has now come to remove the reading glasses, stretch oneself and take a deep breath. We have scanned the panorama of the history of the two oldest civilizations in the world - Israel in detail and India that is Bharat through a study by exception. Considering the mass of historical data and the weight of evidence, brought out thus far, one can venture to suggest certain propositional constructs. History, which deals with the past, is not a dead substance to be discarded into the dustbin. Past determines the present and foretells the future. The events of the past form a foundation on which one resets the edifice of the present and the support for the future. The events of the past are a plot on the space-time continuum as proved by Einstein's Theory of Relativity. Like the tape of a recorder the past events lie buried in a corner of the tape and can be moved to sight by switching the 'Rewind & Play' button, the same way as it can be stored back by pressing the 'Fast forward' button. Thus the past is never lost and can be retrieved through properly documented records. Any civilization worth its name has its roots buried deep in the past through which it draws its sustenance and vitality. The origin and subsequent development of a people like that of a plant depends on three factors. The seed, the soil, and the DNA code. The seed, which has within itself the DNA code and the soil where it is sown, determine the genus and species of a nation. These are basic characteristics, which any external influence can alter only to a minor degree but cannot totally erase.

We have observed that the Hindu Indian and the Judaic Israeli civilizations are the oldest in the world. While the former dates back to almost 8000 B.C. the latter can also be put around 2500 B.C., a period when most of the civilizations of the world were unknown. Just as no archaeological discovery in Israel has ever controverted a Biblical reference, so also the latest finds in India have not contradicted the calendar of events starting from early Vedic period (8000 B.C.) to Mahabharat (3100 B.C.). While in Israel every single event and place in its long history has been validated by textual and archaeological evidence, in India, though there is abundance of textual evidence our archaeological efforts have been extremely limited. Old monuments have decayed and disappeared due to crass negligence and indifference to their preservation. It was left to a British Viceroy Lord Curzon to enact a law for the preservation of historical monuments, leading to the creation of the Archaeological Survey of India. Being the oldest, India and Israel could only give and not take, and as we shall prove shortly we shall continue to give and lead in the future as well.

There are striking similarities between Hindu and Judaic civilizations. Just as Hinduism enlightened the world through its profound philosophy and thought, Judaism too was commanded by their Lord to act as a 'light unto the nations of the world'. Both believe in a common God of the world and the universality and brotherhood of man; put more succinctly in Hindu thought by "Vasudheva Kutumbkam". The Jews like the Hindus have a profound historic belief in a fusing of national redemption with the redemption of all mankind. Their national movement will not be shorn of universal implications. In the state of Israel as in India there is no difference between the Jews or Hindus and the other human beings. The moral code of their prophets and sages seeks true justice and compassion for the human fraternity in the belief that all men are created equal. Hinduism and

Judaism, like Christianity, believe that God created man in his own image, and he makes no distinction between a white, black, or yellow man. This concept is eternal, all encompassing with no beginning or end, neither body nor form. Just like Hindu seers, from the Prophets to Einstein, Jewish genius has never accepted the duality of matter and spirit. In both civilizations there is a healthy communion of material force with spiritual force. The sages of Mishna, as those of Vedas, while stressing the spiritual mission never disregarded the body or its needs, a profound thought so simply expressed in Hindu lore, *"Bhukhe Bhajan Na Hoi Gopala"*, is the same as in Hebrew thought "if there be no flour, there can be no learning". Toil and God; these words occur both in Jewish and Hindu texts. Hinduism and Judaism being the oldest religions known to mankind had their share of distortions, misinterpretations, malpractices and a rigid, often irrational adherence to rituals, at the cost of the spirit. Many evils crept silently into the praxis of Hinduism as it did in Judaism shearing away the spirit from the form. This led to a reformative outgrowth of new sects in Hindu religion and the birth of a completely new religion of Christianity out of Judaism.

Both civilizations shun violence and are imbued with a deep sense of tolerance, which in the past was sometimes misinterpreted as weakness. The so-called militant Zionism, a later day product of reaction against constant injustice and oppression, was a brief flicker in the long history of Judaism. Similarly Hinduism took up arms only when attacked and pressed to the wall by the marauding invaders. The emphasis on the supremacy of the spirit does not disregard the importance of military might, but this might depend first and foremost on the spirit. Though Lord Krishna did teach the use of force against evil, the Hindus in their constant search for the highest form of spiritualism often disregarded this maxim, and thereby invited alien attacks. None of the two coveted foreign lands outside what God had granted to them, nor did they indulge into wars of expansion, political or religious. Being the oldest, and endowed with the rich heritage of their past, they developed a deep attachment to the land of their birth. This sentiment has been more visible among the Jews than the Hindus. Since the Jews could hardly stay in the land promised to them by their Lord and were for historic reasons, scattered to almost all corners of the world, their yearning for their homeland was both a subliminal and existential impulse. On the other hand since the Hindus were never exiled from their land, of which they had plenty and never underwent an exodus, they could never develope the same sense of deep attachment to their homeland as the Jews. The stress that Judaism and Hinduism lay upon individual striving for spiritual perfection and communion with God has over the ages instilled a sense of highly individualised behaviour. As a result, the Jewish tribes were constantly quarrelling among themselves even when faced with foreign aggression. As such, even when the invader was numerically inferior he inflicted a heavy loss on the Children of Israel; so much so that their Lord had to admonish them for their sins. A similar attitude plagued the Indian people for a large part of their history when their princes always warring against one another, fell easy victims to the forces of invasion. So much so that one of them secretly wrote to a Muslim invader to come to India and attack his rival in Delhi. We had no dearth of our Jaichands. The same part is being played today by our leftists and armchair secularists, who openly espouse the cause of our hostile neighbour.

There is a strange domestic species in our country called the "opinion makers". These could more correctly be called "opinion givers". This paranoid breed lives under the illusion that all of God's wisdom is stacked in them. These Resident Non-Indians, a hopeless minority, has adopted India bashing as its main source of income. They are the Television anchors, studio hoppers and members of CPI (M) politburo, and they somehow, hog the English print and visual media space out of all proportion to their real worth. These assiduous beavers, gnaving at the very roots of our culture and values, have a distinguished record of weakening our national resolve at critical moments in the post independence era. As the tension with Pakistan mounts and war clouds thicken, the cry goes up "war does not solve anything". Is it an acoplaytical discovery? Even a child knows that war is the last resort, when diplomacy fails. The screaming and breast-beating brigade of these paid prophets of doom makes the leadership waver, and weaken our strength when the moment comes for decisive action against our hostile neighbour, who has adopted cross-border terrorism as an instrument of state policy. These votaries of restraint are the biggest non-movable assets that Pakistan can have in India.

The Indian culture does lay a great stress and high value on family ties. *Manu Samhita* lays down in some details the duty of family members to one another especially the love and regard for the parents. This trait is not much in evidence in the Christian society of the west in general and America in particular. But with the Jews family solidarity and filial ties are almost sacrosanct. The seed of Abraham though widely scattered retains its subliminal unity and respect for family values.

Both nations suffered inequity oppression and torture for centuries; Israel for most of its recorded history, and India from 1300 to 1700 A.D. by Islam and from the beginning of the 19th century till its liberation from the British rule in 1947. Except for a short period of monarchy under David and Solomon the Jews had no kingdom of their own. Being in Diaspora, most of the time in their living memory, they could only dream and aspire for their Promised Land. Both people suffered indignities, privations and miseries under foreign occupation, challenging their very existence. But both rose, phoenix like from the ashes of their past to achieve excellence when opportunity came. Egypt, Babylon, Spain and the European nations tried to erase the very existence of the Jews, just as the Muslims and the British tried to destroy India and Hinduism. But it was the genius and resilience of these people that prevented them from being consigned to the dustbin of history. Both civilizations suffered at the hands of Islam and Christianity; the Jews more from Christianity of Europe and to a lesser extent from a resurgent Islam of the Middle East. The Indian genius rooted in its immanent culture and precious heritage withstood all onslaughts, and instead of being destroyed, swallowed the destroyer in its womb. It was their deep and abiding attachment to their roots that the two civilizations remained unscathed through the triumphs, tribulations and cataclysms of time and history. Both nations struggled and obtained their freedom from the British; India on 15th August, 1947, and Israel on 14 May, 1948. In both cases the spirit though non-violent could standup to aggression and violence. Israel was trampled under the hoofs of the fighting hordes of Assyrian, Babylonians, Persians, Egyptians, Greeks, Romans and Muslims while India had it's share of invaders, starting from Huns, Sakas, Mongols, Turks, Ghazni, Ghor, Mughals and the British. There is no trace of the invaders and their civilizations, but the nations they attacked, that is India and Israel, endure.

Both the nations have been surrounded by hostile neighbours; Israel by the Arabs and India by Islamic countries in the northwest. The situation remains the same today. More on this later. Both states were partitioned against their wish by the British administration creating permanent enemies and hatred that led to disastrous consequences, which persist even today. In both cases the partition was demanded by the Muslims and openly encouraged by the British, who believed in, and ruled by the policy of "Divide and Rule". Despite the partition, a sizable part of the Muslim population left behind in the mother country continued to be a source of instability, owing, as it did, a supra national loyalty to a Pan Islamic Order.

Israel resorted to an armed struggle to gain its independence from the British mandate. India used a unique method of non-violence and civil disobedience against its rulers, under the inspiring leadership of Mahatma Gandhi, the greatest man of his age. Both freedom struggles received tacit diplomatic support from the United States; President F.D. Roosevelt pleaded India's cause with Churchill, as President Truman helped Israel in the proceedings of the United Nations, and virtually midwifed the birth of a new nation.

Let us now look at the differences. A direct outcome of the teaching of our scriptures has been to nurture a spirit of detachment towards the material as against the spiritual. This trait manifested itself in the total disregard of any threats to our national existence and the inviolability of our land. With Israel their land comes first always and every time, their people come next, to serve the cause of their land. Both India and Israel always had insecure borders with hostile Islamic countries, ever on the lookout to sneak into their territory to cause murder and mayhem. While the Palestinians sent suicide bombers into Israel, India's western neighbour encourages, organises and supports cross-border terrorism into India. The Palestinians cannot hope to destroy the state of Israel and thus resort to a guerrilla war of murder and sabotage. The same way Pakistan cannot match India's military might in an open war; so it has changed track and embarked on a policy of subversion and destabilization. Since Pakistan cannot hope to win in a conventional and decisive campaign, it is trying to inflect a thousand wounds to bleed India to death. This effort is doomed to failure. Man to man, Indian and Israeli soldiers are the best soldiers in the world. If Indian armed forces admire and respect any country and its armed forces, it is Israeli. The two can endure much more hardships than any other nation can. India's weaponry is adequate for its defence tasks and they, like the Israelis, are the masters in the art of improvisation. In addition, Israel has achieved much higher levels in the sophistication of it's weapons. Thus, militarily challenged the two countries can proudly hold their own against any likely enemy offensive. However, India could emulate the Israeli philosophy of reprisals, retaliations and retribution against attack on its people and sovereignty. The so called 'secularist', arm chair elites, and literary chatterati of metropolitan India who have not ventured outside their cosy urban homes, have little concern for the unity and integrity of our land and the abiding values of our civilization. To the Jews freedom is the elixir of life. To the above-educated illiterates freedom is a mere convenience. The Jews being so few, a mere fourteen million in the world of which less than five million live in Eretz Israel, there is a high value to human life. India with a population of one billion does not seem to set any store to any depletion in its human resource. Even before independence and more so after, Israel avenged the death of everyone of its sons.

During the British mandate for every Jew killed or hanged the price was an Arab killed or a British hanged. This is a far cry from our country where everyday scores of civilians and soldiers lose their lives, falling to the bullet of Pak-sponsored terrorism, with hardly any ripples in our metropolitan elite. The casualities among our soldiers in fighting terrorism in Jammu and Kashmir alone exceeds the total lost in all the wars we have fought so far, yet these remain only numbers and statistics. We have not been able to put a high price tag on the loss of Indian life. We in India do not mourn our dead as they do in Israel.

Some of our thinking soldiers on the battleline in Jammu and Kashmir often wonder as to whom they are supposed to protect. One part of the answer is clear. The people of India. But how about their leaders? Why do they too deserve to be protected? Unfortunately, with all the rhetoric of our chatteratie democracy has not yet found deep roots in our land. Elections are rigged with the help of money, mafia and muscle power. The specimens that you find as legislators in state assemblies and members of parliament are a shame to any self-respecting citizen. A law unto themselves, they increase their salaries and perks without any compunction with a consensus that is rare. Cutting across party lines they shower upon themselves privileges that a poor taxpayer and even an affluent Indian would envy. And what do they give back in return? Shouting, slogans, yelling at one another, trooping into the well of the parliament, stalling the proceedings and retiring, having done not an iota of useful work. Is this the rabble that the soldier is expected to protect? Our lawmakers, instead of demanding protection from the armed forces, first need to deserve to be protected. Then only would our soldiers serve any useful purpose when they make the highest sacrifice.

We do not rise up to mete out justice to the hijackers as Israelis do. The rescue operation at Entebbe mounted by Israelis to bring back their hijacked citizens from Uganda should have been an example worth emulation during the IC 814 air heist to Kandhar, where our foreign minister ceremonially handed over five of the most dreaded militants to the Taliban. One would wish that Israel's patriotic and aggressive impulse could also rub on the Indian public and its leaders. Israel is a nation and a civilization rolled into one; India is a civilization but it needs to work very hard to become a nation of any consequence. Let us debunk the theory of 'cultural pluralism' being peddled by our effete social scientists. In a vast country of our size there are bound to be minor differences in social mores and community norms from place to place, but the underlying thread of civilizational unity based on our values and a common heritage, runs deep through all parts of our country. Instead of highlighting the parts we should emphasize the whole. This needs a cultural and national renaissance throughout our country as exemplified by the land of Israel. The breast beating of our leftist messiahs of the dalits cannot obfuscate the fact that India is one and its people are one. It is about time that we as a nation define ourselves in terms of the majority community, a task that Nehru failed to complete at the time of independence. Every country in the world has it's share of minorities but that does not change the colour, ethos, value systems and the moorings of that nation. Israel is a nation on the make. The world Jewry rose as one to help the fledgling state to achieve maturity. India is a nation in its own right; its size and population can hardly be ignored and it has no reason to be apologetic on any count.

What of the present and the future? As observers of the present Indian scene we do not find much to admire. In all areas of human activity India seems to be slipping and the slide down has been precipitious and fast. Against a glorious past of ten millennia we had a terrible degradation in almost everything human since 13th century A.D. till independence and even thereafter. Though, plotted on a time scale of the life of civilizations, our degradation is but a brief interlude, we cannot be too complacent. In moments of a highly critical analysis nothing seems to be going right with us. Lack of pride in our past, an attitude of slavishness to the west, lack of a civic sense, self above the country, corruption, caste conflicts, communal violence, fragmentation of society, covetousness, avarice and greed and the proverbial 'Hindu cowardice'. The list is endless. And the Holy Ganga keeps flowing silently along. But that is only one side of the coin. As an Arab saying goes "This too shall pass". We have many positives. A vast country, unlimited natural resources, a vast reservoir of skilled manpower, some of the best scientists in the world; the possibilities are endless. With our rich past and a glorious heritage, together with the wisdom of our sages of yore, God's plenty, and human wealth there is nothing that India cannot achieve. Our technical and technological competence along with that of Israel is one of the best in the world.

Remember that Kurukshetra is not buried deep enough, and can be lived again by pushing the right buttons on the time space continuum. Ours is the only country in the world, where God gave out his gospel in the battlefield of Dharmakshetra of Kurukshetra. Jehovah gave his commandments to Moses at Mount Sinai, a silent mountain. Jesus got his instructions from his Father God, as Mohammed received his revelations from Allah through his angel Gabriel in the wilderness of the desert. We are the only nation spoken to directly by God himself. The spirit of Kurukshetra should not die. We need not be a pacifist nation. Our patience does not have to be unlimited.

The longevity of a civilization does not depend on its material wealth or its military might. It is determined by the depth of its national conscienceness, human resource, and its infinite capacity to withstand adverse weather. India and Israel are not possessed of a jingoistic nationalism but have a deep and diffused cultural identity and unity of thought which is derived from their deep roots in the past—Torah and Talmud for Israel and Vedas and the Sanatan culture for India. This diffusiveness of culture is a strength rather than a weakness, since it can absorb, assimilate, evolve, transform and renew. It's batteries are being constantly charged, it's vitality will grow, and it shall not get ossified into a time warp as some other civilizations did. Such a civilization instead of being linear shall always remain multidirectional. Endowed with a tolerant nationalism as against state-forced values and culture, placing individual above the state, other worldliness and spirituality above avarice and covetousness. India and Israel are bound to outlive and indeed lead all the civilizations of the world. The Romans wanted power and wealth, they got it and disappeared; the Greeks wanted beauty, they got it and left no trace. The Egyptians wanted immorality but lie buried under the pyramids. The Sumerians, Babylonians, Persians, the Mongols, the Huns and so many others strutted on the stage of the world, and are heard no more.

The two countries are strategically located on the northwest and the southeast corners of the militant Islamic heartland. The two together can act as a double pincer to operate from both sides on this heartland. Thus, militarily by virtue of their strategic positioning India and Israel can beat back any offensive by the militant Islam. We have also noted earlier that Israel is the eastern beachhead of the America centric West European Christianity on the Mediterranean Sea. As per the religious factoid, there are five major civilizations in the world—Christian (2 billion), Islam (1.3 billion), Hinduism (900 million), Sinic or Chinese (1.2 billion) and Judaism (14 million). The Chinese civilization, which has been historically content within its old confines, can be counted out from any clash of civilizations. Hinduism poses no danger to anyone outside, but it shall not yield or surrender. That leaves us with Judaic Christianity and Islam as the main contenders. The future portends a clash of civilizations between Islam and the remaining two civilizations. Since Israel is the arrowhead of the Judaic Christian civilization, the immediate clashes will concern only fundamentalist militant Islam as pitched against Hinduism and Judaism. It needs no prescience of mind to foretell the future.

A word about the nuclear dimensions of the Indo-Pak standoff. Much has been said and written about the U.S. concerns on the possibility of a nuclear conflict between the two neighbours. Of course the U.S. stepped into the space vacated by the British Empire and carrying their colonial baggage and adopted the same policy, initiatives and concerns, thereby balancing India and Pakistan against each other. According to this theory any conflict in the region is bound to destabilise South Asia and the Pacific region and could hurt the U.S. interests. The fear of an impatient finger from the ranks of the extremist and fundamentalist Islamic hot-heads pressing the nuclear button is a bit far-fetched. This argument seems to be the chief justification for the U.S. to allow Musharraf, considered to be a moderating influence to continue to rule as a dictator. The reality is somewhat different. Except a suicide bomber no one in his senses wishes to commit hara-kiri. The former as a jehadi, has the lure of Jannat and possibly black-eyed houris in heaven. But the saner and the majority segment of a society does not suffer from such hallucinations. Compared to Pakistan, India has a far superior nuclear capability, including larger number of warheads, efficient delivery systems including even Inter Continental Ballistic Missiles (ICBM), a very mobile response system and a credible second strike capability. Thus, in spite of India's commitment to a "no first use" policy it would be unwise for Pakistan to attempt a pre-emptive strike. This is bound to invite a massive Indian retaliation. While India may suffer only minor bruises, Pakistan will just cease to exist.

Chapter 21

Apocalypse

The world suffered a violent tremour on 11th September, 2001, when the World Trade Centre and the Pentagon building in the United States were bombed by Islamic militants and barely three months later on 13th December, 2001, when the Parliament of India was attacked by the foot soldiers of militant Islam. This has been a watershed in human history and a defining moment for us all. Simple equations and political paradigms of pre 9/11 era simply do not exist. Militant Islam is on the move. Whatever its apologists may say, Islam had always been drenched in blood and it is splashing it everywhere now. The biggest threat to the democracies of the world comes directly from fundamentalist Islam and its weapon is terror. Mr. George W. Bush may couch his words in diplomatic language for reasons of national interest, and may even resort to mealy-mouthed semantics that his fight is against terror and not Islam. Apocalypse is here and now. The *Dar-ul-Islam* is out to conquer *Dar-ul-Harb* and wipe out the infidel. The coalition of Christian states, hastily cobbled up may not provide a permanent answer. Christianity, with its enormous military might, may temporarily deflect and parry the immediate onslaught, but its arrowhead Israeli Judaism will have to act as its shield and permanent protector. This is one of the reasons that Israel has to endure and prevail. Indian democracy is the other enemy that militant Islam needs to destroy in fulfilling its 'God-ordained' mission. Let there be no mistake; the foot soldiers of Jehad mean business. Osama-Bin-Laden and his Al-Quaeda cohorts and their brothers operating in Jammu and Kashmir are only the symptoms of the disease. The disease is more deep rooted and lies in the tenets of Qoran and the praxis of Islam. Whichever way militants Islam strikes, India and Israel shall have to bear the brunt and defeat it. This is a heavy burden indeed. But they are equal to the task. The fundamentalist militants believe in the sword. They shall have it. Those who live by the sword shall die by it. The hand that ploughs can also smite. With their inherent civilizational strength and the call of the times, India and Israel, Lord be praised, shall not only endure but shall prevail. They are destined to lead.

A Select Bibliography

A.L. Basham: *The Wonder Thai was India*

Abram Leon Sachar, (1972 Edition): *Hisory of the Jews* (30 Centuries of Judaism)

Alan Keenam: *The Phoenix of the West—A Study in Pogrom*

Amos Elon: *The Israelis, Founders & Sons*

Arthur Hertzberg: *The Jews in America* (Four Centuries of An Uneasy Encounter)

Arun Shourie : *Eminent Historians*

Bhagwan Singh: *The Vedic Harappans*

Boden, Professor of Sanskrit at the University of Oxford: *Modern India and The Indians*

Chaim Herzog: *Heroes of Israel* (Profile of Jewish Courage)

David Ben Gurion: *Israel—Years of Challenge*

David Frawley: *The Myth of the Aryan Invasion of India*

David King: *The Gun & The Olive Branch, The Root of Violence in the Middle East*

Dhammapada-Authors unknown

Dr. A.K. Majumdar: *Concise History of Ancient India* Vol. - I

Dr. F. W. Foester: *The Jews-A Christian View*

Harsh Narain, Jaory Daboshi, Ram Swarup, Sita Ram Goel: *Hindu Temples - What Happened to them* (A Preliminary Survey)

Hoag Levins: *Arab Reach-The Secret War Against Israel*

Jacob Beller: *Jews in Latin America*

James Parker: *The Conflict of the Church & The Synagogue*

K.D. Sethna: *Karpasa in Pre-Historic India: A Chronological and Cultural Clue*

K.D. Sethna: *The Problems of Aryan Origins*

Koenraad Elst: *Indigenous Indians: Agastya to Ambedkar*

Maharshi Valmik: *The Ramayan*

Manusamhita-Authors unknown

Mark Tessler: *A History of the Israeli Palestinian Conflict*

Max J.Demont: *The Jews, God & History-A Modern Interpretation of a Four Thousand Years Story*

Max Muller: History of Ancient Sanskrit Literature

Menachin Begin: (Prime Minister of Israel in 1997 and President in 1987) *The Revolt*

Monier-Williams: *Sanskrit-English Dictionary*

N.S. Rajaram: *The Politics of History: Aryan Invasion Theory and the Subversion of Scholarship*

Oden Meeker: *Israel: Old Land New Nation.*

Perceival Spear: *India, A Modern History*

Robert St. John: *Jews, Justice & Judaism*

Robin Wright: *The Sacred Rage*

Roderick Micleish: *Israel and Arabs at War*

Shrikant G. Talageri: *The Aryan Invasion Theory : A Reappraisal,*

Shrimad Bhagwad Gita

Sita Ram Goel: *Hindu Temples, What happened to them- Islamic Evidence Vol. - II*

Samuel P. Huntington: *The Clash of Civilizations & the Re-making of a New World Order*

Subhash Kak: *The Astronomical Code of the Rigveda*

The Brahrnanas-Authors unknown

The Holy Bible

The Puranas-Authors unknown

The Upanishads-Authors unknown

Thomas A Idinopelos: *Jerusalem Blessed, Jerusalem Cursed*

Thomas J. Archdeacon: *Becoming American: An Ethnic History*

Thomas S.L. *From Beirut to Jerusalem*

Ved Vyas: *The Mahabharat*

Ved Vyas: *The Four Vedas*

Ze'ev Schiff R Ehud Ya'ari *Intifada-The Palestinian Uprising* (Israel's Third Front)

Index